Culture and Customs of Italy

Recent Titles in
Culture and Customs of Europe

Culture and Customs of Spain
Edward F. Stanton

Culture and Customs of Germany
Eckhard Bernstein

Culture and Customs
of Italy

CHARLES KILLINGER

Culture and Customs of Europe

GREENWOOD PRESS
Westport, Connecticut • London

Library of Congress Cataloging-in-Publication Data

Killinger, Charles L.
   Culture and customs of Italy / Charles Killinger.
      p. cm.—(Culture and customs of Europe)
   Includes bibliographical references and index.
   ISBN: 0–313–32489–1 (alk. paper)
   1. Italy—Civilization—20th century. 2. Popular culture—Italy—History—20th century.
I. Title. II. Series.
   DG451.K54 2005
   945.092—dc22   2004028234

British Library Cataloguing in Publication Data is available.

Library of Congress Catalog Card Number: 2004028234
ISBN: 0–313–32489–1

First published in 2005

Greenwood Press, 88 Post Road West, Westport, CT 06881
An imprint of Greenwood Publishing Group, Inc.
www.greenwood.com

Printed in the United States of America

The paper used in this book complies with the
Permanent Paper Standard issued by the National
Information Standards Organization (Z39.48–1984).

10 9 8 7 6 5 4 3 2 1

For Pam, Valentina, Marco, and Dante

Bookcomp, Inc.

Contents

Series Foreword	ix
Preface	xi
Acknowledgments	xiii
Chronology	xv
1 The Land, People, and History	1
2 Religion and Thought	41
3 Marriage, Gender, and Family	71
4 Holidays, Saints' Days, Festivals, and Food	91
5 Leisure Activities and Sport	119
6 Literature	137
7 The Performing Arts	155
8 Art, Architecture, and Design	177
9 Cinema and Mass Media	199
Glossary	221
Bibliography	227
Index	235

Series Foreword

THE OLD WORLD and the New World have maintained a fluid exchange of people, ideas, innovations, and styles. Even though the United States became the de facto leader and economic superpower in the wake of a devastated Europe after World War II, Europe has remained for many the standard bearer of Western culture.

Millions of Americans can trace their ancestors to Europe. The United States as we know it was built on waves of European immigration, starting with the English who braved the seas to found the Jamestown Colony in 1607. Bosnian and Albanian immigrants are some of the latest new Americans.

In the Gilded Age of one of our great expatriates, the novelist Henry James, the Grand Tour of Europe was de rigueur for young American men of means, to prepare them for a life of refinement and taste. In a more recent democratic age, scores of American college students have Eurailed their way across Great Britain and the Continent, sampling the fabled capitals and bergs in a mad, great adventure, or have benefited from a semester abroad. For other American vacationers and culture vultures, Europe is the prime destination.

What is the New Europe post–Cold War, post–Berlin Wall in the new millennium? Even with the different languages, rhythms, and rituals, Europeans have much in common: they are largely well educated, prosperous, and worldly. They also have similar goals and face common threats and form alliances. With the advent of the European Union, the open borders, and the euro and considering globalization and the prospect of a homogenized Europe, an updated survey of the region is warranted.

Culture and Customs of Europe features individual volumes on the countries most studied and for which fresh information is in demand from students and other readers. The Series casts a wide net, inclusive of not only the expected countries, such as Spain, France, England, and Germany, but also countries such as Poland and Greece that lie outside Western Europe proper. Each volume is written by a country specialist, with intimate knowledge of the contemporary dynamics of a people and culture. Sustained narrative chapters cover the land, people, and brief history; religion; social customs; gender roles, family, and marriage; literature and media; performing arts and cinema; and art and architecture. The national character and ongoing popular traditions of each country are framed in an historical context and celebrated along with the latest trends and major cultural figures. A country map, chronology, glossary, and evocative photos enhance the text.

The historied and enlightened Europeans will continue to fascinate Americans. Our futures are strongly linked politically, economically, and culturally.

Preface

THE OPPORTUNITY to write a book on Italian culture seemed from the outset both exciting and daunting. After all, many believe that Italy gave birth to modern Western culture and that its gift to the world of the creative arts is both pervasive and unsurpassed. Equally challenging was the realization that the great diversity of habits and traditions of the Italian peninsula defy facile generalization, to the point that one can argue the coexistence of Italian "cultures"—even languages. As the task evolved, the need to focus on the postwar era rendered the project more manageable, and the job of addressing issues of popular—as well as formal—culture made it infinitely fascinating to write.

Nonetheless, even 30 years of studying, teaching, and traveling in Italy can hardly instill a sense of worthiness to such a task. Fortunately, others have provided a wealth of description and scholarly analysis in each of the various subfields of Italian culture and customs. Thus, when primary research and firsthand observations proved inadequate, the abundant work of scholars and writers provided the resources to fill in gaps in the manuscript. To the many students of Italian culture whose work I consulted, I owe a substantial debt; within the confines of the possible, I have acknowledged their contributions.

From the start, the book relied on several basic assumptions. As part of a series, the framework would follow a systematic organization, progressing from a broad summary of major geographical, historical, and cultural features, to an orderly treatment of the most important cultural categories, and culminating in a brief treatment of contemporary political and social trends.

From the start, there was a commitment that the habits and features of ordinary life would occupy an important place alongside the "high" arts—thus "customs" and "culture" cohabit this space. It was readily apparent that the abundantly rich and colorful legacy of Italian life would sustain this effort and would prove capable of carrying the text even when its author faltered.

Acknowledgments

A number of friends and colleagues contributed generously to this project. To all, I wish to express heartfelt gratitude. Sherry Graber, Todd Deery, Brad Camp, and Pam Killinger each provided advice on multiple chapters; their careful reading proved invaluable. Richard Crepeau, John Reich, Luigi Ferri, Tricia Henry Young, Jack Chambless, Scott Perry, George Koller, Pauline Koller, and Richard Sansone gave unselfishly of their time and expertise. Jared Graber's advice and support were essential, as was Pam Killinger's understanding and encouragement. Since a project of this scope requires a wide range of resources, it would have been impossible without the expert assistance from librarians Paulette Smith, Judi Delisle, Catherine Katz, and Nuria Curras. Curt Harmon and Angelique Smith provided expert technical advice. Valentina, Marco, and Dante contributed comic relief, entertainment, and companionship. Timely and thoughtful scrutiny from James Reed proved indispensable. Throughout, Wendi Schnaufer maintained a steady editorial presence and patient guidance.

Chronology

753 BC	Traditional founding of Rome.
509	Romans expelled King Tarquin the Proud.
494	Plebeians challenged patricians in First Secession.
450	Twelve Tables codified Roman law.
390	Gauls defeated Roman army at River Allia.
264–241	Romans defeated Carthaginians in First Punic War.
218–201	Romans defeated Carthaginians in Second Punic War despite Hannibal's successes.
149–146	Rome won Third Punic War, severely punishing Carthaginians.
118	Romans added province of Southern Gaul.
91–88	Roman "Social Wars".
60	First Triumvirate of Pompey, Julius Caesar, and Crassus formed.
49	Julius Caesar crossed Rubicon from Gaul to Rome to confront Pompey.

46	Roman Senate made Caesar dictator for 10 years.
44	Conspirators murdered Caesar.
43	Second Triumvirate of Octavian, Antony, and Lepidus formed.
31	Octavian defeated Antony and Cleopatra at Battle of Actium.
27 BC–14 AD	Augustus reigned.
41–68	Julio Claudian dynasty.
68–96	Flavian dynasty.
96–192	Antonine dynasty.
284–305	Diocletian reigned as emperor.
306–337	Constantine the Great ruled as emperor.
313	Constantine issued Edict of Milan legalizing Christianity.
410	Visigoths under Alaric took Rome.
489	Ostrogoth Theodoric invaded peninsula.
535	Byzantine emperor Justinian invaded.
773	Charlemagne led Frankish armies into peninsula.
800	Pope Leo III crowned Charlemagne "King of Franks" in St. Peter's Basilica.
827	Arabs invaded Sicily.
1025–1091	Normans invaded Sicily.
1176	Lombard League defeated Frederick Barbarossa at Battle of Legnano.
1183	Peace of Constance acknowledged autonomy of Italian cities.
1266	Charles of Anjou defeated Germans at Battle of Benevento and became King of Naples and Sicily.
1282	Sicilians expelled Angevins in Sicilian Vespers.
1305–1377	Papacy moved to Avignon.
c. 1306	Giotto painted frescoes in Arena Chapel, Padua.

c. 1320	Dante published *Divine Comedy.*
1347	"Black Death" ravaged Italy.
1348–1353	Boccaccio published *Decameron.*
	Petrarch published *Canzoniere.*
1413–1417	Donatello sculpted *St. Mark* and *St. George.*
1418	Brunelleschi chosen to construct *Duomo* in Florence.
1430	Turkish fleet defeated Venetians.
1434	Medici family of bankers seized power in Florence.
1454	Italian League formed at Peace of Lodi.
1469–1492	"Lorenzo the Magnificent" ruled Florence.
1475	Botticelli painted *Adoration of the Magi.*
c. 1478–1482	Botticelli painted *Primavera* and *Birth of Venus.*
1494	French invaded Italy, initiating two centuries of foreign occupation of peninsula.
	Savanarola began moral crusade in Florence.
1495–1506	Leonardo painted *The Last Supper* and *Mona Lisa.*
1504	Michelangelo completed *David.*
1505–1509	Michelangelo painted Sistine Chapel ceiling.
1509–1511	Raphael painted *School of Athens.*
1513	Machiavelli published *The Prince.*
1527	Spanish sacked Rome and captured pope.
1559	First Index of Forbidden Books in 1559 marked Counter-Reformation.
	Treaty of Cateau-Cambresis affirmed Spanish dominance of peninsula.
1564	Guicciardini published *History of Italy.*
1599–1602	Caravaggio painted life of St. Matthew, *Conversion of St. Paul,* and *Crucifixion of St. Peter.*
	Bernini sculpted *Fountain of the Four Rivers,* Rome.
1764	Beccaria published *Of Crimes and Punishments.*

1765–1790	Grand Duke Peter Leopold governed Tuscany.
1773	Jesuit order expelled.
1796	Napoleon Bonaparte invaded Italy.
1798	Napoleon divided Italy into his Cisalpine, Ligurian, and Roman republics.
1801	France acquired Italian territory from Austria in Treaty of Lunéville.
1806	Napoleon's army occupied Naples, driving Ferdinand IV into exile.
1814	Metternich convened Congress of Vienna.
1818	Leopardi published *All'Italia*.
1827	Manzoni published *I promessi sposi*.
1829	Rossini composed *William Tell Overture*.
1831	Revolutions erupted throughout the peninsula.
	Giuseppe Mazzini founded Young Italy.
1832	Pellico published *Le Mie Prigioni*.
1835	Bellini composed *I Puritani*.
1843	Gioberti published *Il Primato*.
1844	Cesare Balbo published *Le speranze d'Italia*.
1846	Pius IX (Pio Nono) elected pope.
1848	Revolutions swept through the peninsula.
	King Carlo Alberto issued *Il Statuto*, Piedmontese constitution.
	Austrians defeated Carlo Alberto's armies at Custoza.
1849	Austrians defeated Piedmontese at Battle of Novara; Carlo Alberto abdicated in favor of his son, Vittorio Emanuele II.
	Mazzini organized government of Roman Republic.
	French forces crushed Roman Republic.

1850	French restored Pope Pius IX to Vatican.
	Cavour joined Piedmontese cabinet.
1854	Cavour led Piedmont into Crimean War against Russia.
1859–1860	Second War for Independence.
1860	Garibaldi's "Thousand" volunteers invaded Sicily.
	Garibaldi accompanied Vittorio Emanuele II on triumphal march through Naples.
1861	Italian parliament declared Kingdom of Italy.
1866	Austria ceded Venetia to Italy at Peace of Prague.
1868	Vatican decreed *Non Expedit,* prohibiting Catholics from participating in Italian politics.
1870	Italian troops occupied Rome, completing *Risorgimento.*
1871	Parliament passed Law of Papal Guarantees; Pius IX refused, declaring himself a "prisoner in the Vatican".
	Verdi composed *Aida.*
1882	Italy signed Triple Alliance.
1887	Verdi composed *Otello.*
1890	Mascagni composed *Cavalleria Rusticana.*
1891	Pope Leo XIII issued encyclical *Rerum novarum.*
1892	Italian Socialist Party founded.
	Leoncavallo's *Pagliacci* premiered.
	Giolitti served first term as prime minister.
1896	Ethiopians defeated Italians in Battle of Adua.
1896–1900	Puccini composed *La Boheme* and *Tosca.*
1899	Giovanni Agnelli organized Fiat.
1900	King Umberto assassinated.
1904	Puccini composed *Madame Butterfly.*
1906	Carducci became first Italian to win Nobel Prize for literature.

1909	Marconi won share of Nobel Prize.
	Futurist Manifesto issued.
1911	Giolitti expanded franchise.
1914	Italy maintained neutrality in World War I.
	Mussolini, expelled from the Italian Socialist Party (PSI), launched *Il Popolo d'Italia*.
1915	Italy signed Pact of London; declared war against Austria.
1917	Italian army routed at Caporetto.
1918	Italian army drove Austrians into retreat at Vittorio Veneto.
1919	D'Annunzio occupied Fiume.
	The *Partito Popolare* (PPI) and PSI won sweeping support in national elections.
	Mussolini formed *Fascio di Combattimento* at Piazza San Sepolcro (Milan).
1919–1920	"Red Biennium" ("the red years") brought food riots, lawlessness, industrial conflict and spreading violence, raising the specter of revolution.
1920	"Occupation of the factories".
1921	Fascist "punitive raids" attacked peasant leagues, and Socialist Party, labor, and newspaper offices.
	Mussolini elected to Chamber of Deputies, 1 of 36 Fascists.
	Pirandello published *Six Characters in Search of an Author*.
1922	Fascist March on Rome.
	Mussolini established Fascist Grand Council.
1924	Mussolini's national list won decisive victory in national elections.

Matteotti crisis brought Mussolini's government to the brink of disaster when Unitary Socialist (PSU) deputy Giacomo Matteotti was found murdered.

Italy acquired Fiume.

1925   Mussolini made himself "Head of Government".

1926   Mussolini removed managers of *Il Corriere della Sera* and *La Stampa,* shut down opposition papers.

1929   Lateran Accords signed.

1935   Italy invaded Ethiopia.

1936   Mussolini declared Italian Empire.

Italy formed "Axis" with Germany, sent troops into Spanish Civil War.

1937   Mussolini reorganized propaganda agencies under Ministry of Popular Culture.

Italy withdrew from League of Nations.

1938   Mussolini replaced Chamber of Deputies with Chamber of Fasces and Corporations.

Manifesto of Fascist Racism.

1939   Italy and Germany agreed to "Pact of Steel".

1940   Mussolini declared war on France and Britain, invaded France and Greece.

1943   Allied forces invaded Sicily.

Fascist Grand Council voted to remove Mussolini from power.

King Vittorio Emanuele III appointed General Badoglio head of military government.

Italian government announced armistice with Allies.

German commandos rescued Mussolini, transported him to Lake Garda to establish Salò Republic.

Allied forces landed south of Rome.

1944   Allied troops liberated Rome.

1945	Mussolini and mistress captured and executed by partisans.
1945–1948	Neorealist films directed by De Sica, Visconti, Rossellini, and others.
1946	Italian voters voted to replace kingdom with republic.
1947	Publication of Gramsci's prison letters and notebooks.
1948	Christian Democrats won first parliamentary elections.
	Italy joined Organization for European Economic Cooperation (OEEC).
1948–1952	U.S. Marshall Plan assistance provided to rebuild Europe.
1949	Italy joined North Atlantic Treaty Organization (NATO).
c. 1950–1958	Italy's "Economic Miracle".
1953–1957	Fellini directed *I vitelloni, La Strada,* and *Nights of Cabiria.*
1957	Italy joined European Economic Community (EEC).
1961–1964	Pasolini directed *Accatone, Mamma Roma,* and *The Gospel According to St. Matthew.*
1962	Pope John XXIII called Second Vatican Council.
1963–1968	Christian Democratic Party and Italian Socialist Party (DC-PSI) Center-Left coalition.
1964–1971	Bertolucci directed *Before the Revolution* and *The Conformist.*
1968	Student movement spreads through Italy.
1969	"Hot Autumn": militant strikes among northern workers.
1970	Divorce legalized.
c. 1970–1979	Terrorism of "years of lead."
1973	Communist Party (PCI) leader Berlinguer announced "historic compromise" with progressive political groups.
1975	Family Law of 1975 established gender equality.

1977	Workplace antidiscrimination law passed.
1978	Polish-born Karol Wojtyla elected Pope John Paul II, first non-Italian in 455 years.
	Red Brigades kidnapped former prime minister Moro.
	Comprehensive national health service established.
	Abortion legalized.
1981	Republican Spadolini became first non-Christian Democrat (DC) prime minister in 35 years.
1982	*Mafia* murdered General Dalla Chiesa.
1983–1987	Socialist Craxi governed.
1987	Maxi-trial of nearly 500 alleged *mafiosi* in Palermo, Sicily.
1991, 1993	Referenda radically modified proportional system of elections.
1992	*Mafia* murdered Falcone and Borsellino.
1992–1994	DC, PCI, and PSI dissolved.
1993	*Tangentopoli* ("kickback city" or "bribesville") scandal shook Italy, encompassing major political and business leaders and mobilizing a drive for fundamental change.
1994	Center-Left *Progressisti* and Center-Right *Polo delle Libertà* coalitions emerged.
1996	Prodi and D'Alema led Center-Left *Ulivo* coalition to victory.
1997	Fo named Nobel Laureate in Literature.
1998	Italy met Maastricht Treaty standards, gained admission to European Monetary Union.
2001	Berlusconi and Center-Right *Casa delle Libertà* coalition elected to power.
2002	Currency conversion from lira to euro.
	Physical chemist Giacconi awarded Nobel Prize in physics.

Red Brigades claimed responsibility for murder of labor law professor and government adviser Biagi.

Bossi-Fini law tightened immigration restrictions on non-EU citizens.

2003   Highest appeals court cleared 7-time prime minister Andreotti of ordering a mafia hit on a journalist in 1979.

Death of Gianni Agnelli, one of Italy's major industrialists and head of family empire including Fiat.

18 Italians killed in suicide bombing in Nasiriya, Iraq, Italy's worst single military loss since World War II.

2004   Berlusconi set the record for the longest-lasting government in the history of the Italian republic.

Financial collapse of Parmalat, a major food conglomerate with worldwide investments.

Death of cycling champion Marco Pantani.

2005   Italian security agent killed by U.S. troops in Baghdad while rescuing Italian journalist.

Berlusconi announced plans to begin withdrawing the 3,000 Italian troops from Iraq.

1

The Land, People, and History

THE LAND AND ITS INFLUENCES

THE LONG, NARROW ITALIAN PENINSULA extends into the Mediterranean Sea between Spain and Greece in the shape of a boot, divided east and west by the spine of the Apennine range and partially separated from the rest of the European mainland by the Alps. The Alpine range that transcends Italy's northern border with France, Switzerland, and Austria features some of the highest peaks in Europe, including Monte Bianco (Mont Blanc, 15,771 ft.) and Monte Rosa (15,203 ft.). To the east, the Dolomites (a subrange of the Alps) rise along the Austrian border, cresting at Monte Marmolada (10,965 ft.). From the Ligurian coast in the northwest to the Adriatic coast in the northeast, the Italian frontier arcs along the borders with France, Switzerland, Austria, and Slovenia. At the tops of the great Alpine valleys, passes such as the Little and Great St. Bernard, the Simplon, and the St. Gotthard accommodate travel to France, Spain, and Austria. Thus the Alps have not obstructed trade, travel, or other communication with the rest of Europe, nor have they prevented invasion of hostile forces from Hannibal to Hitler. Today, railroad lines and auto tunnels such as the Mont Blanc and San Bernardino further ease travel to France, Switzerland, and Austria.

From the Alpine border to the toe of the boot in Calabria, the peninsula stretches about 750 miles to the south. The Italian Republic includes the large islands of Sicily and Sardinia and a number of smaller islands, the largest of which is Elba and the most remote, Lampedusa, only 70 miles from the north coast of Tunisia. Across the Adriatic Sea from Venice lie the Balkans, a mere 50 miles distant. Together, the Republic covers approximately 116,000 square miles, about three-quarters the size of California. Bordered by the Ligurian, Tyrrhenian, Ionian, and Adriatic Seas, Italy counts more than 4,600 miles of coastline, including several superb natural harbors, particularly Genoa, Naples, Venice, and Palermo. The expansive coastline and its seaports have in turn oriented Italy toward the outside world and have provided bountiful economic opportunities, especially evident in the case of Venice, which has for centuries excelled as a commercial hub. In addition to opportunity for maritime trade, Italy's location in the western Mediterranean Sea has bestowed on it a strategic importance that has outweighed its real military strength. The Italian peninsula also includes two independent states: Vatican City, at 109 acres the smallest sovereign state in the world, governed by the Pope; and San Marino, a small, mountainous republic south of Rimini near the Adriatic coast.

Although less dramatic than the Alps and the Dolomites, the Apennine mountain range has exerted greater influence on Italy's history and culture, particularly by hindering internal transportation and communications. Roughly 80 miles wide at an average height of 4,000 feet, the Apennine range extends 800 miles from Liguria in the northwest down the center of the peninsula, bending through the toe of the boot, under the narrow Straits of Messina to emerge in Sicily. The highest of the Apennine peaks are in the Abruzzi region: Monte Carno (9,560 ft.) in the Gran Sasso chain and Monte Amaro (9,170 ft.). The range includes at least three active volcanoes, Mount Vesuvius (Monte Vesuvio), near Naples, Mount Etna in Sicily, and Stromboli in the Lipari islands.

Northern Italy is known for its picturesque lakes, particularly Garda (the largest), Maggiore, and Como. The southwest shore of Lake Lugano likewise is Italian. Also in the North are the rivers Adda, Isonzo, Tagliamento, Ticino, Piave, and Po, the latter watering the broad and fertile plain of the Po River valley. Italy's best known rivers, the Tiber that flows through Rome and the Arno that connects Florence and Pisa, cross the center of the peninsula from the Apennines to the Tyrrhenian Sea. However, among all of Italy's rivers, only the Po affords a major transportation artery. And although the Romans developed a widespread system of roads, the decline of the empire left many towns unconnected, retarding trade and reinforcing the tradition of local self-sufficiency. Only in the twentieth century have Italians developed an extensive infrastructure and a national market for goods. In part as a result of its mountainous topography, Italy has traditionally been a place of localized politics, economy, culture, and customs. To understand Italy is to understand its great local and regional traditions, a feature that has challenged the creation of a modern nation state and led some to emphasize the importance of local over national characteristics.

Not only have the Apennines historically interfered with the development of a unified culture, isolating one town from another, but the mountains and their foothills have limited the availability of land suitable for growing grains and grazing livestock. Consequently, except for the fertile valley of the Po River in the North, the southern plain of Puglia, and the sloping hills of Sicily where grains grow in abundance on large estates, Italian farmers have typically found themselves restricted to small plots for grazing sheep and cultivating grapes, olives, and cheese as marketable crops. Complicating agricultural production are the marshes that historically dominated parts of central Italy, requiring major reclamation efforts in draining and irrigation to be productive.

THE REGIONS AND REGIONAL IDENTITIES

The Italian Republic is divided into 20 regions, each of which is subdivided into provinces and communes. Five of the 20 (Valle d'Aosta, Trentino-Alto Adige, Friuli-Venezia Giulia, Sicily, and Sardinia) have been awarded special autonomy because of unique circumstances of language and history. Regional divisions are especially significant because of the influence of traditional, local characteristics in shaping the mosaic of Italian culture. Beginning in the northwest, one passes first through Liguria, then to Piedmont, the Valle d'Aosta, and Lombardy.

With deep valleys running from the Alps and Apennines to the sea, and with excellent natural harbors, Liguria provides a profitable commercial outlet for the upper Po Valley and its farms. Liguria's densely populated major cities are ports: Savona, Imperia, La Spezia, and Genoa. Genoa is home to 40 percent of the region's population and employs a large work force in the shipyards, oil terminals, power plants, and other industrial factories. Genoa's twelfth century, Pisan-style San Lorenzo cathedral, housing an important sculpture of the saint by Andrea Sansovino, provides an architectural focus. The Via Garibaldi features several grand palaces with galleries, including the Palazzo Cataldi and the Palazzo Bianco. The coastal beaches of the Italian Riviera, the mild climate, and abundant vegetation have attracted tourists, vacation dwellers, and sailors particularly to the Ligurian towns of Portofino, Rapallo, San Remo, and Santa Margherita. Liguria borders France, Emilia Romagna, Tuscany, and, to the north, Piedmont.

Nestled in the foothills to the Alps, Piedmont (Piemonte) includes soaring peaks, the western shore of Lake Maggiore, and the heavily cultivated, industrialized, and populated plain of the upper Po River valley. Its major cities are

Turin (Torino), Alessandria, and Novara. A city of Roman origin, Turin served historically as capital for Lombards, Franks, Piedmontese, and, briefly, for the newly declared Kingdom of Italy. Much of the city was developed in the seventeenth and eighteenth centuries according to a systematic plan, so that it features wide, tree-lined, and arcaded boulevards. Among its cultural attractions are the medieval church of San Domenico, the Renaissance cathedral of San Giovanni, the Piazza San Carlo, the Savoy Royal Palace (Palazzo Reale), the Academy of Science (housing the Egyptian Museum), and the Museum of the *Risorgimento* (as Italian unification is known) in the Palazzo Carignano. Home to the Fiat auto plant, Turin also hosts its university and a number of other industries, including those in engineering, electronics, textiles, and food. Partly because of its links to northern Europe (it borders France and Switzerland), and partly because of enlightened leadership from its farming and commercial sectors, Piedmont developed by the mid-nineteenth century the most progressive regional economy on the peninsula.

Lombardy (Lombardia) holds the distinction of being Italy's most densely populated region, largely because of the city of Milan, Italy's "second capital" after Rome. Lombardy includes Italy's largest lake, Garda, as well as Lake Como and parts of Lakes Maggiore and Lugano. Sweeping through the central Po Valley, the fertile plains of Lombardy have supported Italy's most productive and prosperous farmers, who, in turn, traditionally produced much of the capital to fuel industrial growth. Its advantageous position on the main trade route from the Mediterranean to northern Europe has contributed to Lombardy's steady presence as a commercial and banking hub.

Milan (Milano) holds the distinction of being Italy's financial and industrial center (producing especially automobiles, steel, and furniture) as well as a world leader in fashion and design. With a sprawling population of 1.6 million, Milan attracts a steady flow of tourists to its major attractions, including its grand, white marble, Gothic duomo; Leonardo da Vinci's "The Last Supper" in the refectory of the Convent of Santa Maria delle Grazie; and La Scala, the world famous opera house. At the center of the city, near the Cathedral, is the popular Galleria Vittorio Emanuele, the nineteenth-century covered shopping center. In addition to a number of old basilicas, Milan houses the Brera Palace and Picture Gallery; the Sforza Palace with its Municipal Museum of Art and adjacent Sempione Park; and the Pirelli tower, Italy's first skyscraper, designed by Pier Luigi Nervi and Gio Ponti. Other important Lombard cities include Como (center of the silk industry), Cremona, Mantua, Pavia (with its famous university), and the industrial centers Bergamo and Brescia.

Trentino-Alto Adige, the Veneto, and Friuli-Venezia Giulia constitute the northeastern regions, sometimes known as the Venetias. Of the four, the

Veneto has traditionally played the most important role in the economic and cultural life of the peninsula, largely because of its major city, Venice (Venezia), unique in its picturesque canals and cafes, its stunning architecture, and its wealth of artistic treasures. Along the Grand Canal are 200 marble palaces, including the Ca d'Oro (golden house), Ca Rezzonico, and Palazzo Pesaro. The canal leads under the Rialto Bridge to the famous Piazza San Marco with its Byzantine-influenced St. Mark's Basilica, Duke's (Doge's) Palace, and the connected Bridge of Sighs. Of architectural and artistic significance are Venice's many churches, including Santa Maria della Salute and San Giorgio Maggiore; and its galleries, especially the Gallerie dell'Accademia, Scuola di San Rocco, and the Peggy Guggenheim Collection of modern painting and sculpture. Although dominating the region culturally and economically, Venice is home to only about 330,000 persons, leaving the Veneto without a city of dominant size.

Among the other important cities of the Veneto are Verona, known for its Roman theater, and Padua (Padova), with its superb university where Dante,

Gondolier, Venice. Courtesy of the author.

Petrarch, Copernicus, and Galileo studied. Spanning the Venetian plain of the eastern Po Valley where the River Po flows to the Adriatic Sea, the Veneto has provided a gate through which trade has for centuries passed between the Mediterranean and northern Europe. The Veneto extends to Lake Garda in the west and into the Alps in its northern reaches. Among its rivers are the Adige, the Tagliamento, and the Po, whose delta forms the Venetian Lagoon, controlled and shaped by the medieval republic of Venice. In the modern era, the Veneto has maintained its traditional economic base of international commerce, fishing, shipbuilding, and tourism, and has more recently developed a number of medium-sized, niche industries (for example, ceramics, glass, furniture, and household appliances).

The Trentino-Alto Adige is a small and sparsely populated, mountainous region dominated by the Dolomite chain and home to a largely Germanic population. Trent (Trento) and Bolzano are the two most important cities, each the capital of a province of the same name. The region of Trent is predominantly Italian-speaking with a commercial economy. The city is home to the Lombard Romanesque Cathedral of San Vergilio where the famous Council of Trent convened in the mid-fifteenth century to restrain Martin Luther's Protestant Reformation. Bolzano, gateway to the Brenner Pass through the Alps, is a bilingual (German- and Italian-speaking) region that has likewise traditionally prospered from trade to northern Europe. The city of Bolzano features two major sites, a Romanesque Gothic duomo and a Dominican Monastery, as well as the Fascist-era Victory Monument designed by Marcello Piacentini.

Friuli-Venezia Giulia lies northeast of Venice, divided by the Tagliamento River that runs from the Alps south through the Friuli plain to the Adriatic Sea. Because of a history of changing national jurisdiction—parts of the region were transferred to Yugoslavia after World War II—the region is one of diverse languages and cultures, with dialects of Venezia, Friuli, and the busy port city of Trieste being spoken. Trieste's economy derives from shipbuilding, shipping, and related industries such as oil refining. The fifth century Basilica of San Giusto rests on the site of a Roman temple on a hill overlooking the busy port. The region's second largest city, Udine, is a rail and road distribution center for trade to Austria and the Balkans.

A large region that virtually crosses the peninsula east to west, Emilia-Romagna derives its name from the Roman road called the Via Emilia. From the broad and fertile Po Valley in the north, Emilia-Romagna rises to the Apennine mountains, connecting north to central Italy, and thus serving as a major hub of road and rail transportation. Known for its bounteous production of wheat, fruits, vegetables, and grapes on an efficient system of cooperative farms, Emilia-Romagna has developed an important industrial base, particularly in processing, packaging, and distribution of foods (Parmigiano-Reggiano cheese, Parma hams), production of automobiles, farm machinery, chemicals, thermonuclear power, and natural gas. Bologna, the region's capital and largest city, is known for its university (founded in the eleventh century, with renowned legal and medical studies), a number of public monuments, and flourishing industrial and commercial sectors. Bologna's most important cultural sites include the imposing Gothic Basilica of San Petronio, dating from the fourteenth century, Giambologna's bronze Neptune fountain, and the Piazza Comunale with its municipal art museum. Other important cities in the region include Ferrara, Modena, Parma, Imola, Piacenza, Reggio nell'Emilia, Rimini, and Ravenna, former capital of the Western Roman, Gothic, and Byzantine empires.

South of Emilia-Romagna is Tuscany (Toscana). A triangular region situated in the center of the peninsula, Tuscany falls from the Apennines in the east through the Maremma marshes to the Tyrrhenian Sea and the islands of the Tuscan archipelago in the west. Most of its rivers (including the Arno, northern Tiber, and Serchio) wind to the Tyrrhenian and are not navigable for long distances. One of Italy's most heavily wooded and mineral-rich regions, Tuscany also is intensely cultivated in many areas, with vineyards and silvery olive groves partitioning the gently sloping hills of the Chianti district and the Val d'Arno. In addition to the chemical, textile, and metallurgical industries, crafts such as woodworking flourish alongside banking and tourism. The region's medieval hill towns, many of Etruscan origin, attract tourists, as do its cities, famous for their Renaissance art.

Florence (Firenze) is Tuscany's most important city, particularly because of its wealth of art and architecture. Notable among Florentine public spaces are the Piazza del Duomo (Santa Maria del Fiore), the Piazza della Signoria (with its Palazzo Vecchio), numerous palaces, including the Pitti, the Medici-Riccardi, the Strozzi, the Uffizi (with its museum) and the Rucellai; and the churches of San Lorenzo (with Michelangelo's Laurentian Library and Medici Chapels), Santa Spirito, Santa Maria Novella, San Marco, Santa Croce, Santa Maria del Carmine (with its elegant Brancacci Chapel) and the Basilica of San Miniato al Monte. Among Tuscany's other prominent cities are Arezzo, Livorno, Lucca, Pisa, Pistoia, and Siena. Tuscany has provided an abundance of distinguished artists, particularly of the Renaissance era, including Leonardo da Vinci and Michelangelo Buonarroti.

Umbria is a small, landlocked, wooded region in the center of Italy north of Rome whose green hills roll from the Apennine range in the east across the valley of the Tiber River to the west. Near the northern border with Tuscany is Lake Trasimene, Italy's fourth largest and the site of a famous ancient battle. Traditionally a region known for agricultural production, especially of

Coppersmith, Montepulciano, Tuscany. Courtesy of the author.

wheat, sugar beets, tobacco, and truffles, Umbria boasts industrial development, particularly the steel, chemical, and textile plants of Terni and the
famous pottery of Deruta. The capital of Umbria is Perugia, a hill town and
market center with a well-known university. It boasts a Gothic cathedral of
San Lorenzo and the Piazza of November 4th, with its Pisano fountain, Pri-
ors' Palace, and National Gallery of Umbria. Other Umbrian cities are Assisi
(with its Basilica of St. Francis), Gubbio, Spoleto (known for its Festival of
Two Worlds), and Todi.

The Marches (Le Marche) is a small region that follows the rugged eastern slopes of the Apennine range down to the Adriatic Sea. Largely mountainous, it includes a coastal plain and a series of seaside towns that attract
tourists to its beaches. Ancona, the regional capital, is a busy port that
houses shipbuilding, fishing, chemical, and metallurgical industries.
Ancona's sites of cultural interest include its Cathedral of San Ciriaco, a
fifteenth-century Merchants' Loggia with a Venetian Gothic facade, its

Medieval tower, hill town in the Chianti district.
Courtesy of the author.

Arch of Trajan, and the National Museum of the Marches in the Palazzo Ferretti.

Lazio or Latium is a region in central Italy stretching from the Apennine range in the east to the coastal plain of the Tyrrhenian Sea and dominated by the city of Rome. Its major river, the Tiber, flows into the Tyrrhenian. Although farming and various industries contribute to the economies of the region, they are overshadowed by the economic influence of Rome as a tourist attraction and a center of administration for both the national government and the Roman Catholic Church. Founded by the Latins on an ancient site on the banks of the Tiber in the eighth century BC, Rome is Italy's largest city at about 2.6 million inhabitants.

The city attracts throngs of tourists to its numerous architectural marvels: magnificent classical buildings, including the Colosseum (Flavian Amphithe-

Courtyard in Florence. Courtesy of the author.

ater), the Pantheon, the Foro Romano, the *fori imperiali* (imperial forums), the Campidoglio, the Ara Pacis Augustae, the Castel Sant'Angelo (tomb of Hadrian), the baths of Caracalla and Diocletian, the Theater of Marcellus, the arches of Titus, Septimius Severus, and Constantine; the palaces *(palazzi)* of the Farnese, Barberini, Borghese, and Farnesina; striking public spaces, including the Piazza di Spagna, Piazza Navona, Piazza S. Pietro, and the Trevi fountain; and renowned churches, including S. Giovanni in Laterano, S. Maria Maggiore, St. Paul Outside the Walls, and, the most celebrated, St. Peter's Basilica. Other cities of Lazio include Tivoli, Albano Laziale, Rieti, Viterbo, Frascati, and the ports of Civitavecchia and Ostia.

The Abruzzi (or Abruzzo) is a sparsely populated, mountainous region that falls along sharp ridges from the highest peaks in the Apennine range down its eastern slopes to the sandy coast of the Adriatic. The rivers of the Abruzzi, including the Sangro and the Vomano, flow into the Adriatic. Traditionally a

Della Robia rondel, Pistoia Hospital. Courtesy of the author.

region of small farming (vegetables, olives, and grapes), the Abruzzi has diversified by developing chemical, clothing, and tourist industries. Notable towns of the Abruzzi are L'Aquila and Pescara. The economy of L'Aquila is based on a thriving crafts sector and the marketing of agricultural products. Its architectural highlights include the fifteenth-century Basilica, a Castle (or "Spanish fort") that houses the National Museum of the Abruzzi, and the popular Fountain of the 99 Chambers.

Molise was, until 1963, part of the Abruzzi. A poor and isolated region dominated by the southern Apennine range, Molise descends to the Adriatic coast but is devoid of a natural harbor. It depends on agriculture, very little of it commercial, a large service sector, and some tourism along the Adriatic beaches. The capital of the region is Campobasso, an agricultural center that boasts several churches, especially the Romanesque San Giorgio, the baroque San Antonio Abate, and the neoclassical Santissima Trinità.

Campania spans an arc along the Tyrrhenian Sea from Gaeta and the Bay of Naples south along the Gulf of Salerno and east to the slopes of the Apennines. The economy of Campania, traditionally based on agriculture and seafaring commerce, has become industrialized along the coastal plain, producing chemicals, processed food, and textiles. Also important is the tourist traffic to such renowned retreats as Sorrento, Amalfi, and the islands of Ischia and Capri, and to the numerous sites that feature architectural remains from the classical era, particularly Paestum and Pompeii.

The history and character of Campania are largely explained by the menacing presence of Vesuvius, one of the world's best-known and most-feared volcanoes, and by the dominance of its densely populated capital, Naples. Naples features an abundance of architectural wonders. The Castel Nuovo is a thirteenth-century fortification surrounded by a moat and entered through a triumphal arch. The Teatro San Carlo is among Italy's best known opera houses. The Capodimonte palace houses Naples's national gallery, featuring works by Titian, Caravaggio, Simone Martini, and Rosso Fiorentino. Collections from Egypt and Pompeii are found in the National Archaeological Museum.

Apulia, Basilicata, and Calabria make up the heel and toe of the Italian boot. Apulia (Puglia) extends narrowly along the Adriatic coast from the promontory of Gargano, along wide, sandy beaches, and past many harbors, including the capital, Bari, and the port city of Brindisi, south along the Salentine peninsula to the Gulf of Taranto. Bari features the Basilica of St. Nicholas, a Romanesque structure begun in the eleventh century, a Romanesque cathedral, an archaeological museum, and the important Laterza publishing house.

The region includes two main rivers, the Fortore and the Ofanto, two large coastal lakes, Lesina and Varano, and extensive caves. The Apulian economy still relies largely on agriculture, especially vegetables, grapes, and olives, irrigated by an extensive aqueduct, and farmed largely by urban populations. The region has industrialized, particularly in the southern "triangle" of Bari-Taranto-Brindisi where steel and chemicals prevail. Tourism has become important, not only drawing vacationers to the Adriatic beaches, but to the interesting interior, and particularly to Alberobello, which contains the unique, ancient, white circular dwellings called *trulli*.

Basilicata (or Lucania) is a small, mountainous region of high pastures and chestnut forests that spans the peninsula from the Tyrrhenian to the Ionian Seas. Its predominantly agricultural economy leaves it sparsely populated and well below the national average in income. The province of Matera has begun to develop industrially, particularly in chemicals. The capital, Potenza, perched high above the Basento River, remains largely an agricultural center. Potenza features its annual "procession of the Turks," a celebration of a miraculous intervention by its patron, St. Gerardo, to save the city from a Muslim invasion. The thirteenth-century duomo is dedicated to the patron saint.

Calabria is the narrow region south of Basilicata (and similar in many ways) that curves in a wooded, mountainous arc between the Ionian and Tyrrhenian Seas along the "toe" of the Italian boot, divided from Sicily by the

Strait of Messina. The region boasts sandy beaches and unspoiled seas along both coasts, each of which is home to numerous seaside resorts. The largely agricultural Calabrian economy, known for its grapes and olives, provides the lowest per capita income of the 20 regions and boasts very few manufacturing enterprises. The major cities of Calabria are Catanzaro, Cosenza, and Reggio di Calabria, wedged between the Aspromonte range and the Strait of Messina and rebuilt after the destructive earthquake of 1908. Catanzaro is famous for its silk industry. Of interest are its church of San Domenico and duomo, dedicated to the Assumption of the Virgin.

Sicily (Sicilia) is the largest of the Mediterranean islands and, when the Aeolian islands are included (Lipari, Ustica, Egadi, Pantelleria, and Pelagie), Sicily is Italy's largest region. Separated from the mainland by the Strait of Messina, Sicily is dominated by the resurgent Apennines and Mount Etna, Europe's largest volcano. The region's rich history reflects a succession of conquerors, leaving a wealth of architectural and artistic treasures that include some of the best preserved Greek buildings on earth. Sicily is the fourth most populous of Italy's regions, densest in the coastal cities of Palermo, Messina, Catania, and Siracusa and the inland areas around Agrigento and Licata. Traditionally relying on the production of wheat and citrus, Sicily has diversified by producing petrochemicals and pharmaceuticals. Tourists are attracted to Sicily's many beaches, inland mountains, and numerous historical sites. Sicily's major cities include Palermo, with its active port and its many notable churches and public buildings; Agrigento, home to spectacular Greek monuments; Catania and its agricultural market at the foot of Mount Etna; the important port of Messina; and the southeastern ancient Greek city of Siracusa, now a bustling port.

Palermo, Sicily's capital and primary port, offers a wealth of architectural and artistic gems. Central Palermo includes the Piazza Pretoria with its dramatic fountain and the Piazza Bellini, with two twelfth-century structures, the Martorana and the church of San Cataldo. The Norman Palace (now the home of the Sicilian Parliament) houses the Arab-Norman Palatine Chapel and the garden of the Villa Bonanno. The twelfth-century Zisa castle provides another example of Arab-Norman architecture. Palermo's Teatro Massimo dates from the seventeenth century and remains a majestic opera house.

Sardinia (Sardegna) is the second largest island in the Mediterranean, resting in the Tyrrhenian and Sardinian Seas, divided by the Strait of Bonaficio from the French island of Corsica to the north. Dominated by the Gennargentu mountains (peaking at over 6,000 feet), Sardinia is an autonomous region that still relies on agriculture, sheep herding, and cheese and wine production, along with newer industries and its tourist trade that thrives along the northern Costa Smeralda. Also of interest to tourists as well as scholars are the inland archaeological sites featuring the *nuraghi,* conical, stone structures that date from the ancient period. For reasons of its history and topography, the larger population centers are found inland, especially around Cagliari and Sassari. Cagliari is the capital, a busy southern seaport founded by Carthaginians that is home to a number of important architectural sites, including its Cathedral of Santa Maria di Castello, the fifth-century Basilica of San Saturnino, and a Roman amphitheater. To the north of the island is the city of Sassari, which thrives particularly as a center for agricultural exchange.

THE PEOPLE

In spite of a legacy of localized traditions, the people of Italy rank among the more homogeneous national groups on the European continent, particularly in terms of language, national origin, and religion. Although dialects vary and the question of the language *(la questione della lingua)* has persisted since the age of Dante, well over 90 percent speak Italian as their first language and about 98 percent of the population is literate. However, as many as 60 percent of Italians continue to use one of the many dialects. In the home, about one-quarter of Italians use both the Italian language and a dialect, while another quarter use a dialect almost exclusively. Among the dialects are Sicilian *(siciliano),* Venetian *(veneto),* Sardinian *(sardo),* Apulian *(pugliese),* Calabrian *(calabrese),* Tuscan *(toscano),* Lombard *(lombardo),* and numerous others. Small pockets of obscure dialects exist as well, some surviving from the ancient and medieval eras. An example would be a Bavarian dialect still spoken in several villages in the Veneto region. In Sardinia, for example, there exist several dialects, but most would be able to speak *sardo* as well as the Italian language. An example of variations in dialect might be the spelling and pronunciation of *andiamo* ("let's go"), first person plural of the verb *andare* ("to go"). Florentines, speakers of standard Italian, would say *"andiamo";* Venetians, *"andemo";* and Piedmontese, *"anduma."*[1]

There also exist a number of regional variants of the Italian language; in other words the national language is marked with distinct regional variations in pronunciation, spelling, and syntax. Since the early fourteenth century when Dante provided Italians with a common vernacular language, Florentine Italian has generally been favored as the literary language and has enjoyed a superior status as a model for pronunciation. However, even Florentine displays its regional earmarks. For example, Florentines will often emphatically substitute the "h" for the hard "c" before a vowel at the beginning of a word, so that *casa* (house) becomes *hasa.* Such usage is often situational and exaggerated. A Florentine might emphasize the aspirate "h" among local friends,

Friends and Pastore Maremmano (sheepdog), San Casciano, Tuscany.
Courtesy of the author.

but shift to the "c" pronunciation in a more cosmopolitan setting. Recently,
because of television and the infusion of technological terms, the linguistic
forms of Milan and Rome have challenged Tuscan for the claim to be the new
national standard. All of the Italian dialects are Romance languages, deriving
from Latin, and can be mutually understood. Scholars of language sometimes
argue that a language such as Italian differs in status from dialects and
regional variants only because one form has been chosen as the official language of the nation. [2]

As a result of immigration patterns and the shifting of northern boundaries
over time, several million Italian citizens speak as their first language something other than Italian. These are not dialects, but linguistic minorities. For
example, Slovenians from the former Yugoslavia inhabit the northeast;
Greeks and Albanians are scattered through the southeast; and French- and
German-speaking minorities, their rights protected in the Republic's consti-

tution, inhabit the Valle d'Aosta and Alto Adige, respectively. Furthermore, recent immigration has begun to diversify the nation and its language. Among the new immigrants to Italy, North Africans (primarily Moroccans and Tunisians), Albanians, and former Yugoslavs dominate, with smaller numbers of other Europeans, North Americans, sub-Saharan Africans, Asians, and Pacific Islanders making up a population of approximately 1.3 million foreign residents.[3] Increased rates of immigration and higher birth rates among immigrant communities, combined with extremely low birth rates among Italians, suggest that long-term trends will diversify the nation even more.

As a convincing indication of religious homogeneity, recent statistics suggest that 85 percent of Italians profess themselves Roman Catholics, although only about 35 percent attend mass regularly. The Church retains a significant place in local customs, particularly because of saints' days and such rituals as baptism, first communion, and marriage. Ironically, in a nation whose history has been so dominated by the Vatican, many Italians have maintained a uniquely skeptical attitude toward the organized Church, particularly with respect to papal decrees on such issues as birth control, divorce, and abortion.

THE HISTORY

Italy is distinguished by a long and glorious past dominated by Romans and the city states of the medieval and Renaissance eras. The history of Italy dates from at least the second millennium BC when various groups of Indo-European peoples migrated across the Mediterranean Sea to settle in villages in the Po River valley and along the coasts of the peninsula and the nearby islands. The great cultural diversity of the peninsula included Greeks who settled on the Adriatic coast and in eastern Sicily by the eighth century BC and Celts who crossed the Alps into northern Italy two centuries later. Of all the non-Indo-European speaking peoples, the Etruscans stand out because of their great influence. A people of obscure origin, the Etruscans had developed an advanced civilization that by the eighth century BC began to dominate the hill towns of central Italy between the present-day cities of Florence and Rome. Although they never unified the region politically, the Etruscans did introduce a degree of cultural unity in their art work, aristocratic social structure, language, technology, customs, and economic systems.

Italian history reached another turning point when the Etruscans extended their influence to the eventual site of Rome. Ideally located amid the hills next to an island in the Tiber River, along the natural "salt route" that crossed the region of Latium, the site had been inhabited since before 1000 BC. According to ancient myth, brothers Romulus and Remus founded Rome in

753 BC. Archaic Rome was ruled by a series of kings said to be four Etruscans followed by three Romans. One of the Etruscans, Tarquin the Proud, helped to make Rome the largest and most important city in the central peninsula. In doing so, Tarquin so abused his power that a group of Roman aristocrats banished him from the city.

In the place of King Tarquin, the Romans developed a political system that became the Roman Republic. It featured two consuls and a series of magistrates who served one-year terms. Through much of the first century of the Roman Republic, a class conflict known as the "struggle of the orders" pitted the plebeians, the lower order or class, against the dominant patrician aristocracy whose interests were represented by the Senate. The plebeians won a series of concessions, including a written legal code (the Twelve Tables, 450 BC) and the right to marry patricians.

While the plebs were gaining concessions, Romans were busy fighting to maintain order in the surrounding area, threatened by tyrants and private armies. Although Romans extended their power throughout much of the south and center of the peninsula, Samnites, Sabines, and other Iron Age peoples repeatedly imperiled the peace. In the fourth century, Gallic invaders swept south to Latium. At the river Allia in 390, the Gauls delivered the first major defeat to a Roman army, then proceeded to sack the city.

Once recovered, the Romans extended their influence through much of the peninsula in a series of more aggressive military campaigns of the fourth and third centuries. When their legions defeated the Samnites and the Tarantines and took the Greek cities of the south by 260 BC, Rome solidified control of virtually the entire peninsula, which they began to refer to, for the first time, as "Italia." The victorious Romans acquired slaves as captives in military victories, and the growing slave population led to the development of larger estates, owned by aristocrats, displacing many small farmers and driving them to the city to join the ranks of the plebs.

In 264 BC, Rome fought Carthage in the first of three Punic (Phoenician) Wars that began when Carthage challenged Roman expansion in order to protect its commercial holdings. In 219, after extended conflict, the Carthaginian general Hannibal invaded Italy from Spain, using his elephants to cross the Pyrenees and Alps into northern Italy. Hannibal won numerous engagements, but he failed to wrest the allegiance of the conquered peoples from the Romans. In 211, the Romans began a campaign of retaliation that culminated in the decisive victory by Roman general "Scipio Africanus" at the Battle of Zama in 202. In the Third Punic War in 149, the Romans destroyed Carthage, took a North African province, expanded to the Balkans, and added provinces in Asia and southern Gaul. Julius Caesar won all of Gaul 50 years later in a series of military conquests. In 30 BC, Octavian added Egypt as a province by winning the Battle of Actium, providing Rome the largest and longest-lasting empire in history.

The celebrated military victories and the great wealth they afforded in turn brought major changes. Roman generals and the Senate basked in newly won prestige. At the same time, the spoils of victory overwhelmed the primitive Roman economy as enormous amounts of gold inflated prices and several hundred thousand new slaves drove down wages. Many peasants, displaced by slave labor, drifted to cities in search of work, while the middle class of businessmen and bankers grew in response to opportunities provided by the new wealth. The growth of an urban lower class in turn created new economic demands. When the Gracchus brothers sponsored radical land reform, both were considered serious threats by conservatives in the Senate. In 133 BC, a mob loyal to the Senate killed Tiberius Gracchus; his brother Gaius and 3,000 supporters met a similar fate 12 years later.

The violence surrounding the land reform campaign was accompanied by numerous slave revolts. While Roman legions were busy quelling the slave revolts, most notably the one led by Spartacus, the "Social Wars" of 91–88 BC erupted in the provinces as non-Roman citizens demanded full rights. These widespread disturbances paved the way for a number of ambitious generals to enter the political scene, each armed with battle-hardened, loyal legions. Among the generals were Marius, Sulla, Pompey, and Julius Caesar.

Marius and Sulla in turn seized power, until Sulla's eventual retirement led to a power struggle among three generals—Pompey, Crassus, and Julius Caesar—who formed a secret Triumvirate in 60 BC. While Caesar was leading his legions through Gaul, Crassus died on a military campaign in Asia in 53. When Caesar heard that Pompey and the Senate had stripped him of power, he marched his troops from Gaul across the river Rubicon to Rome, pursuing Pompey as he retreated and defeating him at Pharsalus in Greece. After campaigning through Egypt and annexing new territory, Caesar returned triumphantly to Rome where the Senate, in 46 BC, reluctantly made him dictator for 10 years.

When Caesar consolidated his power by taking numerous offices for himself and accepting the loftiest honors, the Senate regarded him as arrogant and as a threat to revolutionize Rome. Members of the Senatorial faction plotted against Caesar, and on the Ides of March (March 15) 44 BC, a group of conspirators including Cassius and Brutus stabbed Caesar to death, shouting that they had restored the Roman Republic. In fact, what followed were 13 more years of civil conflict.

Caesar was succeeded in power by his young grand nephew, heir, and adopted son, Octavian. After participating in the Second Triumvirate to bring stability, Octavian convinced the Senate to remove Antony. The next year, 31 BC, Octavian defeated the Egyptian fleet at the Battle of Actium and pursued Antony and Cleopatra to Egypt where in 30 BC both committed suicide. When he added Egypt as a province, Octavian—or Augustus as he would be known when the Senate conferred that honorary title—returned to Rome to consolidate his power there, already in command of much of the Mediterranean region.

Augustus reigned for 44 years, during which he presided over a restructuring of the Roman Empire in the name of the virtues and values of the old Republic. He called the product of his reforms the Principate, and he called himself *princeps,* or "first among citizens." While strengthening his grip on power, Augustus launched an ambitious program of urban reforms, building and repairing temples, roads, theaters, markets, aqueducts, and a drainage system. At the same time, he addressed the needs of the local population by managing the distribution of food and providing entertainment at the new amphitheater.

To buttress his power, Augustus assembled a huge professional military force of 60 legions that engaged in peacekeeping operations in Africa, Asia, the Rhine and Danube frontiers, the Alps, and the Adriatic coast. At its height, Augustus's Principate included perhaps 50 million people and provided the Mediterranean world with an extended period of peace and prosperity known as the *pax Romana.*

Augustus was succeeded by a series of dynasties: The Julio-Claudians, AD 14–68; the Flavians, AD 68–96; and the Antonines, AD 96–192. Although the Julio-Claudians followed Augustus's policies, all of them ruled in the name of the Roman Empire, abandoning Augustus's deference to the Senate and to the old Republic. The military became even more active, interfering regularly in the political process, and only one, Claudius, ruled with distinction.

The emperors presided over numerous religious groups, including the emperor cult, the mystery cults, Jews, and Christians. Although discriminated against, Jews reached an agreement of coexistence with Roman authorities. Such was not the case with Christians, who were viewed by Romans of the first century as a greater political threat. In about 30 BC, Pontius Pilate, the prefect of the Palestinian province of Judea, tried and executed Jesus. Jesus's followers redoubled their commitment, while Roman authorities continued to regard them as a new, exotic sect until the emperor Nero singled them out for abuse.

The suicide of the cruel, young tyrant Nero in AD 67 plunged Rome back into civil war. The emergence of the 60-year-old general Vespasian 18 months later marked the advent of the Flavian dynasty (AD 68–96). Vespasian's sons Titus and Domitian followed him, the latter winning notoriety as an abusive tyrant. After the murder of Domitian, the general Trajan established the

Antonine dynasty (AD 96–192), destined to restore respect to the emperors and extend peace to the Empire. After Trajan had established a superb reputation for governing, his great nephew Hadrian introduced a series of reforms and tightened Rome's provincial government. His design and construction of the Pantheon reflected great advances in Roman public architecture and building methods in the Antonine era. Antoninus Pius sustained the dynasty's reputation for wisdom in governing while abolishing most anti-Semitic policies. His successor, Marcus Aurelius, a philosopher of peace, ironically found himself drawn into ominous warfare on a wide-ranging front, from northern Italy, to the Rhine and Danube rivers, to North Africa.

Marcus Aurelius's death in 180 left the government in the hands of his degenerate son, Commodus, whose own murder in 192 led to a deepening crisis and ultimately to what has been called "the fall of the Roman Empire" in the West. By the mid-third century, much of the centralized political structure had broken down in Italy, replaced by less formal, more localized cultures influenced by the immigrating Germanic tribes. Prosperity declined as well, reducing many areas to subsistence levels. Meanwhile, disturbances on the frontiers forced Roman legions to fight both Germanic tribes and Persian armies, in turn intensifying political instability in Rome as armies overthrew emperor after emperor.

After a century of conflict and decay, the emperors Diocletian and Constantine introduced a range of administrative and economic reforms that breathed new life into the Empire. Included were Constantine's religious reforms, legalizing Christianity, and discriminating against Jews. Most important was Constantine's shift of the capital eastward to the city he bestowed with his name: Constantinople. The Byzantine Empire (as it was now called) would prosper and endure for 1,000 years, while in the west, Italy would be reduced to the level of a province like Gaul or Spain.

The fourth century brought some mild economic recovery to the peninsula, while a number of cities enjoyed a degree of cultural renewal. As the Christian Church expanded, cathedrals often added schools, so that classical language and literature were nurtured. In the second half of the century, the emperor Valentinian moved the capital of the west from Rome to Milan.

When Roman political power dispersed in the period known as the Middle Ages or medieval era, the peninsula began to develop along decentralized lines that we now recognize as Italian. Political power would not again be unified throughout Italy for more than 1,400 years. In a number of urban areas, a middle class of merchants and bankers emerged to dominate the cities and their environs. Especially important was the rise in central and northern Italy of the autonomous communes that maintained commercial activity. Among the most active in international trade were the port cities of Venice, Genoa, and Pisa.

The bulk of the peninsula was subjected to a series of outside conquerors—Ostrogoths, Lombards, and Franks. In the same period, the Church organized around the Bishop of Rome as pope (father of the Church) and became an international force. People living in Medieval Italy did not yet use the term "Italy" and did not think of themselves as "Italian"; their identities and loyalties remained local.

The seizure of power in 476 by the Germanic king Odoacer marked the end of the Roman Empire. Thirteen years later the Ostrogoths claimed power in the peninsula, only to be defeated and displaced by the troops of the Byzantine emperor Justinian in 536. In the process, Justinian subjected Italy to devastating warfare, famine, and chaos, leaving the place so weakened and defenseless that a Lombard force of mounted warriors swept down from the north and overwhelmed Italy in 568. Unable to govern, the Lombards abandoned the Roman aqueducts, drainage systems, and roads.

When Pope Stephen II protested Lombard expansion, Pippin III, King of the Franks, led a campaign to drive the Lombards out of northeastern Italy and granted to the pope the territory that would constitute the Papal States. When the Lombards violated the settlement, the Frankish chieftain Charlemagne invaded in 773, took the Lombard capital of Pavia, and declared himself king of the Lombards. His successors in the Carolingian dynasty claimed much of northern and central Italy for about 150 years until the German king Otto I crossed the Alps in 951 and proclaimed himself king of Italy. The Germanic kings would maintain weak and uneven control until about the year 1000.

In the medieval south, Byzantine emperors controlled political power. Many of the ports now served as hubs of international trade throughout the Mediterranean, while small farming prevailed inland. Arab forces invaded Sicily in 827 and advanced to the southern mainland in the 840s. Sicily thrived under Arab rule until the Byzantine counterattack at the end of the century drove them out and essentially returned southern cities to local autonomy.

The revival of trade by the mid-eleventh century and the related development of the northern communes set Italy apart from much of Europe and spurred the general expansion of the European economy that would follow. In turn, prosperity led to the growth of population, freeing some peasants to migrate to the cities, drawn by new opportunity. The communes threw off imperial control and gained autonomy, usually dominated by a newly prosperous class of merchants, bankers, and lawyers at the expense of the bishops and counts who had previously dominated. However, the communal system proved unstable and particularly vulnerable to challenges from within, as rival families built fortified towers and fought openly in the streets.

The resurgent medieval German (or Holy Roman) Empire forced the Italian communes to cooperate. When Frederick I (*Barbarossa*) invaded northern Italy and destroyed Milan in 1162, the northern communes banded together in the Lombard League and defeated Frederick at the Battle of Legnano (1176), forcing the Holy Roman Emperor to concede the autonomy of the communes in the Peace of Constance (1182).

By the twelfth and thirteenth centuries economic expansion gave rise to significant developments in Italian cities. Merchants, tradesmen, and professionals organized guilds that influenced the politics of the communes. The guilds, in turn, encouraged the broadening of political participation in the name of the *popolo* ("the people," or ordinary town folk). Universities such as the renowned University of Bologna developed to shape a secular culture, derived from Roman sources, that laid the groundwork for the emergence of the Renaissance. By the middle of the thirteenth century most communes organized as republics, each dominated by a chief executive *(podestà)*.

By the second quarter of the thirteenth century, the expansion campaign of *Barbarossa's* grandson, Emperor Frederick II, ran afoul of Popes Gregory IX and Innocent IV. Frederick II launched an invasion from his home in Sicily, provoking an extended conflict with the popes that spread to northern cities. In each city, factions battled: Guelphs backed the pope; Ghibellines supported the emperor. The Guelphs generally prevailed, except in the Romagna. At the Battle of Benevento in 1266, the French armies of Charles of Anjou, supporting Pope Urban IV, defeated the German armies of Manfred, illegitimate son of Frederick II. The failures of Frederick and Manfred ended the attempt to impose unity on the Italian peninsula until the Piedmontese succeeded in doing so 600 years later.

What survived in Italy as the medieval era drew to a close was a cultural pattern that might be recognized as Italian. In contrast with much of Europe where the system of rural manors prevailed, an urban culture thrived in Italy, dominated by an aristocracy whose influence came from banking and trade with the outside world. Italy remained connected with its classical roots, not just in formal education, but in the more tangible presence of Roman roads, ports, and law. Education and literacy spread as the economy grew, providing the means to support the emergence of a substantially new culture known as the Renaissance.

During the fourteenth and fifteenth centuries, Italian artists, architects, and writers turned to classical themes for inspiration, while Italian writers began to use a formal language modeled after the writing of the Florentine poet Dante Alighieri. A transitional figure born in the medieval era, Dante penned the epic masterpiece *Divine Comedy* (c. 1320), which anticipated the Renaissance in its language and its criticism of the politics of the church.

Dante's writing also reflects the turmoil of his native Florence from which he was forced into exile in 1301. The political conflict of Dante's Florence exemplified widespread power struggles in many northern and central cities, as aristocratic despots known as *signori* seized power, usually supported by leading local merchants. As the German emperors lost interest in conquering Italy, *signori* such as the Visconti family in Milan, the Medici in Florence, and the Este in Ferrara strengthened their hold on cities throughout the peninsula. At the same time, popes lost much of their power through political partisanship. In 1305, the new French pontiff, Clement V, moved the papacy to Avignon where it remained until 1377 when Pope Gregory XI returned to Rome, ending the period known as the "Babylonian Captivity." The disputed election of Pope Urban VI in 1378 prompted the selection of a second pope, Clement VII. For 35 years, the Church remained split in the "Great Schism" until reunified at the Council of Constance.

The famine, plague, and warfare that engulfed much of Europe by the mid-fourteenth century hit Italy hard, especially because its cities had been growing and prospering as commercial and banking centers for 200 years. As conflict disrupted trade, food prices soared and hunger spread, weakening the population to the pandemic known as the "Black Death," which ravaged the continent and spread through Italy in 1347–48, killing perhaps one-third of its population. Afterward, plagues recycled through the peninsula, striking Florence eight times before the end of the fifteenth century. As a result, the economy suffered, the *signori* generally tightened their grip on political power, and religious changes swept through the peninsula as Italians despaired. Most notably, the number of Dominican and Franciscan preaching friars increased, as did the growth of confraternities committed to civic charity.

By 1400, as fighting among them continued, five Renaissance city-states dominated the peninsula: Milan and Venice in the north; Florence in the north-center; the Papal States in the center; and the Kingdom of Naples in the south. Each city assembled a fighting force including some combination of a communal army, supporters of the bishop, leading nobles, local guilds, and mercenaries paid by revenues from taxation. By the second half of the century, Turkish aggression and the heavy toll taken by the warfare drove the five cities to create the Italian League at the Peace of Lodi (1454).

In each case the *signori* provided patronage that financed Renaissance artists. Best known are the Medici of Florence, the Visconti of Milan, and several popes, including Leo X (son of Lorenzo "the Magnificent" de' Medici),

Julius III, and Pius IV, known respectively for their support of the artists
Raphael and Michelangelo. In Florence, the Medici also supported the brilliant Renaissance humanist writer Pico della Mirandola, while local cloth
merchants commissioned Brunelleschi's design and construction of the
famous duomo (cathedral). The prosperity of Florence and its patronage for
painters, architects, and sculptors brought the city to the height of Renaissance brilliance in the fifteenth century. Among other notable Florentines of
the Renaissance were Leonardo, Masaccio, Donatello, Ghiberti, Ghirlandaio,
Piero della Francesca, Michelozzo, and the writer Niccolò Machiavelli. In
The Prince (1513), Machiavelli boldly rejected the conventions of humanism
in favor of a more modern analysis of power and thus represents a transition
from the Renaissance to the early modern era.

By 1500, political changes moved the focus of the Renaissance from Florence to Rome. The Medici family's loss of power combined with the moralistic campaign by the Dominican preacher Savanarola drove artists and
intellectuals such as Leonardo, Michelangelo, and Raphael to Rome where
the Vatican offered generous subsidies. Pope Julius II commissioned
Michelangelo to paint the ceiling of the Sistine Chapel, and Julius's successor,
Leo X, appointed Raphael chief architect of St. Peter's Basilica.

In 1494, French armies of King Charles VIII invaded northern Italy,
beginning the Italian Wars, a half century of assaults on Italian territory.
From Milan, the French moved south, challenging the Spanish and the
papacy and forcing them into a coalition. The French were badly beaten in
1513 at the Battle of Novara and again in 1525 at the Battle of Pavia, the
most important single engagement in the half century of warfare. In 1529,
the Treaty of Cambrai made Charles V king of Italy, affirming Spanish control of much of the peninsula. After several other failed campaigns, the
French abandoned Italy except for the city of Turin, bringing to a close the
damaging Italian Wars.

The French invasions proved disruptive in many ways. Other invaders followed, slowing economic and political progress and subjecting Italians to two
centuries of foreign occupation. By the mid-sixteenth century, Spain had
established control of Sicily, Naples, Sardinia, and Lombardy, and indirect
control of much of the remaining peninsula. The Spanish Empire would
maintain this dominance for 150 years during which conditions generally
worsened because of warfare, economic recession, the smothering influence
of the Catholic Counter Reformation, and the conservative cultural values
brought by Spanish aristocrats.

In the first half of the seventeenth century, conflict raged, especially in
northern Italy. As a result, the banking, textile manufacturing, shipbuilding,
and agricultural sectors further deteriorated, forcing Italian merchants to

import finished products from northern Europe, while exporting raw materials, olive oil, and wine. Suffering spread, the plague returned, and population declined. In the rural areas, aristocrats acquired more land, reducing small landholders to tenant farmers and day laborers. Farming techniques relapsed, lowering productivity and forcing Italians to import grain.

By the eighteenth century, shifts in European diplomacy began to alter patterns of foreign presence in the Italian peninsula. In the Treaty of Aix-la-Chapelle (1748), the European powers created a formula that helped to stabilize the area. The Austrians displaced the Spanish in northern Italy and reached a rough equilibrium with their French rivals for about a half century. This rivalry enabled the Piedmontese to attain the status of a sovereign kingdom (1713) and to acquire the island of Sardinia (1720) and the western part of the Duchy of Milan (1748). It was largely the Piedmontese drive for expansion that led the dukes (now kings) of Savoy to promote reforms designed to acquire vast amounts of uncultivated and untaxed land. The Savoy dynasty modernized schools and provided protective tariffs for Piedmontese businesses, in turn feeding the king's revenues and enabling him to strengthen his government and his army.

Like the Piedmontese dynasty, the Austrian Habsburgs promoted reforms in their own interest. Enlightenment ideas spread through northern and central Italy, particularly in Lombardy, Tuscany, and in the cities of Bologna, Modena, and Parma. In contrast, the Papal States remained commercially and agriculturally retarded. In the southern Kingdom of the Two Sicilies (Naples and Sicily), a number of Italian intellectuals of the Enlightenment *(Illuministi)* advocated fundamental reforms in the face of staunch tradition. After limited success, the reformers encountered stiff resistance when the French Revolution frightened the King of the Two Sicilies into abandoning his support for even moderate reform.

The French Revolution of 1789 and its Napoleonic aftermath provided Italy the first significant opportunity to achieve both domestic reform and national unification. Initial Italian enthusiasm for the French Revolution waned as the movement radicalized in late 1792. The spread of war between France and the Austrian coalition spilled into Italy, disrupting the extended peace. In 1796, the French dispatched the Corsican general Napoleon Bonaparte into northern Italy where he defeated Piedmontese and Austrian forces and established French power. In the Treaty of Campo Formio, France affirmed its control of northern Italy, in turn handing Venezia to the Austrians. By 1798, Napoleon had divided all of Italy north of Naples into three republics, driving the pope into exile. Committed to using Italy and its resources to support his military campaigns, Napoleon suppressed revolutionary fervor while centralizing his administration. In the interest of effi-

ciency, Napoleon swept aside many medieval traditions, including many of
the church's privileges and title to much of its land.

After seizing and consolidating power in France, Napoleon renewed his
military campaign by defeating Austrian troops in a series of battles and forcing the Austrians to relinquish northern Italy to France in the Treaty of
Lunéville (February 1801). Until Napoleon abdicated in 1814, he controlled
the entire Italian peninsula (except for Sicily and Sardinia). By imposing
sweeping reforms in administration, infrastructure, education, and civil law,
Napoleon created new opportunities for economic development and an
expanded middle class. However, his heavy-handed methods, military con-
scription, and reintroduction of the death penalty alienated many Italians.

During the Napoleonic era, Italian nationalism appeared in a number of
guises, some inspired by the nationalism of the French Revolution, some
reacting against Napoleon's autocratic methods. The most important was the
Carboneria, whose members were called *carbonari,* a name probably derived
from their habit of meeting secretly in caves around charcoal fires. A number
of Italian writers advocated forms of nationalism as well, but Napoleon's
defeat in Russia and his abdication in April 1814 dealt a serious setback to the
nationalists' efforts by enabling the Austrian foreign minister, Prince Klemens
von Metternich, to restore the old rulers to power and to snuff out nationalist movements.

After the Congress of Vienna of 1814–15, Metternich managed to establish either direct or indirect control of most of the peninsula. However,
because the Savoy dynasty was "legitimate," Metternich allowed Piedmont
(known as the Kingdom of Sardinia) to add Genoa and to remain the only
territory independent of Austrian domination. Throughout much of the
peninsula, Napoleonic modernization was abandoned as privileges were
restored to the aristocracy. Nonetheless, some of the reforms remained in
place, and Italian nationalism and liberalism continued to evolve, if only
gradually and unevenly.

Economic problems and clandestine political movements fueled local
insurrections, but ideological disagreements and disorganization rendered
them ineffective. Failed uprisings occurred in Naples, Palermo, Piedmont,
and Lombardy in 1820–21; and in Parma, Modena, and the Papal States in
1831. In the midst of failure, the young Giuseppe Mazzini fled to France
from his home in Genoa to found *Giovane Italia,* or Young Italy, whose purpose was to fight for "independence, unity, [and] liberty for Italy." Mazzini
was destined, even in exile, to provide a lasting intellectual and spiritual
energy to the independence movement, advocating mass revolution to produce a democratic republic. After an insurrection misfired in 1832, Mazzini

fled under penalty of death to Switzerland (1833), then England (1837) where, except for several covert trips to Italy, he lived the rest of his life.

Several northern moderates advocated alternatives to Mazzini's radical democratic vision. Among them was Vincenzo Gioberti, whose *On the Moral and Civil Primacy of the Italians (Il Primato)* proposed that the papacy lead the drive for unification. Several others, including Cesare Balbo, urged Carlo Alberto, King of Piedmont, to expand his territories in order to create a federation of states. By the mid-1840s, Balbo's cousin Massimo D'Azeglio emerged to lead a public campaign in support of Italian nationalism, while rejecting violent revolution. At the same time, the newly elected pope, Pius IX (Pio Nono), introduced reforms in the badly governed Papal States, while Carlo Alberto fashioned economic reforms in Piedmont.

All were overwhelmed by the Europe-wide depression of the 1840s and the staggering revolutions of 1848 to which the suffering contributed. The Italian revolutions began in Sicily and Naples and spread through the peninsula, forcing major concessions from the governing authorities. In Piedmont, King Carlo Alberto issued a constitution *(Il Statuto),* as did King Ferdinand II of Naples, the Grand Duke of Tuscany, and Pope Pius IX. Soon every Italian region was granted a constitution, except for Lombardy and Venezia where the Austrians refused. When the revolution in Vienna drove Metternich into exile, his entire European system staggered. All the governments in Italy were shaken, allowing Italians to throw off outside rule. In the "Five Days of Milan," supporters of the federalist Carlo Cattaneo forced the Austrian troops to abandon the city, opening the way for Carlo Alberto to move his Piedmontese troops into Lombardy, encouraged by moderates such as Count Camillo Benso di Cavour, to upstage the Mazzinian radicals. In Venice, Daniele Manin led Venetians in overwhelming Austrian forces there. Sensing opportunity, Mazzinians seized power in Rome. With the assistance of Giuseppe Garibaldi, sailor and international freedom fighter, Mazzini declared the Roman Republic, forcing Pope Pius IX to flee the city. By January 1849, revolutionary governments seized power in Tuscany, Modena, and Parma.

After initial successes, the Italian nationalist surge of 1848 faltered. Austrian forces defeated the Piedmontese at the battles of Custoza and Novara, leading the humiliated king to abdicate in favor of his son, Vittorio Emanuele II.

Partly because the new governments could not cooperate, Austrian and Bourbon forces methodically reversed the revolutions, restoring themselves to power. In Rome, a French invasion force of 20,000 overwhelmed the Republic and restored Pius IX to power, while the Bourbons reclaimed power in the Kingdom of the Two Sicilies.

With the failure of both Gioberti's plan for an enlarged papal state and Mazzini's revolutionary republic, Cavour and the Piedmontese moderates seized control of the *Risorgimento*. By modernizing railways, banking, commerce, the tax system, and governmental administration, Cavour (prime minister in 1852) made Piedmont a model of efficiency.

Wary of unifying the peninsula but spurred by events, Cavour pursued expansion through diplomacy. He seized the opportunity to order Piedmontese troops into the Crimean War, then won a seat at the peace table in 1856, thrusting Piedmont onto the European diplomatic agenda and befriending French Emperor Napoleon III. Two years later at the resort of Plombières, Cavour secretly won Napoleon's approval to support the Piedmontese campaign to drive Austria out of northern Italy.

When the Austrians delivered an ultimatum to Piedmont, Cavour refused, initiating the Second War of Italian Independence in April 1859. The combined Piedmontese and French forces defeated the Austrians at the battles of Magenta and Solferino, securing Lombardy for the Piedmontese. Napoleon III then signed the Peace of Villafranca with the Austrian emperor and left the conflict. Devastated and unwilling to accept a treaty that left Austria in control of Venezia, Cavour resigned.

Improving diplomatic conditions and a burgeoning drive for independence in central Italy convinced Cavour to return to power in January 1860 to lead the unification drive. He won plebiscites (direct ballots) in Tuscany and Emilia that brought both into a new Kingdom of Italy in March, while insurrection raged in Sicily where Mazzini lieutenant Francesco Crispi summoned Garibaldi. In May, Garibaldi steamed from Genoa with his "Thousand" volunteers sworn to fight for "Vittorio Emanuele and Italy." Garibaldi's Red Shirts swept through Sicily, defeating the Bourbon forces and inspiring rebellion, as Garibaldi declared himself "dictator of Sicily."

Afraid that Garibaldi might convert the South to a democratic republic, Cavour ordered the Piedmontese army south, occupying the Papal States and adding them to the Kingdom of Italy. In October, King Vittorio Emanuele II and Garibaldi met at the Volturno River where the wounded guerrilla commander agreed to accompany the king in a triumphal march through Naples, after which Garibaldi retired to his farm at Caprera. In March 1861, the new Parliament met in Turin and declared Vittorio Emanuele II King of Italy. Cavour died shortly thereafter, failing to achieve his ambition of incorporating Rome or Venice into the new kingdom.

Changing conditions in Europe enabled Cavour's successors (known as "The Right" for their relative conservatism) to pursue unification. By allying with Prussia in its victory over Austria in the Seven Weeks' War (June–July 1866), Italy acquired Venezia at the Peace of Prague (August 1866). When

Prussia went to war with France four years later, Napoleon III withdrew his troops from Rome, enabling Italian troops to occupy Rome in September 1870, completing the *Risorgimento*.

The newly unified Kingdom of Italy faced numerous obstacles, a reality captured by the famous statement attributed to Massimo D'Azeglio: "We have made Italy; now we must make Italians." One of the daunting issues became known as the Roman Question, the relationship between church and state. When the government relocated to Rome, Pope Pius IX reacted by issuing the *Non Expedit*, prohibiting Catholics from participating in Italian national politics. Under pressure, the Parliament issued the Law of Papal Guarantees as a concession, but Pius IX rejected the offer and proclaimed himself a "prisoner in the Vatican." Other problems included widespread poverty and underdevelopment, allegations of corruption in the new government, and a perception that Piedmont had "conquered" the peninsula, leaving power in the hands of a northern elite.

Most persistent was the Southern Problem. Soaring southern expectations remained unfulfilled, while confusion contributed to a wave of crime known as the "Brigands War." The Italian government responded by dispatching half its troops south, suspending civil liberties, and seizing control of local governments. It was during this campaign that the army reported confronting a criminal organization known as the *mafia*. Although the military effort failed to resolve the Southern Problem, it did harden the regional stereotypes: northerners viewed the South as poverty-riddled and lawless; southerners in turn regarded the Kingdom of Italy as a heavy-handed northern elite that governed by sheer force alone.

In 1876, the Left won control of Parliament, bringing to power two former Mazzinians, Agostino Depretis and Francesco Crispi, who would dominate the Left for the remainder of the century. Although the Depretis government failed in a number of its initiatives, they did expand the vote and introduce legal reforms. When the Right supported some of his measures, Depretis welcomed them, saying they had been "transformed." Consequently, a number of the cabinets of this era included both Right and Left, a phenomenon known as *"trasformismo,"* indicating that decisions were made by a series of deals among an elite of middle-class politicos who had little concern for differences in policy or for ordinary Italians.

Depretis's former Minister of Interior Francesco Crispi (governed 1887–91 and 1893–96) dominated Italian politics in the last decade of the century. Crispi achieved notable reforms, not only in expanding the political system, but in public health and charitable organizations. However, Crispi's reputation was sullied by his use of excessive force in the face of an eruption of socialist and anarchist radicalism. Especially troublesome to Crispi was a wave of peasant insurgency in his native Sicily, known as the *fasci Sicliani*. When prime minister Giovanni Giolitti's attempt to suppress the *fasci* led to the deaths of 92 Sicilian peasants, Giolitti's government fell at the end of 1893, returning Crispi to power. Crispi suspended civil government, dispatched 40,000 troops to Sicily, dissolved the new Italian Socialist Party (PSI), and purged the rolls of many of the poorest voters.

Even more damaging to Crispi's reputation was his foreign policy. He strengthened Italy's ties with Germany in the Triple Alliance, then instigated a military buildup that alarmed France and led to a tariff war. Ambitious to establish an empire, Crispi urged the invasion of Ethiopia, then acquired the colony of Eritrea on the Red Sea, only to be rebuffed and forced out of power after the Ethiopians defeated Italian troops in the Battle of Adua.

In the wake of humiliating defeat, rising bread prices intensified suffering and led to mob violence in 1898. The worst caused 80 deaths when the army fired into a crowd in Milan. In response to the *fatti di Maggio* (events of May), as the violence was labeled, the government of Antonio Di Rudinì arrested PSI leaders, censored the press, and closed universities. Di Rudinì's government gave way to General Luigi Pelloux, who announced in June 1899 that he intended to govern by royal decree. Rebuffed by wide-ranging opposition, Pelloux resigned, replaced by the caretaker Giuseppe Saracco. A few days later, in July 1900, Gaetano Bresci, an Italian anarchist from New York, assassinated King Umberto, bringing to a close a turbulent era in Italian history.

Vittorio Emanuele III inherited the throne at his father's death and would occupy it through two world wars and the Fascist era. For the first two decades of the new century, the dominant political figure was five-time prime minister Giovanni Giolitti. Industrial development and expanding markets brought new prosperity to the peninsula, closing the economic gap with northern Europe. A northern industrial-commercial "triangle" connected the cities of Milan, Turin, and Genoa, expanding the middle class and raising incomes. At the same time, the North-South gap widened, while emigration from the South continued at an alarming rate.

The Socialist Party pressured Giolitti to pursue changes; in turn the prime minister seized the opportunity to utilize selective reforms for political purposes—to consolidate his moderate base and isolate his more extreme critics. After stepping in and out of power twice, realigning his coalitions, supporting banking and tax reform, and appealing in turn to Catholics, businessmen, and moderate socialists, Giolitti returned to power in 1911 to make his most important contribution. The election law of 1911–12 expanded eligible voters from 3 to 8 million and enfranchised all military veterans and males over 30. However, in spite of sweeping changes, particularly in the cities of the

North, a small leadership class continued to dominate national political power.

In the midst of social and cultural change, a tide of nationalism swept the country into a war in Libya. The nationalist movement, led by Enrico Corradini, Luigi Federzoni, and the Italian Nationalist Association, argued that Italy must pursue its destiny—domination of the Mediterranean Sea and completion of the *Risorgimento* by conquering the "unredeemed" territories of Trieste and the Trentino. In an effort to exploit the nationalist surge, Giolitti declared war in September 1911, bombarded and occupied the Libyan coastline, and in November proclaimed Italy's annexation of Libya. Although the military offensive boosted Giolitti's popularity, its benefits proved marginal.

At its 1912 Congress, the Socialist Party turned markedly to the left, led by a fiery young revolutionary from the Romagna, Benito Mussolini. In response, the agile Giolitti turned to the right for support, pledging his supporters in the "Gentiloni Pact" to oppose socialism and divorce in return for Catholic support. In the face of opposition, Giolitti once again resigned, handing government to Antonio Salandra and his foreign minister, Sidney Sonnino, whose job it would be to lead Italy through an escalating European crisis.

As war grew ever nearer, an increasing number of Italians expressed doubts about the wisdom of fighting alongside Germany and Austria, their Triple Alliance partners. Because the Triple Alliance was viewed as defensive, Italy remained neutral when Austria declared war on Serbia in July 1914. At the same time, the British and French, appealing to Italy's imperial aspirations, secretly offered Italy a place in their Triple Entente.

Italy's initial decision to stay out of World War I ignited a divisive debate known as the "interventionist crisis." Salandra proclaimed that Italy's decisions would be guided by *sacro egoismo* (sacred self-interest). Debate raged in the press. In the PSI newspaper, *Avanti!*, Benito Mussolini advocated war as a means of revolution. Expelled from the party as a result, Mussolini launched his own newspaper, *Il Popolo d'Italia*, to carry on his campaign. A number of groups that supported Italian entry into the war—Futurists, nationalists, and democrats opposed to German militarism—clashed openly with antiwar forces in the disturbances labeled "Radiant May," while Salandra and Sonnino negotiated secretly with the British. Without consulting Parliament or the military, Sonnino signed the secret Pact of London of April 1915 by which the Entente powers agreed to reward Italy with territory in return for her entry into the war within three months. Salandra resigned in the face of mounting opposition, but when the king could not find a suitable replacement, Salandra returned and won the support of Parliament for war against Austria.

Unprepared for war, Italy suffered staggering losses, defeat, and humiliation. After 200,000 Italian casualties in the 1915–16 campaign against Austrian forces in the area northeast of Venice, Salandra resigned in favor of 78-year-old caretaker Paolo Boselli. In October 1917, German troops reinforced an Austrian attack at Caporetto, driving 700,000 Italian soldiers into frantic flight.

For Italians, Caporetto proved the low point of the war and the cause of widespread finger-pointing. But as Allied armies drove the Central powers into retreat on the western front, Italian forces recovered lost territory, crossing the river Piave and capturing the village of Vittorio Veneto. The victory at Vittorio Veneto provided cause for celebration and stands as a monument to the resilience of the Italian people. At the same time, the victory inflated Italians' expectations to be rewarded with territory by the terms of the Treaty of London.

The devastation of World War I aggravated a climate of political instability in 1919, as left-wing socialists called for a Soviet-style revolution. In reaction, the squads of the new Fascist movement, organized among socialists, syndicalists, Futurists, and *arditi* (special forces) in Milan, dispensed their own rhetorical and physical fury, aimed chiefly at socialists. When the Italian delegation arrived at the Paris Peace Conference with high expectations for territorial gains, they found their ambitions frustrated. In reaction to the major powers' refusal to grant them Fiume, the Italian delegation walked out, setting the stage for the nationalist movement to label Italy's war effort a "mutilated victory." Economic suffering in turn inflamed political instability, as food riots and industrial violence led to a general period of conflict known as the "red biennium" ("the red years") of 1919–20. In September 1919, the poet and wounded veteran Gabriele D'Annunzio led a march on the contested city of Fiume, employing symbols, including black shirts, that the Fascist movement would adopt.

The 1919 general elections held in the midst of the "red biennium" yielded victory to the two mass parties, the PSI (156 seats) and the new Catholic democratic party, the *Partito Popolare* (PPI, 100 seats). When the two could not cooperate, Giolitti returned to power for his fifth term as prime minister. In the fall of 1920, Soviet-style "Factory Councils" took control of industrial plants in Milan and Turin. The spreading insurgency of the "occupation of the factories" convinced businessmen, landlords, and growing numbers of the middle class to turn to Fascist squads to counter the threat of a Bolshevik revolution. In turn, Mussolini exploited those fears while expanding the Fascist movement from its original, radical roots to perhaps 250,000 members by the time Giolitti called for new elections in 1921. The Fascists (Mussolini included) won 36 of the 535 seats in the Chamber of Deputies (lower house of Parliament), while the PPI gained seats and the left held its ground, leaving Giolitti's liberal coalition ruling with only a minority of seats. Unable to reorganize a strong coalition, Giolitti once again resigned, replaced by moderate socialist Ivanoe Bonomi.

Sensing opportunity, Mussolini created the Fascist Party (PNF), appealing to moderates and conservatives while distancing himself from the radicalism of the early movement. Nonetheless, squads of Fascist "Blackshirts" intensified their violent attacks. Bonomi's resignation led the king to appoint the indecisive Giolitti loyalist Luigi Facta prime minister, while Mussolini bolstered his support from businessmen, the church, and the military. At the Fascist congress of October 1922, party leaders laid secret plans to seize power by marching on Rome, a significant risk, because the Italian army could easily overpower them if ordered into action by the king. However, when the Facta cabinet requested martial law in the face of growing evidence of Fascist insurgency, the king refused, leading Facta to resign. After negotiations, the king named Mussolini to head a coalition cabinet. Safely in power, the Fascists completed their March on Rome on October 30, 1922, striking out at their opponents in another wave of violence.

Having seized control, Mussolini spent the next three years bolstering his power, cultivating an image of respectability while at the same time condoning Blackshirt violence. In the process, he implemented a series of changes that began to define the Fascist state. He created the Fascist Grand Council (1922); made it easier for the PNF to claim a majority (Acerbo law, 1923); extended favors to the Vatican; and convinced the manufacturers' association to negotiate with the new Fascist unions (Palazzo Chigi Accords, 1923), which led to banning strikes, lockouts, and non-Fascist unions (Palazzo Vidoni Pact, 1925).

In April 1924, in a climate of fraud and violence, voters supported the Fascist coalition of candidates who captured 374 of the 535 seats in the Chamber of Deputies, enabling Mussolini to consolidate his power more fully. Shortly after reprimanding Mussolini from the floor of Parliament, Unitary Socialist leader Giacomo Matteotti disappeared (evidence later implicated Mussolini). Two months later, the discovery of Matteotti's body showered criticism on Mussolini, forcing his hand. On January 3, 1925, Mussolini took "full responsibility for what has happened," defiantly challenging Parliament to impeach him.

Two days later, Mussolini dropped all appearance of operating democratically and moved to create an authoritarian state. He cracked down on the press, outlawed political opposition, replaced each local government with an appointee known as a *podestà;* took over as Secretary of the Interior; created the secret police (OVRA) and a Special Tribunal to punish political crimes; and took control of the civil service and the professions.

To publicize the regime's expansive claims to progress, the Duce (leader, from the Latin *dux*) initiated a propaganda campaign, glorifying Fascist themes such as the "Battle of Grain" (to make Italy self-sufficient in food supply). To impart values, the Fascists created such organizations as the Balilla (clubs for young Italians), GUF ("Fascist University Youth"), and the Dopolavoro ("leisure time organization"), featuring sporting events and entertainment. By the mid-1930s, Fascist propaganda had degenerated into a "cult of the Duce," which Mussolini dramatized by striking heroic poses before the cameras. The regime also utilized architecture for propagandistic purposes, especially to invoke the glories of Italy's past. However, in painting and other visual arts, overt censorship was minimal. In 1937, Mussolini centralized all propaganda efforts under the authority of the Ministry of Popular Culture and began the next year to outlaw films from Hollywood in an effort to stimulate Italian production. In 1939, the new School Charter committed the education system to developing Fascist values.

In spite of its cultural rhetoric, the Fascist state focused most significantly on fundamental economic change. The centerpiece of Fascist economics was the Corporate State, an attempt to reorganize industry and labor into new units called "corporations." Mussolini formalized corporativism by establishing the Ministry of Corporations in 1926. The regime created 22 corporations in 1934, then in 1938 replaced the Chamber of Deputies with a Chamber of Fasces and Corporations. The Corporate State's achievements are unimpressive, and since the Great Depression led the government to take control of a number of industries, any accurate assessment remains difficult.

Relations with the church provided another important focus of the Fascist regime. In the Lateran Pact of 1929, Mussolini reached an agreement with the church that protected Catholic schools and granted autonomy to the Vatican state. In return, the church's stamp of approval provided legitimacy to the Fascist state. However, it was neither cultural, economic, nor religious policies, but foreign policy that would put the Fascist regime to the ultimate test.

In the 1920s, with Germany in a state of utter ruin, Italy maintained relatively better relations with Britain than with France. Then, frustrated by the Versailles settlement, Mussolini began to side with the war's losers in an unsuccessful attempt to destabilize diplomacy. In 1932, Il Duce took over the foreign ministry in an attempt to infuse Italian foreign policy with a more dynamic, nationalistic drive.

Adolph Hitler's arrival in power in January 1933 put Mussolini on notice. In his opposition to the diplomatic status quo, Hitler was a potential collaborator, while his ambition to control neighboring Austria made him a menace. Hitler thus forced Il Duce to tread carefully between the German and Franco-British camps. At the same time, Hitler's presence provided Mussolini the opportunity to pursue his own imperialist agenda in Ethiopia: to avenge the 1896 defeat at Adua, build popular support, and acquire natural resources and a "safety valve" for Italian settlement. The Italians invaded in October 1935. In the face of ineffective League of Nations sanctions, Italian troops took Addis Ababa in May 1936 and declared the Italian Empire a few days later. Distanced now from England and France, Mussolini steered his diplomacy toward Germany.

The next month, Italian forces entered the Spanish Civil War. Galeazzo Ciano, Mussolini's son-in-law and the newly appointed, pro-German Foreign Minister, convinced the Duce to support the rebel forces of Francisco Franco against the Spanish republican government. When Germany similarly threw its support to Franco, the Duce moved to collaborate with German diplomacy in what he dubbed "the Axis." Influenced by his 1937 trip to Germany, Mussolini took Italy out of the League of Nations, separating it further from the western democracies. The next year, although Italy had little history of persecuting its small Jewish population, the Fascists introduced the *Manifesto of Fascist Racism* (1938).

Mussolini at first stood aside as Hitler expanded, absorbing Austria and the German-speaking Sudetanland of Czechoslovakia in the spring of 1938. However, at the Munich Conference, the Duce became convinced that England and France lacked the resolve to stop Hitler. When Italian forces invaded Albania, the British pledged to protect Greece, leading Mussolini to consult with Hitler. The outcome was the "Pact of Steel" of May 1939, by which Italy and Germany committed to mutual support in the event of war. In September, World War II began as Hitler's *Blitzkrieg* assault of Poland brought Britain and France into the conflict.

Rapid Nazi successes led the ambivalent Duce to declare war on France and Britain on June 10, 1940. Unprepared, Italian troops nonetheless invaded France, the Suez, Greece, and Albania. The French quickly signed an armistice with Germany; Italians forces were driven out of Suez by the British, out of Greece by the Greek army, and rescued by Hitler in Albania. In the larger war, Mussolini supported Hitler's 1941 invasion of Russia with 200,000 troops and declared war on the United States after the attack on Pearl Harbor. When the British and American armies won the control of North Africa and the Russians held at Stalingrad, the Allies decided to strike at the Axis by invading Italy. By that time, opposition to Mussolini had developed within government and military circles, based primarily on Italy's dismal performance and dwindling resources.

On the night of July 24–25, 1943, the Fascist Grand Council voted to remove Mussolini from power. The king appointed General Pietro Badoglio head of a military government and ordered Mussolini quietly arrested. On September 8, amid confusion, Badoglio announced an armistice with the Allies and fled Rome alongside the king, just ahead of German troops. Four days later, German commandos rescued Mussolini and transported him to Lake Garda to establish the Salò Republic, a last-ditch attempt to maintain Fascism on the peninsula. Liberated after 20 years of repression, anti-Fascists formed a vigorous resistance movement, centered in the Committees of National Liberation (CLNs) in Rome and Milan. Most active were the communist partisans who created a heroic legacy by liberating cities from German and Fascist forces.

In a relentless battle to liberate Italy against a tenacious German enemy, Allied forces slugged their way northward. As civil war raged, they liberated Rome in June and Florence in July, 1944. When Germany finally collapsed the next spring, partisans forced the surrender of the last German troops in Italy and captured Mussolini. On April 27, 1945, Mussolini and his mistress were executed and hanged in a public square in Milan, lowering the curtain on the Fascist era.

In the aftermath of war, the advent of the Cold War dissolved the triumphant Grand Alliance and engulfed Italian politics. The British and American governments backed the Catholic Church and its new Christian Democratic Party (DC) to counter the Soviet-influenced Communist Party (PCI). On June 2, 1946, Italian voters chose to abandon the Savoy monarchy in favor of a republic and selected delegates to write a new constitution. The Constituent Assembly produced a document that created a weak presidency, a bicameral legislature elected by universal suffrage, and an independent court system.

In the first elections of the new Italian Republic, held in April 1948, the DC soundly defeated the combined parties of the left by a margin of 48.5 percent to 31 percent, giving the DC an absolute majority of seats in the Chamber of Deputies. For 40 years, with support from the United States, the DC held onto power in various combinations as the governing party, leaving Italian national politics competitive in name only. Thus, in spite of averaging more than one change of government per year, Italy would remain, throughout the second half of the twentieth century, one of the more stable governments in Europe.

Another reality of postwar Italy was the "Economic Miracle" of the 1950s and 1960s. Mired in the devastation and suffering of World War II, Italy began to reconstruct its economy largely as a result of U.S. aid and European integration. The Marshall Plan (1948) stimulated growth in the industrial sector and encouraged Italy to lower tariffs and join the Organization for European Economic Cooperation (1948) and the European Coal and Steel Community (1951). As a result, Italy's industrial production virtually doubled in the 1950s, outstripping France, Britain, and the United States. By the 1960s, Italy was a major industrial power.

The elections of Pope John XXIII and U.S. President John F. Kennedy enabled the DC to pursue an "opening to the left," bringing the PSI into the governing coalition of Aldo Moro in 1963. This center-left coalition lasted until 1968 when voters rejected the PSI, driving them out of the government. At the same time, student-led insurrections swept Europe, demanding educational reform, an end to the Vietnam War, and a wide-ranging leftist agenda. Shortly thereafter began the era known as "*anni di piombo*" (the years of lead) when extremist groups of the right and left engaged in a campaign of violence intended to create disorder. When PCI leader Enrico Berlinguer distanced himself from Moscow in his "historic compromise" with other progressive parties in 1973, he alienated part of the communist left, producing splinter groups. The most notorious was the Red Brigades, which conducted a campaign of "kneecappings," abductions, and assassinations that culminated in the daylight kidnapping of former Prime Minister Moro, whose corpse was later found in the trunk of a car.

By the mid-1980s, relative peace returned to the peninsula, partly because police and prosecutors turned arrested terrorists into police informants. By that time, a bloated public sector combined with falling revenues to strap the economy with large budget deficits at the same time that inflation soared and unemployment spread. However, a general European recovery combined with lower oil prices and increased productivity in the work force to produce remarkable growth, especially in small and medium-sized producers. Still, as Italy moved into the 1990s, serious problems threatened its ability to meet the Maastricht standards to qualify for the European Monetary Union (EMU). In 1998, after an austerity program managed by Carlo Azeglio Ciampi as prime minister and treasury minister, Italy overcame its currency, debt, and deficit problems and gained entry into the EMU.

With the end of the Cold War, spreading political scandals profoundly transformed Italian politics. The most direct result of the collapse of the Soviet Union was the dissolution of the PCI and the reorganizing of its constituents into the more moderate Democratic Party of the Left (PDS) and the hard-line Rifondazione Communista (Communist Refoundation, or RC).

Communist Party poster, "Kiss with your eyes closed, vote with your eyes open," Panzano in Chianti. Courtesy of the author.

Already suffering from the demise of the PCI against which it had defined itself, the DC was rocked by allegations of pervasive scandal. *Tangentopoli* ("kickback city" or "bribesville"), as it became known, led to a series of investigations by magistrates in Milan. Labeled *Mani pulite* ("clean hands"), the probe quickly involved former prime ministers Bettino Craxi (PSI), Giulio Andreotti (DC), Arnaldo Forlani (DC), and Giorgio La Malfa (Republican), as well as prominent businessmen such as Cesare Romiti (Fiat). *Mani pulite* revealed a massive labyrinth of bribes required of businessmen that in turn maintained the parties in power over decades, blocking change and contributing to huge deficits. By the spring of 1993, the investigations had pointed to one-third of the members of Parliament and had forced the resignation of many in the cabinet of Giuliano Amato (PSI).

Public outrage over the widely publicized scandals led both to irresponsible allegations and a growing mandate for fundamental reform focused on changing the system of proportional representation. Reformers maintained that the proportional system of elections made it impossible for a party to achieve a majority of seats, thereby empowering the party leaders (called secretaries) to trade favors for power. In 1991 and 1993, voters overwhelmingly passed referenda to replace the proportional system with winner-take-all elections in local government and three-fourths of the seats in Parliament. These changes were so profound as to lead some to herald a "Second Republic."

Among the changes were new political alignments that replaced the old party system. The remnants of the DC reformed as the *Partito Popolare* (PPI, the DC left) and the *Alleanza Nazionale* (AN, including much of the old DC right wing). More important was the emergence of two broad coalitions that promised the possibility of American- and British-style competing parties: the center-left *Progressisti* ("Progressives") and the center-right *Polo delle Libertà* ("Liberty Pole"), shaped by media baron Silvio Berlusconi. Berlusconi won a stunning victory in the 1994 general elections but governed a mere seven months before Umberto Bossi of the *Lega Nord* (Northern League) withdrew his support and toppled the government. In 1996, the reorganized center-left, now the *Ulivo* ("Olive Tree"), won control of the government, only to be brought down when RC leader Fausto Bertinotti pulled out of the government of Romano Prodi. Former communist Massimo D'Alema then governed until resigning in the spring of 2000.

Gianfranco Fini and Mirko Tremaglia, *Alleanza Nationale* rally, Bergamo. Courtesy of Crystal Espinosa.

Political demonstration, Bergamo. Courtesy of Crystal
Espinosa.

The general elections of 2001 matched two coalitions from 1996. Berlusconi, running under the banner of his renamed *Casa delle Libertà* ("House of
Freedoms"), won a resounding victory over *L'Ulivo* candidate Francesco
Rutelli, taking a majority of both houses of Parliament. By mid-2004, Berlusconi's government had lasted more than three years, thereby establishing a
new longevity record for the republic. The possibility that Berlusconi might
preside over a period of relative stability may provide him the opportunity to
implement his campaign promises to lower taxes and government expenditures, reform pensions, and expand the infrastructure without increasing the
debt. Enthusiastically pro-American, the dynamic Berlusconi has proven a
strong supporter of the policies of U.S. president George W. Bush. Until the
spring of 2005, that support did not waver, in spite of widespread popular
opposition to the war. However, in March, 2005, shortly after Italian security
agent Nicola Calipari was killed by American troops while rescuing Italian
journalist Giuliana Sgrena, Berlusconi announced the "progressive reduc-
tion" of Italian troops in Iraq.

NOTES

1. Brian Richardson, "Questions of Language," in *The Cambridge Companion to
Modern Italian Culture,* ed. Zygmunt Barański and Rebecca J. West (Cambridge:
Cambridge University Press, 2001); Tullio de Mauro, "Linguistic Variety and Lin-
guistic Minorities," in *Italian Cultural Studies,* ed. David Forgacs and Robert Lumley
(New York: Oxford University Press, 1996), 88–101; Anna Laura Lepschy, *The Ital-
ian Language Today,* 2nd ed. (London: Routledge, 1992); Derek Aust with Mike
Zollo, *Italian Language, Life and Culture* (London: Hodder and Stoughton, 2000).

2. Richardson, "Questions of Language," 63–65.

3. "Gli stranieri regolarmente presenti in Italia," http://www.istat.it.

2

Religion and Thought

BECAUSE ITS CHURCHES maintain a commanding presence in every city and village in the peninsula, it might be assumed that Roman Catholicism dominates Italian culture. While that influence is substantial, and while an overwhelming majority of Italians consider themselves to be Catholics, Italian culture is much more secular and diverse than outward appearances might suggest. In part, this diversity derives from two largely secular, historical forces that converged with the Christian tradition to shape Italian culture: the Roman Empire and the Italian Renaissance. In contemporary Italian culture, several strands of religious and secular traditions remain prominent. Secular philosophers trust in human reason—confidence in the rational powers of the individual—which provides an especially durable connection to Roman and Renaissance thought, as well as to the Enlightenment. And while the Italian Enlightenment (that era characterized by emphasis on experience and reason) is less well known than the French or English, it too made an impact, particularly in the works of Cesare Beccaria, Pietro Giannone, and Antonio Genovesi. The secular tradition celebrates the ability of the individual to discover truth by means of logical analysis. In twentieth-century Italy, this tradition is best represented by two very different philosophers, Benedetto Croce and Antonio Gramsci. More recently their influence has diminished, giving way to a great dispersal of new strains of thought, much less certain of the validity of rational analysis, including neorealism, existentialism, the postmodern theories of hermeneutics and semiotics, and a range of avant-garde experimentation. Among the major proponents of those schools of thought have been filmmakers Federico Fellini and Pier Paolo Pasolini and authors Dario Fo and Umberto Eco.

Equally powerful in the Italian tradition is the unique presence of the Holy See (Vatican City), headquarters to a religion that claims 1 billion adherents worldwide. The Vatican, like Roman and Renaissance monuments, has imposed its own momentous influence on Italian religion and thought. The papacy has maintained an important political force—even when it was ordering Italian Catholics to boycott elections—by its ability to persuade Italian leaders and to dominate the Christian Democratic Party (DC) until its recent collapse. Furthermore, a number of modern popes have articulated strong doctrinal positions that reverberate throughout the peninsula via the church's numerous channels of communication. However, it may surprise many that the church's positions on moral and social issues have not been automatically accepted—in fact have been widely defied—by a population that is at least nominally Catholic.

In contrast to the secular traditions that rely on reason, analysis, and human experience to reveal truth, the pious tradition of the church turns to the spiritual realm and to the pope, whose authority is said to descend directly from St. Peter, to provide understanding. This tradition offers a rich legacy of philosophical and theological writings as well, especially in the work of St. Thomas Aquinas (known as Scholasticism), St. Augustine, and, more recently, in the authoritative doctrinal decrees by a series of twentieth-century popes and Vatican councils. Among the most important prelates have been Popes John XXIII and John Paul II. In its theology the church has condemned much of modern philosophy as futile. Italian existentialists such as Enzo Paci and Luigi Pareyson have similarly rejected rational explanations of the universe. Other contemporary Italian philosophers have looked back to the writings of Aquinas to shape a school of thought known as neo-Scholasticism.

It is also particularly true in Italy that other strands of religious thought and practice persist, some of them drawn from pagan rituals, mysticism, and the cults of saints, particularly those connected to a local village. These threads of Italian religion often exist on the fringes of Roman Catholicism, viewed as Catholic by their practitioners, but not always accepted as legitimate by the Vatican. And while a number of these elements of religion and thought are found outside Italy as well, there are distinct Italian forms that influence the way Italians pursue understanding and view the world.

BENEDETTO CROCE AND ANTONIO GRAMSCI: TWO INTELLECTUAL TITANS

The two Italian thinkers who exercised the greatest influence on contemporary thought—both in Italy and around the world—were the Neapolitan idealist Benedetto Croce and the Sardinian Marxist Antonio Gramsci.

Gramsci died in a Fascist prison in 1937 at age 46; Croce, who lived well into his eighties, participated in the spirited postwar debates until shortly before his death in 1952. It is ironic, then, that these two men could so dominate the postwar era, in very different ways and largely in opposition, unsurpassed by subsequent Italian thinkers. The reasons for their great influence are found in their own individual lives and work. In the case of Gramsci, the durability of his thought came from its highly original application of Marxist theory to Italian culture and from his own place in Italian memory as an inspirational "martyr." Croce likewise occupied a distinguished historical reputation as the leading independent voice in Italy during the Fascist era, one who inspired many young opponents of the regime. His thought remained resilient because he applied his singular brand of philosophical idealism and historicism (see p. 45) to politics, science, aesthetics, and culture, more or less consistently, for over a half century. It has been written that Croce "exercised a kind of benevolent dictatorship over Italian literary and philosophical life. Not since Goethe had any single individual dominated so completely the culture of a major European country."[1] Paradoxically, the disciples of Gramsci did double service. They not only reinvigorated their mentor's work, but by attacking Croce as nemesis, they kept the more conservative philosopher's theories alive as well, although greatly diminished in reputation.

BENEDETTO CROCE: "QUIETIST" RESISTANCE, IDEALIST PHILOSOPHY, AND HISTORICISM

Benedetto Croce's impact was accentuated by the fact that his life spanned a vast portion of the history of the modern Italian state—forged in his infancy and recreated shortly before his death. Born in 1866, Croce would participate in the intellectual life of Italy through the Liberal period, two world wars, and the intervening era of Fascist dominance. After studying in Rome with philosopher Silvio Spaventa, Croce moved to Naples where he lived his adult life amid his vast personal library. Independently wealthy, he founded the philosophical review *La Critica* ("Criticism") in 1903, which provided him a ready outlet for his ideas for almost a half century. Croce used the review to revitalize Italian culture, establish a set of cultural standards, and develop a new generation of intellectuals. Thus Croce advanced a cultural agenda with strong, although indirect, political implications.[2] And although he was not drawn instinctively to politics, he did lead the Liberal Party, a moderate party of intellectuals, was appointed Senator (a lifetime position) by Prime Minister Giovanni Giolitti in 1910, and later served as minister of public instruction in Giolitti's final government (1920–21).

The volume of Croce's work is vast. His early work on Marxism, aesthetics, Hegelian idealism, and historiography had solidified his reputation as a major Italian thinker well before Benito Mussolini took power in 1922 and began to establish his Fascist state.[3] Although at first Croce regarded Fascism as a promising movement, he quickly became disillusioned. As a result, he distanced himself from the regime and from his former associate and *La Critica* coeditor Giovanni Gentile when Gentile emerged as Fascism's primary philosopher. In fact it was as a voice of passive dissent, expressed indirectly in *La Critica* and elsewhere, that Croce became known for his "quietist" and "serene" anti-Fascism. In 1925 Croce published his "Manifesto of Anti-Fascist Intellectuals" to counter Gentile's "Manifesto of Fascist Intellectuals." Four years later, Croce addressed the Senate in opposition to Mussolini's Lateran Pact with the Vatican, voted against it, and walked off the floor in protest.

During the Fascist era, although many dissenters were driven into exile, Croce remained immune from Fascist repression. When Mussolini ultimately fell from power as the Allies began to liberate Italy in 1943, Croce emerged from his "quietist" resistance to participate actively in the Liberal Party. He subsequently served in two cabinets and the Constituent Assembly (which wrote the new constitution) and was reappointed Senator-for-life. His political identity in the immediate postwar era solidified his place in the pervasive debates over the nature of Fascism and the future of the post-Fascist state. At the same time, Croce's advocacy of the monarchy and the support given him by the British and Americans made him a prime target of socialists and communists. Additionally, he had never expressed support for democracy or organized politics and had shown open contempt for democratic values as overly abstract and simplistic. Consequently, Croce was viewed as the leading "conservative" intellectual force in Italy, even after his death, as Marxists attacked his work in their quest to dominate postwar culture.

Croce never held a political presence except in this indirect way; his place was always in culture, not politics. Similarly, Marxists never achieved political power, but they did win the culture wars against Croce and his conservative (if unorthodox) idealism. Victimized by a rhetorical onslaught in universities, journals, and the popular press throughout the postwar era, Croce's ideas became largely discredited. However, the mere fact that they endured, even as objects of ridicule, testifies to the depth of their impact.

The most important of Croce's ideas were his own original forms of idealism and historicism. Like many Italians, Croce passed through a phase of Marxism in the 1890s. He later believed that through Marx he had reexamined some of his own abstractions and had incorporated some Marxist insights into his own theories of history. However, he ended by dismissing

Marxism for its "economic reductionism," or its tendency to reduce history merely to its economic components, while dismissing other factors.[4]

Even more misguided than the Marxists, according to Croce, were the positivists who, inspired by the French philosopher Auguste Comte, insisted that all knowledge must be based only on observation. Partly to reject positivism, Croce proclaimed a "rebirth of idealism."[5] His idealism developed from several sources: the German idealist G.W.F. Hegel,[6] one of Hegel's Italian proponents, Francesco De Sanctis, and the eighteenth-century Italian philosopher Giambattista Vico.[7] From Hegel, Croce formed an understanding of philosophy as the historical development of concepts, always grounded in a particular historical occurrence. Croce's idealism also grew from his aesthetics[8]—a focus on the universal human spirit, intuition, and imagination—which, he argued, constitute a peculiar form of knowledge and reveal themselves in history. Furthermore, Croce believed that only in history could truth be discovered. Accordingly, he severely narrowed the importance of both science and religion as paths to truth and turned from his early idealist philosophy to historicism, the belief that only a knowledge of history can lead to an understanding of human affairs and a comprehension of the present.

Although Croce's historicism derived naturally from his early emphasis on history, it developed a unique quality, a radical form that he labeled "absolute historicism." He distinguished his brand from the German historicism of Hegel, because the Germans, he concluded, had simply not gone far enough. Croce believed that concepts such as liberalism or justice, for example, cannot be understood in the abstract, outside their historical context or without reference to time and place. In fact Croce's historicism called for abandoning abstract values and forsaking the search for objective truth. In history, by responding creatively to unique historical circumstances, each individual might find reality. That reality, however, consists not of separate historical "facts," but of an accumulation of human responses to all previous events.[9]

In his historicism, Croce rejected both Hegel and Marx (although he had learned from them) because of their pursuit of general laws of history. According to one scholar, the core of Croce's historicism consisted of "faith in history, liberal political action, and historical knowledge."[10] Together, they constituted for him a kind of secular religion, one he differentiated from both Roman Catholicism and the secular humanism and natural law of the Enlightenment. And while he rejected natural science as a path to truth, he likewise dismissed as futile the social sciences, philosophy, and romanticism as well. History was for Croce everything: the indispensable source of all knowledge, the fundamental building block of all cultures, the unfolding saga of liberty and individual creativity, the one bond that allowed the individual to connect with something greater, and the most potent inspiration for action.

Among Croce's most important works were his writings in history and historiography (the study of historical interpretation). In his *History of Italy from 1871 to 1915*[11] and *History of Europe in the Nineteenth Century*,[12] Croce made a strong case for "history as the story of liberty" and classical liberalism as the driving force behind civilization's progress. In both books Croce idealized the nineteenth century—and particularly the late century when both Italy and Germany unified—as a positive period trapped between the eighteenth-century excesses of the Enlightenment and French Revolution and the twentieth century's futile pursuit of socialism, positivism, and, by implication, Fascism. By celebrating the "liberty" of the pre-Fascist period in Italy, Croce thus indirectly criticized the repression of the Fascist regime. However, both works conveyed a moral tone that was better received in the earlier century than after the fall of Fascism, when the books seemed antiquated to many.

In fact, Croce's major historical works have been criticized as superficial in their moralistic generalizations and lacking in the kind of analysis that modern historians demand. Furthermore, the picture Croce painted of Italy in the Liberal (pre-Fascist) era as a developing political system seemed to imply that all Italians had to do in overthrowing Fascism was simply to return to the politics of the past. Fascism had represented merely a "parenthesis" in Italian history. That idea infuriated not only Marxists, but numerous political factions who together believed that the rise of Fascism had been precisely the fault of a corrupt and self-serving political elite, the very same political class that had commanded power in the Liberal era. Thus Croce was charged not only with writing poor history, but also history with a political purpose. The Marxists claimed that Croce had emphasized smooth transitions in history at the expense of conflict and revolution. Even liberals found fault with Croce—and he with them—over the liberals' commitment to laissez-faire, free-market economics. According to Croce, no economic system enjoyed any degree of inherent superiority over any other. His historicism led him to believe that, within a liberal political structure, people should be free to choose an economic order—capitalist, socialist, or mixed—fitting their particular historical moment.[13]

Such arguments over the history of the pre-Fascist and Fascist eras necessarily dominated the highly-charged contests over political and cultural influence immediately after the World War II. Among those who most forcefully challenged Croce's history in the postwar era were followers of Antonio Gramsci and his theories. In fact, in many ways, Gramsci and Croce continued to influence Italian postwar thought long after their deaths and to the end of the century.

ANTONIO GRAMSCI AND THE INFLUENCE OF IDEOLOGY ON POSTWAR POLITICS AND THOUGHT

Historian Massimo L. Salvadori has written that the Italian Resistance movement (1943–45), while failing to dominate postwar politics, produced a powerful influence on postwar Italian culture.[14] The successful Italian Resistance to German occupation and the Italian partisans' triumphant overthrow of the remnants of the Fascist state took on legendary proportions in the immediate aftermath of World War II. As Italians celebrated Allied victory and the liberation of the peninsula from two decades of Fascist rule, communists stepped forward to claim credit. Although that claim has recently been challenged, the heroism of the Resistance movement nonetheless yielded a mythology that provided Italian Marxists a hallowed place among the various groups that emerged from a generation of suppression. Removing constraints produced a burst of anti-Fascist thought that gave a fresh voice to numerous reinterpretations of Italian history and culture. The dominant voice belonged to Antonio Gramsci, one of the founders of the Italian Communist Party (PCI) who had languished in an Italian prison cell for two decades. The much-celebrated, posthumous publication of the six volumes of his *Prison Notebooks*[15] between 1948 and 1951 established Gramsci as the most influential Italian intellectual of the postwar era.

The combination of Gramsci's impact and the heroism of communist partisans catapulted the Italian left to a position of cultural prominence in the wake of World War II. The PCI, well organized, with extensive trade union ties and covert support from the Soviet Union, emerged as a force to be reckoned with. But in spite of PCI leader Palmiro Togliatti's efforts to portray the PCI as a patriotic, trustworthy party, they could not convert their enormous cultural influence to political power. Allied victory gave way almost immediately to the Cold War so that many Italian voters tended to associate the PCI with the Soviet Union, influenced by an effective propaganda campaign by the anti-communist Christian Democrats (DC) and the Vatican, supported by the U.S. government's funding and intense political and economic pressure.

In April 1948, the PCI went down to emphatic defeat in the first general election of the new Italian Republic, winning along with its partners in the Popular Democratic Front only 31 percent of the votes. The victory by the DC (a near majority of 48 percent) proved durable, as the party would manage to control Italian political power through various arrangements for a half century. However, if the Communist Party failed to control the political arena, Marxist intellectual influences maintained their dominance more or less intact until the 1990s, when the Soviet Union and the PCI (the

DC as well) collapsed, and new conservative political forces emerged, including the Northern leagues and the reinvented Fascist Party (*Alleanza Nazionale,* or AN).

Marxist influence over Italian culture took many forms, most prominently in the application of Gramsci's theories. What made Gramsci's work so powerful were its originality and its pertinence to the Italian experience. Instead of simply restating Marx and Lenin, Gramsci introduced new points of analysis of Italian history and society and an entirely fresh point of view. For example, he introduced new critiques of class structure, intellectuals, and political leadership, all of which appealed to a generation searching for answers to explain the failures of its political system and the frailty of a once-proud culture that had collapsed in the face of the Fascist regime. Consequently, a generation of new Italian intellectual leaders—professors, editors, publishers, moviemakers, and writers—captivated by Gramsci's persuasive work, thronged to the PCI and applied Gramscian analysis to a wide range of Italian historical, cultural, and social issues. In contrast, moderates and conservatives, fairly or not, were weakened by association with the Fascist culture of the previous decades. Partly by default, this left Marxist intellectuals holding a virtual monopoly over Italian formal culture.[16]

One of Gramsci's compelling arguments was to call for a "new culture" that would integrate the "high" or formal culture of the intellectual class with the "popular" culture of the masses. The new cultural agent, Gramsci asserted, should be the political party that would imbue the masses with the new Italian Marxist culture; in turn, Gramsci viewed culture as a means by which the party could produce political revolution. In that spirit, the young poet and Resistance fighter Giame Pintor wrote in his last letter of November 1943: "We musicians and writers must...contribute to the liberation of all.... [An intellectual] must know how to take his post in a combat organization."[17]

Because his adaptation of Marxism was an attempt to apply theory to Italian politics, Gramsci invariably tied his thought to political action. In both the political and cultural domains, Gramsci believed that Italian communists would prevail, primarily because their unique ability to address society's problems provided them the upper hand. This conquest would not be achieved by force, however, but by convincing Italians that the communist program surpassed all others. Gramsci called this peaceful domination of political and cultural authority "hegemony." His reading of history and of Marx convinced him that culture is always bound to class interests, and that at any given time, one social class or another maintains hegemony. Gramsci argued that Italian communists, grounded in the lower classes (the industrial working class, or proletariat, and the peasantry) and operating with a superior set of ideas, would replace the middle class that had established its hegemony during unification and maintained it through the Fascist era. In order to do so, communists would have to supplant the middle-class ideology (system of thought) with its own Marxist ideology.[18]

Furthermore, Gramsci called for new leadership from workers and peasants. Intellectuals such as Croce, who spoke in politically neutral language, were in fact the voices of the prevailing middle class who contributed to middle-class hegemony. To counter the traditional intellectuals, Gramsci advocated the advent of a new group of "organic" intellectuals, drawn from the lower classes, speaking for them, and contributing to Marxist hegemony.

Palmiro Togliatti, Neorealism, and the "Italian Road to Socialism"

Because Gramsci had summoned a sweeping and innovative world view—and because his 1937 death in prison robbed Italian Marxists of their most original thinker—numerous debates and polemics developed over interpretation of his theories. Political primacy in this important debate belonged to Palmiro Togliatti, who succeeded Gramsci as head of the PCI and returned to Italy in 1944 from exile in Moscow. Togliatti professed that Gramsci had proclaimed an "Italian road to socialism," a unique pursuit of the classless society through peaceful, cultural means. In order to dominate, Italian Marxists would first have to establish hegemony over cultural institutions such as the universities and the press. Togliatti's version of Gramscian theory was emblematic of what became known as Euro-communism, a unique ideology by which Marxist goals would be achieved gradually, without resorting to violent revolution. Part of the continuing debate over Gramsci's theory focuses on the extent to which he committed to Marxist-Leninist goals such as the dictatorship of the proletariat and the political preeminence of the party.

One of the most powerful examples of Marxist cultural influence came in the form of neorealism. Toward the end of the Fascist era, this extraordinary cultural and intellectual movement began to develop. Shaped by the Resistance experience and a profound humanism as much as by Marxist theory, neorealism burst into full bloom by the mid-1940s, particularly in film, literature, and painting. The result was that a number of left-wing artists and writers emerged to set the standards in "high" culture and to provide the Italian left with a cultural supremacy that endured for nearly a half century. Among the notable neorealists were filmmakers Roberto Rossellini, Luchino Visconti, and Vittorio De Sica; painter Renato Guttuso; and writers Italo Calvino, Carlo Levi, Elio Vittorini, and Vasco Pratolini. Although they did not work by a formula and did not fully agree on ideology or the tenets of art and creativity, the neorealists did share several common approaches. They celebrated the heroism of ordinary Italians in the Resistance movement and shared a commitment to use their art for social purposes. In doing so, they portrayed images of social injustice and economic suffering and thus provided a Marxist analysis of Italy's political and economic system and an indirect attack on middle-class ideology. Neorealist intellectuals were so influential in the postwar era that, as one scholar notes, "Neorealism became the obligatory point of reference" in Italian formal culture.[19]

As influential as neorealism became, it did not equip the left to meet the rapidly advancing demands of a new popular culture. One of the major problems faced by the Italian Communist Party was that its cultural policy focused on "high" or formal culture—literature, drama, and film—because Togliatti and the party leadership, in contrast to Gramsci, remained suspicious of mass culture. This put the party at some disadvantage by the 1960s as Italy opened up to a wide range of new influences from popular culture, particularly American movies and television. One who challenged Togliatti's cultural policy was Pier Paolo Pasolini. A poet and a member of Italy's "high" culture, Pasolini embraced Gramsci's idea of the "organic" intellectual. Realizing the limitations of traditional literature, he moved first to dialect poetry and then to filmmaking and journalism. As a result, Pasolini became one of the most notable cultural figures of the postwar period.

Pasolini was not alone in challenging the place of Togliatti and the PCI in Italian culture. A number of independent voices surfaced, first from the left. Prominent among them was the communist Elio Vittorini. In September 1945, Vittorini introduced *Il Politecnico,* the most influential Marxist review of the era. In his journal, Vittorini ranged widely from literature and art to politics and sociology, calling on intellectuals to commit to radical cultural change, hoping to shape and empower a new culture that would provide a context for political action. In demanding that intellectuals and culture maintain their independence from the political party, and in distinguishing between cultural and political commitment, Vittorini provoked the wrath of Togliatti. The two consequently engaged in a continuing, highly publicized polemic over the responsibility of Marxist intellectuals to the PCI and to the Marxist revolution. Whereas Togliatti established realism and neorealism as the party's preferred modes of artistic expression, Vittorini gave exposure to numerous experimental genres. Even though Vittorini's journal ceased publication after 27 months, *Il Politecnico* remains emblematic of an emerging struggle between Italy's left-wing intellectual and cultural elites.

Neorealist impact on Italian thought and culture was dramatic, yet it could not last in the face of fundamental change. And although left-leaning intellectuals continued to dominate Italian formal culture, by the 1950s they had become more independent and diversified in voice as the PCI's influence waned. Among the reasons for greater individuality of thought were the impact of Gramsci's letters, the great turmoil that shook international communism on the death of Soviet leader Josef Stalin in 1953, and the 1956 speech delivered by his successor Nikita Khrushchev in which he lashed out at Stalin as a brutal despot. As Khrushchev signaled a more flexible international communism, Italian Marxists were encouraged to move in their own directions. Many had given up in their attempt to reach workers through mass culture and reverted to an effort to manipulate "high" culture.

AVANT-GARDE EXPERIMENTATION: FEDERICO FELLINI AND UMBERTO ECO

As Marxist domination of Italian culture diffused, the Economic Miracle introduced important new influences in the 1950s. Most powerful were the advent of commercial television and cinema and the expanded efforts by Italian publishing houses. Italian television, filled with images of the new material prosperity and heavily dependent on American programs and format, seemed well beyond the reach of leftist intellectuals and provided a romanticized version of contemporary capitalism that socialists were unable to match. At the same time, Federico Fellini and other Italian directors began to move beyond neorealism to explore on the big screen the dark side of the new prosperity, employing such cultural themes as banality, vulgarity, decadence, and hypocrisy, while probing the inner depths of fantasy, alienation, and madness.

Other writers, visual artists, and filmmakers initiated an avant-garde movement in the late 1950s and into the next decade. Many shared a common attack, boldly examining and manipulating language, time, and space. Among them, Pasolini experimented with his own poetry and his journal *Officina,* while a number of poets, novelists, musicians, painters, architects, and other artists pushed the limits of their respective forms, most notably the experimental Milanese cluster known as *"Gruppo 63."* Destined to prominence among the avant-garde were the writer Umberto Eco, who pioneered the application of semiotics (the study of symbolic language) to Italian culture, and the innovative film director Michelangelo Antonioni. Vittorini coedited with Italo Calvino *Il menabò,* a journal that gave exposure to a variety of new forms and inquiries into Italian society and culture and, particularly, to wide-ranging critiques of the growing pressures of commercialization and modernization.

The combined impact of the great diffusion of Italian thought in the 1950s and 1960s led away from the postwar paradigm; the polemic by the disciples of Gramsci against the philosophy of Croce now was largely relegated to memory. Nonetheless, Gramsci's work remained a powerful influence and a source of inspiration for many left-leaning Italian intellectuals who, in spite of their various experiments, often retained an ideological affinity with their neorealist predecessors. By the end of the turbulent sixties, the center of the debate over Italian thought and culture had moved noticeably to the left. That movement seemed to crystallize in response to the tumult and violence of 1968, especially the escalation of the war in Vietnam, the Maoist cultural revolution in China, and violent clashes between university students and police in Paris.

THE IMPACT OF 1968: PIER PAOLO PASOLINI AND DARIO FO

Those worldwide events made the year 1968 a symbol of cataclysmic change. In Italy, the protest movement had actually begun the previous year and lasted a decade, much longer than elsewhere. The protests generated a spreading wave of violence known as the "*anni di piombo*," carried out by both left- and right-wing extremist factions. At the same time 1968 brought to the forefront a series of "New Left" movements, some of them in direct rejection of the PCI. These groups dramatized cultural conflict, not only between ideological factions, but between generations as well. Most of the demonstrators embraced a "youth" culture that rejected both communism and Roman Catholicism, the dominant strains of the existing culture, in favor of a blend of countercultures that now moved aggressively onto the public stage. Prominent among them were students, feminists, environmentalists, and gay activists. Their demands were iconoclastic in that they rejected the ideas and cultural norms of the past and impatiently refused to work within the existing political system. They called for "revolution" and envisioned a bold new world. Their immediate impact on elections was marginal. However, these countercultural forces redefined the boundaries of Italian politics as well as mainstream culture, and by their effective use of radio and television, influenced the means by which ideas were communicated. Just as young protesters learned to manipulate the electronic media in the United States and France, so they did in Italy.[20] And although many of their ideas were not inconsistent with the agenda of the PCI, the success of the "New Left" and the youthful protesters at capturing attention weakened the cultural monopoly of the Marxists, creating an opportunity that the new conservatives eventually would seize.

The influences of 1968 shaped Italian thought and culture through the 1970s and 1980s. However, as the student militants and their cohorts broke down traditional cultural norms and reoriented thought, they enjoyed far more success in the cultural realm than in electoral politics. Among the cul-

tural changes was a rethinking of gender issues and a subsequent transformation in the way Italians viewed women in the family, workplace, and society.
In that sense, the 1968 protests paved the way for a departure from the past
and for the successful campaigns to protect women on the job and to legalize
divorce and abortion.

A number of intellectuals responded individually to the changes. Pasolini
criticized the student protests, distancing himself from the left, and produced several highly controversial films until his murder in November 1975.
Playwright Dario Fo moved from mainstream to "alternative" theater *("piccolo teatri")* and into the role of a subversive intellectual. He wrote, produced, and acted in a number of plays, most prominently *Mistero buffo
(Funny Mystery)* in 1969 and *Morte accidentale di un anarchico (Accidental
Death of an Anarchist)* in 1972. Clearly a transitional figure, Fo was recognized as a leading independent intellectual, imaginative and improvisational,
whose work provoked government censorship and eventual condemnation
from many sources. The tone of Fo's anticlerical, antiauthoritarian satire
linked him back to the Marxist left of the immediate prewar era, and one of
his theater ensembles was associated with the PCI. However, his satire and
overt criticism of the party's bureaucracy brought the wrath of the communist press, driving him further toward an independent direction. His 1977
television performance of *Mistero Buffo* was condemned by the Vatican as
blasphemous, and his criticisms of the Vietnam War and of U.S. President
Lyndon Johnson led the United States to deny him a visa. Twenty years after
the infamous television performance of *Mistero Buffo*, in retrospective recognition of the importance of his innovative work, Fo was awarded the Nobel
Prize for literature.

Pasolini and Fo were only two examples of the profound changes that
influenced Italian intellectuals in the 1970s and 1980s. In the realm of theory
and philosophy, Emanuele Severino (*L' essenza del nichilismo, The Essence of
Nihilism,* Milan, 1982) and Gianni Vattimo (*Il soggetto e la maschera, The
Subject and the Mask,* Milan, 1974) emerged at the forefront of a generation
of thinkers who would champion what would generally be referred to as postmodernist thought.

THE POSTMODERN ERA IN ITALIAN THOUGHT: ENZO PACI AND LUIGI PAREYSON

The postmodern era in Italian thought may be traced from the late 1970s
publication of two influential works, Italo Calvino's *Se un notte d' inverno un
viaggiatore* (*If on a Winter's Night a Traveler,* Milan, 1979), and Umberto Eco's
vastly popular *Il nome della rosa* (*The Name of the Rose,* Milan, 1980). In each

instance the writers utilized a narrative framework in which to introduce a series of issues that have become central to postmodern thought, in particular semiotics and reader reception theory (the belief that no thought is complete until processed by a reader). Also important in developing postmodernism in Italy was Gianni Vattimo's *Il Pensiero debole* (*Weak Thought,* 1983) in which he made the case for subjectivity in contrast to the absolute certainty found, for example, in Marx's economic determinism.[21]

In fact, it may be possible to identify an "Italian School" of postmodern thought, in spite of the realization that much of Italian cultural influence has been in the form of visual images rather than written language. According to some modern Italian philosophers, Italy paid a price for its tradition of historicism that endured through the work of Croce: it withdrew into a conservative, constructed ("imaginary") past, and thus, ironically, defaulted on its role as cultural and intellectual force in European thought.[22] Among those philosophers who debunked Croce's "absolute historicism" were Italian pragmatists and existentialists. The pragmatists, inspired by the American philosopher John Dewey, repudiated Croce's historicism and idealism by arguing that the meaning of a doctrine is to be found only in its results, and that knowledge can thus be obtained only through experimental inquiry. The Italian existentialists, in the tradition of Danish philosopher Søren Kierkegaard, rejected Croce from a very different position, asserting that the universe cannot be understood rationally, nor can truth be found deductively, because the universe is not intelligible, leaving the individual to make authentic choices in his or her own pursuit of truth.

Most important among the Italian existentialists were Enzo Paci and Luigi Pareyson. Paci's existentialism, like Croce's idealism, focused on history, but moved in a path that brought him closer to Marx than to Croce. Paci also pursued phenomenology (*Diario Fenomenologico, Phenomenological Diary,* Milan, 1961), influenced by the German mathematician Edmund Husserl, in attempting to describe and analyze experience and consciousness. In contrast, the existentialism of Pareyson (*Studi sull'esistenzialismo, Studies on existentialism,* Milan, 1943) was derived from the spiritualist tradition in Italian thought, dating to the work of the fifth-century theologian Augustine of Hippo, and somewhat analogous to the Christian existentialism of twentieth-century theologians Karl Barth and Paul Tillich. Pareyson viewed existentialism as a personal philosophy that, while rejecting any possibility of objective truth, recognizes that the individual's relationship with God will animate his or her search for truth. Skeptical of theoretical, empirical, and technological paths to understanding, both Paci and Pareyson contributed to the movement that rejected rational explanations of both the individual and the universal.

The 1980s brought a new generation of Italian philosophers, who had begun to concentrate on hermeneutics (the theory of subjective interpretation of texts), which led to exchanges with other European thinkers influenced by the works of the German philosophers Martin Heidegger and, especially, Hans-Georg Gadamer. The leading figures in Italian hermeneutics were Vattimo, Pier Aldo Rovatti (*Abitare la distanza, To Live at a Distance*, Milan, 1994), Aldo Gargani (*Crisi della ragione, Crises of Reason*, Turin, 1979), and Mario Perniola (*Dopo Heidegger. Filosofia e organizzazione della cultura, After Heidegger: Philosophy and Organization of the Culture*, Milan, 1982). This circle of Italian philosophers shared a certain life experience that separated them from their predecessors who had participated in the traumatic events of World War II, the Resistance movement, and the reconstruction of the continent; instead, they had been shaped more by the watershed events of 1968 and the violent ideological struggles of the "*anni di piombo*" that followed. In fact, Italian hermeneutics is sometimes viewed as a response by leftist intellectuals to the failure of both ideology (Gramsci) and historicism (Croce) to provide adequate paths to truth and understanding. The movement is also seen as a search for an alternative to the reliance on reason that has characterized Western thought since the Enlightenment.

Over the past several decades, Italian postmodern thought has clustered around ideas that both symbols (in semiotics) and text (in hermeneutics) are understood only as the observer or reader constructs a subjective interpretation. Umberto Eco emphasizes the dialogue between author and reader. Semiotics, according to Eco, establishes the right of the reader to interpret, in the sense that the meaning of every message depends on the reader's interpretation. Eco argues that, far from being revolutionary, reader-oriented theory fits within the mainstream of interpretation of text that dates from Aristotle and provides an important alternative to dictionary-style interpretation.[23]

Those in semiotics and hermeneutics who emphasize the importance of interpreting text continue to be challenged by the neo-Scholastics, producing lively dialogue within contemporary Italian thought. The neo-Scholastics take their inspiration from Scholasticism, the medieval thought, especially of Thomas Aquinas, revived in Italy in the late nineteenth century and again after World War II. Among the neo-Scholastics who attempt to adapt the philosophy of medieval Christianity to a contemporary context is Emanuele Severino. Severino emphasizes what he considers a fatal flaw in Western culture, dating from classical Greek thought. In the continuing philosophical debate about the conflict between Being and Becoming, Severino contends that Westerners have embraced the idea of Becoming, wherein things originate in nothingness and are ultimately reduced to nothingness. In Western thought, writes Severino, "truth...appears only at the end of a process. But the truth of Being neither rises nor sets, and in its eternal Appearing lies the essence of man."[24] The fundamental Western cultural belief in Becoming produces great anguish, according to Severino. To compensate for the agonizing dread of nothingness, Western Christian culture has constructed a deity and a system of enduring values.

Among the important points of disagreement between the theories of hermeneutics and neo-Scholasticism are fundamental questions of the impact of technology. While hermeneutics proposes engagement with technology in order to impose ethical constraints, neo-Scholastics view technology as more diabolical, intrinsically bound to dominate and ultimately destroy Western culture.[25]

By the 1990s, with the death of many of the prominent writers of the postwar era, the familiar dialectics between Marxists and Croceans, positivists and neorealists, neo-Scholastics and existentialists, Vittorini and Togliatti, had disappeared. As yet no clearly-defined schools of Italian thought have emerged to replace them; instead greater diffusion within the postmodern framework characterizes Italian thought at the advent of the new century. This scattering of thought is made more emphatic by the prominence of non-print communications, particularly radio and television, which have required new skills and further displaced left-wing intellectuals, many of whom disdained the mass electronic media. In the process of this recent dispersion of ideas, moderates and neoconservatives have thrived, particularly in the context of political ideology and on the coattails of the meteoric rise to political power by the media mogul Silvio Berlusconi.

Berlusconi's rise was both accommodated and accompanied by a new independent conservatism in Italian political thought that challenged the very assumptions on which the Italian left had maintained its postwar influence for nearly a half century. Led by the voluminous research by the University of Rome historian Renzo De Felice, historians and journalists attacked the heroic tradition of the Resistance and the anti-Fascist movement. De Felice had originally revived the reputation of Mussolini in his carefully documented, multivolume biography.[26] Although the implications were subtle at first, the reassessment of the Duce filtered into the popular media and contributed to the fortunes of neo-Fascist political forces. The idea gained acceptance that left-wing intellectuals had exaggerated the evils of the Fascist regime and glorified the mythology of the partisan fighters for the benefit of the communist movement. In attempting to discredit the Resistance movement, the neoconservatives challenged the very legitimacy of the left to dominate Italian intellectual life, claiming that Italian Marxists had been mere puppets of Moscow. This ongoing struggle to reinterpret Italy's past has taken center stage in a wider contest for political and cultural influence waged by

Italian conservatives. The outcome of this encounter of ideas holds portentous implications for Italy's future.

ITALIANS AND RELIGION: THE "ROMAN QUESTION"

Italians maintain a unique relationship with the Roman Catholic Church by virtue of the presence of the Vatican, the world capital of Catholicism, within the environs of Rome. As a result, the church has played an important role in Italian culture and politics throughout history. During the *Risorgimento* (the nineteenth-century unification movement), the philosopher-priest Vincenzo Gioberti called for the papacy to lead the drive for nationhood. Not only did Gioberti's plea go unanswered, but Italian unification ultimately succeeded only at the expense of the church. In 1864, sensing the challenge from Count Camillo di Cavour and his secular Piedmontese supporters who led the *Risorgimento*, Pope Pius IX issued the *Syllabus of Errors,* which denounced modern civilization and proclaimed it an erroneous belief that "The Roman Pontiff can, and ought to, reconcile himself, and come to terms with progress, liberalism and modern civilization."[27] In the same spirit, Pius followed four years later by issuing his *Non expedit,* ordering Italian Catholics to boycott the political life of the new Italian state. In 1879 Pius called the First Vatican Council, which issued the powerful dogma of papal infallibility (that when teaching on faith and morals in his official capacity, the pope's words are a perfect reflection of God's advice) on all matters of doctrine. In September of that year, after French Emperor Napoleon III withdrew his garrison from Rome during the Franco-Prussian war, Rome fell to the new Italian kingdom.

From the outset of the new Italian state, it was clear that there would be no official Catholic political party during Pius's era, as a tone of frigid hostility settled in. Having lost the Papal States to the new Kingdom of Italy, Pius excommunicated the Piedmontese leaders who had annexed church territory. This issue of church-state relations was labeled the "Roman Question," and would continue to trouble the new state, particularly because the church discouraged participation in elections in a culture where building national political awareness and patriotism already faced enormous barriers of illiteracy, apathy, rural alienation, localism, and poverty. When Pius proclaimed himself a "prisoner in the Vatican," the new Italian government passed the Law of Papal Guarantees, granting the papacy numerous concessions equivalent to those afforded a foreign head of state, while allowing the pope to retain the Vatican and other properties on a tax-exempt basis. While the pope refused to accept the law, both he and the Italian government benefitted, the Papacy by unofficially reaping the privileges, the state by relieving diplomatic pressure to improve relations with the Vatican.

When the "Left" took power in 1876, they continued to honor the concessions. However, they ridiculed the Vatican in Parliament and the press, while sponsoring anticlerical legislation. Parliament confiscated church property that was sold at auction, closed some religious orders, and required military service for priests. They instituted a public school system to offset the influence of religious schools, civil marriage that required an official public ceremony in addition to a church wedding, and legal separation of marital partners upon certification by civil courts. At the same time, some religious orders found ways to keep their property, the church maintained their hospitals, and the public schools taught the Roman Catholic catechism. Thus, while the church maintained some of its prerogatives, the new Italian state provided its citizens secular alternatives. Partly as a result of that ambiguity, church-state relations provided a continuing source of contention for at least a half century.

When Pope Leo XIII began his pontificate in 1878, he determined to regain the church's former dominance of Italian society. To that end, he redirected the church's social doctrine so as to address the changing realities of Italian life, particularly in light of industrialization and the rise of Marxist socialism. He issued his famous encyclical *Rerum novarum* in 1893, establishing the church's axiom of harmony between the working class and the business class based both on a just relationship and the mutual acceptance by each class of its social status.

The election of Pope Pius X in 1903 led to some weakening in the application of his predecessor's *Non expedit* prohibition and the engagement of the church in the political process on the side of moderate and conservative political interests. At issue was the strengthening of the socialist movement in Italy, regarded as a direct threat by the Vatican in an age of increasing industrialization and urbanization. Catholics voted in growing numbers, so that in the general election of 1913, Prime Minister Giovanni Giolitti thought it necessary to appeal to them in order to maintain his Liberal coalition's hold on power. Shaped by Giolitti and Count Ottorino Gentiloni, the Gentiloni Pact assured Catholic votes for Giolitti's Liberal candidates in return for Giolitti's support for religious education in public schools and opposition to divorce legislation.

Pius XI's election to the papacy in 1922 coincided with Mussolini's rise to power and led to some accommodation between church and state. For example, one of the few non-Fascist organizations to survive Mussolini's consolidation of power was Catholic Action, which Pius had used to mobilize the Catholic faithful. In 1929, when Mussolini normalized relations with the church in the Lateran Accords, Catholic Action was granted an exemption, enabling the group to exceed 2 million members in the 1930s.

The Lateran Accords included three major provisions. They first recognized the sovereignty of the Holy See (Vatican city) in return for the pope's acceptance of Rome as capital of the Italian state. In order to win the pope's support, Mussolini negotiated an agreement to accept Catholic instruction in public schools, grant state recognition of church weddings, and condone the Catholic Action group. And finally, the church was compensated for its loss of territory at the time of unification in return for agreeing to accept the loss as permanent.

The pontificate of Pope Pius XII (1939–58) marked a significant change in Italian culture because he was committed to the renewal of Catholic power in Italy through the creation of a new Catholic political party. In the midst of the chaos that accompanied the Allied invasion of the peninsula in 1943, with the Duce overthrown and the king having fled Rome, Pius XII emerged as a force in Italy, attempting to negotiate with both Allies and Germans. In his 1943 encyclical *Mystici Corporis,* Pius declared the church the "mystical body of Christ," claiming greater legitimacy than any other organization, including the Italian government. Furthermore, Pius pressed to maintain control over the crucial issues of life, death, and morality by holding the line on such matters as divorce and contraception, while calling for censorship of the cinema. At the same time, Pius used his resources to counter Italian communism by sponsoring an aggressive and pervasive political agenda: a new Catholic labor union organization to offset the communist-dominated unions, an even stronger Cold War partnership between the church and the United States, and a call to the faithful to rally behind the campaigns of the DC—which the Vatican dominated.[28]

Pius XII's program was enormously effective in reestablishing the presence of the church in postwar Italy. The church achieved its greatest success by building a powerful political party (the DC), which managed to control Italian politics for most of the next five decades. In that impressive success are also to be found seeds of failure, as Patrick McCarthy points out. In calling for a democratic system while simultaneously exercising autocratic control of the DC, the Vatican undercut the development of grassroots, competitive democracy and set itself up for blame when the DC ultimately was destroyed by scandal. And by tying its fortunes to the United States, the Vatican unintentionally contributed to the popularization of American culture and the massive infusion of American money via the Marshall Plan. Consequently, at the very time when Pius had managed to strengthen the presence of the church in Italian life, Italian society was quickly changing to adopt many characteristics of modernization that the church had opposed throughout the history of modern Italy. And by focusing its energies on anti-communism, the church had unwittingly aided the growth of consumer capitalism, which it came to view as an even more dreadful enemy.[29]

In many respects, the achievements of Pius XII harkened back to the era of Leo XIII (1878–1903). In fact, the church's basic ideology remained consistent for almost a century, from the *Risorgimento* era to the Second Vatican Council of 1963–65. For nearly a century, among its many social doctrines, the Vatican invariably advocated the family, the subordination of women, and the acceptance of social status, while rebuking atheists and communists. The church decreed that God had created the family for the purpose of perpetuating life and as the natural unit in which a wife should serve her husband. Furthermore, one should obey God's will and accept one's station in life, while accepting the pope as the only legitimate interpreter of God's word. Atheists and communists, products of the devil's work, would join sinners in eternal damnation.[30]

These principles of Catholic culture were disseminated to the Italian population through bishops and priests in more than 25,000 parishes throughout the country, but also through the Catholic press and numerous Catholic organizations, including Catholic Action, the Christian Democratic Party, and farmer and labor organizations. Thus the Vatican maintained remarkable consistency, discipline, and centralized authority in influencing Italian culture throughout most of the first century of the existence of the Italian state.

POPE JOHN XXIII AND THE SECOND VATICAN COUNCIL

In spite of Pope Leo XIII's historic determination to regain the Church's former influence in Italian society, that society had been changed fundamentally by modern forces of Fascism, World War II, the Cold War, and, notably, by the Economic Miracle. By the time 77-year old Venetian Cardinal Angelo Roncalli was elected Pope John XXIII in 1958, practicing Roman Catholics had become a minority in Italy.

John XXIII would be noted for several initiatives, the most important being the Second Vatican Council and the movement of the DC government toward a center-left coalition. The Second Vatican (or Ecumenical) Council (1962–65) reshaped the Italian Church by changing the liturgical language from Latin to Italian; shifting power from the Papal Curia (council) in Rome to the bishops, who were now provided a voice through the new bishop's council; and creating a more humble church that he called "the people of God," which welcomed believers as well as nonbelievers.

In retrospect, Roncalli's influence was perhaps greatest in reorienting the church in broad, conceptual terms and in opening the church—to voices of dissent within and to the world beyond Rome. Believing that the church was losing touch with the masses, he preached a social gospel, redefining his role along New Testament lines in the image of Christ as a "good shepherd" leading his flock. In that respect, John's papacy marked a sharp break with his predecessors who had delivered a much sterner, more authoritarian message. John's optimistic view of the fundamental goodness of mankind led him to preach a message of hope, forgiveness, and redemption and to launch the church on a path known as "Progressive Catholicism." Likewise, John's ecumenism encouraged dialogue with Third World countries—particularly to combat oppression and poverty—as well as with other faiths and ideologies. This was particularly evident in his famous encyclical *Pacem in terris* (Peace on Earth, 1963), addressed to "all men of good will," in which the pope distinguished between the belief and the believers. All non-Christians were, above all, children of God who deserved to be engaged in dialogue, despite their adherence to false beliefs.[31] Furthermore, *Pacem in Terris* reoriented the Vatican's foreign policy away from the anti-communism of Pius XII and toward world peace.

It was this emphasis on dialogue that persuaded Pope John to relinquish the church's historic effort to reconquer Italian society and to loosen the reins on the Christian Democratic Party (DC). Free of papal domination, the DC reached out to the center-left to ally with the Socialists (PSI), augmented its already significant political influence, and distanced itself further from the Vatican. As a result, the DC began to develop numerous clienteles (dependent interest groups) independent of the Vatican, a trend that would ultimately engage the party in a web of destructive corruption. Ironically, however, though the party freed itself from papal control, it was firmly tied to the Catholic Church in Italy.

A number of bishops of the Italian Catholic Church greeted the changes initiated by the Second Vatican Council with alarm and resistance, blaming the reforms for a steady decline in attendance at services and growing confusion in the church's message. When the moderate Cardinal of Milan Giorgio Montini was elected Pope Paul VI on the death of John XXIII in 1963, the job of completing and implementing the Second Vatican Council fell to him. He followed his predecessor's lead in reaching out to the Third World, addressing the United Nations, and thus moving to free the church from its Euro-centered past and its link with Italy. He further distanced the church from its Italian heritage by widening the Vatican's breach with the DC, implying that a Catholic could be expected to choose among many parties. However, on doctrinal matters, his vocal support of the church's ban of contraception made him appear more conservative than John and placed the Vatican in distinct opposition to a rapidly modernizing and secularizing Italian population that included many practicing Italian Catholics who openly opposed the church's positions. The evidence of the change came in the Italian Parliament's legalization of divorce in 1970 and the 59 percent of the voters who defeated the 1974 referendum, backed by the Vatican, that would have overturned the new divorce law.

THE INFLUENCE AND LIMITS OF RELIGION IN ITALIAN SOCIETY: POPE JOHN PAUL II

When in 1978 the Polish Cardinal Karol Wojtyla was elected Pope John Paul II, the first non-Italian in over 450 years, it was clear that the church was presiding over a largely secular Italian culture. In fact, Italy had never been as uniformly Catholic as the church's pervasive presence suggests. From a figure of 69 percent in 1956, self-reported church attendance fell to 48 percent in 1968, 35.5 percent in 1972, and about 30 percent by the end of the century (only 19 percent in Milan and 15 percent in Rome). At the same time, Catholic Action fell from 3.6 million members in 1962 to 800,000 in 1973, while the Catholic labor union folded, and a number of dissident groups appeared, denouncing the church as elitist.[32] By the 1990s, although more than 80 percent of Italians described themselves as Catholics, fewer than half attended confession regularly or believed in heaven and hell, and only one-third supported the church's ban on contraception. As is the case with most all cultural factors, regional differences exist. Protestant sects have spread, especially in the north. In all of Italy, the northeastern region of the Veneto is the most heavily Catholic, but its birth rate is also among the lowest in all the regions, indicating the futility of the church's ban on contraceptives. The Vatican's influence in elections has diminished as well. One scholar concludes that by the 1990s no more than 15 percent of the Italian electorate were receptive to the church's influence.[33]

Even though a clear majority of Italians claimed to have attended mass in the 1950s, knowledgeable Italians understood that even then many were merely nominal Catholics, drawn to the church by the traditional rites of passage—baptism, the marriage ceremony, and the funeral mass. Since about 98 percent of contemporary Italians have been baptized (a figure that has held steady) and more than 80 percent still are married in the church, it seems clear that, whatever the impact of greater secularization, the church remains the sole guardian of these rituals. Furthermore, public opinion surveys have indicated that Italians remain somewhat more religious in their views of life than the European norm.[34]

Still other Italians were said to relate to the church through superstition, such as belief in the evil eye (*malocchio,* the belief that some persons cast a curse by looking at a victim), supernatural powers of a local saint, or witch-craft. Theologians trace such superstitions more often to pagan rituals than to the church, but the fact remains that many Italians associate such magic with Christianity.

Certain aspects of Italian Catholicism remain extraordinarily appealing to parishioners and have sustained the church as it has struggled to maintain its strength in an increasingly secular world. One such phenomenon is the bian-nual event in Naples when the blood of San Gennaro liquefies. Each September and May, Neapolitans and pilgrims gather at the Treasure Chapel of San Gennaro to await the miraculous transformation into liquid form of the brown, powdery substance, said to be the blood of their fourth-century patron saint. Participants believe that San Gennaro holds the power to pro-tect Naples. Thus in 1980, when Mount Vesuvius devastated parts of the city, many Neapolitans blamed the Second Vatican Council for the restrictions it had placed on the San Gennaro celebration, unwavering in their faith in their patron saint. In some ways, this incident reveals the durability of the cult of saints and local, popular traditions that continue to inspire devotion among some of the very Catholics who ignore Vatican decrees and dismiss the church hierarchy as authoritarian.

A comparable phenomenon is the extraordinary popular support for the late Capuchin friar and mystic known as Padre Pio that led to his canoniza-tion in 2002, an event in St. Peter's square attended by hundreds of thousands of devotees. Padre Pio had been the object of an enormous cult following that even intensified after his death in 1968. "Never before in the history of Chris-tendom has the cult of a saint expanded so rapidly and so intensely," writes one authority.[35] Pio's followers claimed that he exhibited stigmata similar to the wounds that Jesus suffered on the cross. However, many in the church questioned not only the stigmata, but claims of his miracles and reports that he wrestled with the devil. His cult following and reports of his experiences at the monastery of San Giovanni Rotondo triggered investigations by the Vat-ican, which then ordered him to celebrate mass in private and avoid exposing his stigmata. Pope John XXIII, who was critical of cults, renewed the investi-gation, weighing charges of fanaticism and financial irregularities. As a result, Padre Pio remained an outcast, taking his place on the fringes of Italian reli-gious culture alongside weeping Madonnas, others who claimed stigmata, and paranormal experiences. At the same time, Pio's devotees rallied to defend him from the Vatican, so that his rejection by the Holy See actually contributed to the myth that enveloped him and brought support from some Catholics opposed to the reforms of the Second Vatican Council. At the same time, Pio's prophecies and visions attracted Catholic fundamentalists, reminding them of the tradition of Our Lady of Fatima, which features a similarly zealous cult based on the mythology surrounding a miraculous appearance of the Virgin Mary in a small town in Portugal in 1917. Such appeal suggests a strong need among some Italian Catholics to find charismatic figures who preach a traditional Catholic message.[36]

It was the direct intervention of Pope John Paul II, who as a young man had traveled to Padre Pio at San Giovanni Rotondo for confession, that reversed the Vatican's position and led ultimately to his sainthood. Significant here is the grassroots adherence to the charismatic friar, known as "the people's saint," over the opposition of the Vatican and, even more emphatic, the subsequent reversal of Vatican policy to embrace the grassroots traditions. The questions that surrounded his paranormal experiences have been closed by the church. Padre Pio has taken on the status of an Italian national saint in the tradition of Francis of Assisi and Antony of Padua. Confirming the point at Pio's beatification, Wojtyla pronounced Padre Pio a "son of Italy."[37]

The very choice of a non-Italian pope indicated that the church was continuing to move outward from its traditional base (there are currently more non-European than European cardinals). In turn, Wojtyla put the finishing touches on the Vatican's separation from the DC, consistent with the Second Vatican Council's reorientation of the church away from its European focus. In 1995, Cardinal Camillo Ruini, president of the Conference of Italian Bishops, acknowledged the new reality by announcing that, with the dissolution of the DC, there would no longer be a single Catholic party in Italy. In fact, Catholic political unity had long been an illusion, with only about half of DC members attending mass regularly (while a full 10 percent of Italian communists attended church services). With the collapse of the DC and the "first republic" in the early 1990s, Catholic voters split their votes, about 18 percent siding with the *Partito Popolare* (Popular Party, or PPI), the DC's major successor, while about 30 percent supported Berlusconi's Forza Italia movement, with others distributing their votes among smaller parties. In the European elections of 2004, the UDC (*Unione dei Democratici Cristiani,* or Union of Christian Democrats) showed substantial progress.[38]

The charismatic new pope traveled widely, more than all his predecessors combined, using his journeys to reach out to Catholics worldwide and to acknowledge that he accepted the validity of other religions. Of greatest symbolic importance were his 1985 visit to the main Jewish temple in Rome, his 1986 invitation to world religious leaders to join him at St. Francis Basilica in Assisi, and his visit to the Wailing Wall in Jerusalem in May of 2000 when he asked forgiveness for the church's role in the Holocaust.[39] In part because of Wojtyla's global vision, the Italian church now has diminished in importance within world Catholicism. When Pope John XXIII was elected in 1958, one-third of the College of Cardinals were Italian; as of 2003 the Italian component had dropped to one-fifth of the total. Furthermore, many young Italian Catholics were drawn to non-Italian, international forms of Catholicism, and particularly to the new, radical "liberation" theology of Latin America.

While opening the church to new geographical horizons, John Paul II took a consistently firm stand on doctrinal issues that has served to redefine the church, leaving Italians with clear-cut choices, resolving some of the ambiguities of the period following the Second Vatican Council. Consequently, Wojtyla brought a certain calming effect to the church, recentralizing Vatican authority and quieting dissent. In the broadest theological terms, the pope took a position against excessive reliance on science, technology, or reason, subordinating all to faith. His stand on social issues was uniformly conservative, leaving no room to doubt the church's opposition to contraception, abortion, fertility treatment, biotechnological research, noncelibate clergy, ordination of women, and homosexuality. The pope's adroit use of the media to showcase his charismatic presence enabled him to present the Vatican's positions effectively. In the process, he won the admiration of many Italians but failed to convince them to accept his social and moral doctrines, as indicated by the fact that fewer than one-third of Italian voters supported the church's position on the 1981 referendum that would have reversed the 1978 law legalizing abortion.[40] On the other hand, Wojtyla did not lead the church down a path of comprehensive conservatism. He did not support the surge of neoconservative, free-market economics, making a point that free-market forces cannot satisfy human needs, speaking out on behalf of laborers and the poor, and advocating debt forgiveness for the Third World. Nor was the pope unaware of women's issues. While standing firm against a feminist social agenda and reinforcing the church's traditional commitment to a domestic role for women as mothers, he supported women's rights in the workplace and apologized for any fault the church might bear for past transgressions that enforced inferior status for women.[41]

At the same time, speaking both as head of the Catholic Church and as Bishop of Rome, Wojtyla took an active interest in Italy and Italians. On several occasions, the pope admonished the *mafia*. In his first such public reproach in Agrigento, Sicily in May 1993, he passionately proclaimed: "The *Mafia* offends against God!"[42] The pope's passionate message inspired priests in Palermo to stand up to the *mafia*, which promptly retaliated by gunning down the Rev. Giuseppe Puglisi and car-bombing two Roman churches. Two years later, the pope took his message to the Sicilian *mafia's* home turf in Palermo, chastising Italians in a powerful speech: "Do not kill! No man, no human association, no *Mafia* can change or trample the right to life, this most sacred right of God."[43] Although the pope repeated his rebuke of the *mafia*, some remain skeptical, questioning the church's commitment.

Palermo mayor Leoluca Orlando walked out of a reception for the pope during the 1995 visit to protest the presence of a bishop accused of having mob ties.

In addition to the problem of organized crime, Pope John Paul II regularly addressed a range of other Italian issues. He emphasized the Vatican's support for the rights of workers, denounced racism and xenophobia, and called on Italians to welcome immigrants. And in addressing the Italian Parliament in November 2002, the pope asked Italians to commit to reversing the "grave threat" of the declining birthrate; to uphold the "rights of the family as the natural society based on marriage"; to address the problems of unemployment, poverty, and immigration; and to guard against a "secularist culture" and "a consumerism indifferent to spiritual values."[44]

Among the church's positions that have generated the greatest enthusiasm among Italians was the pope's consistent objection to the use of military force, in opposition to the Gulf War, the 1998 Allied bombing of Iraq, the NATO bombing of Serbia, and the 2003 U.S.-led invasion of Iraq. In the 1990s, notes Donald Sassoon, "the Church became a rallying point for many of those who took a pacifist position."[45] However, on this issue, as on others, the Vatican holds no monopoly, even among Italian Catholics. The *Pax Christi* peace movement has criticized the church, not only for alleged favoritism that priests have shown to jailed *mafiosi*, but for selective invocation of the peace doctrine.

On a similar international theme, Wojtyla's call for debt relief for Third World countries has resonated among parts of the Italian electorate. An even more appealing humanitarian stand on which the pope has won widespread support among Italians is his consistent and vocal opposition to the death penalty, which Italy has not used since 1947 and abolished in 1994. John Paul II pled for mercy at Italian vigils on behalf of death row inmates[46] and took a strong stand in his 1995 encyclical *Evangelium Vitae* (The Gospel of Life) in which he declared the church's near total opposition to the death penalty.[47]

What appears to have happened to Italian Catholic culture is that it has reinvented itself. Even under the powerful leadership of Pope John Paul II, the Vatican continued to surrender its earlier attempt to reconquer Italian society. In place of the historic monopoly held by the Vatican has emerged a more diverse Italian Catholicism. And although the church has even encouraged such diversity, Wojtyla held the line on dogma, claiming that the church retains sole access to truth.[48]

At the same time, a majority of Italians refuse to accept the papacy's exclusive claim to moral truth. About one-third of Italian Catholics refuse to believe that disobeying the church's moral teachings constitutes a mortal sin.

No longer the dutiful followers of an authoritarian, politically dominant Vatican and its political party, Italian Catholics, liberated by the Second Vatican Council and the demise of the DC, have regrouped in numerous voluntary Catholic associations and affiliated with various political parties. One such lay group is the Association of Christian Workers (ACLI). Another is *Opus Dei* (God's Work), known as a secretive, worldwide, conservative Catholic lay organization with strong ties to Vatican inner circles. Another is *Comunione e Liberazione* (Communion and Liberation, CL), which originated in 1954 among students in Milan and now counts 70,000 members, primarily in north and central Italy. A hard-line, grassroots pressure group that opposes many aspects of progressive Catholicism, modernization, and globalization, CL illustrates the resiliency of independent Catholic groups in a period when the Vatican has lost influence and the Christian Democratic Party has collapsed.

Defiant of much of the church's social policy, Italian Catholics nonetheless remain connected to the church by rituals, by a still ubiquitous clergy of nearly 200,000, by an extensive Catholic press, and by the church's many social and charitable arms in which large numbers of Catholics volunteer their time. In more than 4,000 centers around the country, Catholic volunteers administer to the homeless, AIDS victims, drug addicts, and refugees. One recent phenomenon seems to illustrate rather dramatically the durability of Catholic traditions. The BBC reported in November 2003 that competing shows of religious fiction, depicting the lives of saints and popes, are running away with ratings on Italian television. On a spring weekend of 2003, over 35 percent of Italian households watched a dramatic rendition of the life and death of the 12-year-old martyr, Saint Maria Goretti.[49]

Italians hold varying views on the pontificate of John Paul II. Applauded for his stand in opposition to the death penalty and the wars in Bosnia and Iraq, criticized for his views on women, birth control, abortion, and divorce, the late pope remains in death, as he was in life, primarily a symbol of courage and an object of affection and respect. In many ways, this Polish prelate represents a diluting of the importance of Italy, having focused more dramatically than his predecessors on the church's global mission. Like millions of others, many Italians await with eagerness the emergence of a post-Wojtyla Vatican.

NOTES

1. H. Stuart Hughes, *Consciousness and Society* (New York: Alred A. Knopf, 1958), 201.

2. David Ward, "Intellectuals, Culture and Power in Modern Italy," in *The Cambridge Companion to Modern Italian Culture,* ed. Zygmunt Barański and Rebecca J. West (Cambridge: Cambridge University Press, 2001), 85.

3. Benedetto Croce, *Materialismo storico ed economia marxistica* (Milan: Sandron, 1900); Croce, *Estetica come scienza dell'espressione e linguistica generale: Teoria e storia* (Milan: Sandron, 1902); Croce, *Saggio sullo Hegel seguito da altri scritti di storia della filosofia* (Bari: Laterza, 1906); Croce, *Teoria e storia della storiografia* (Bari: Laterza, 1917); Croce, *Storia della storiografia italiana nel secolo decimonono* (Bari: Laterza, 1921).

4. Croce, *Materialismo storico;* David D. Roberts, *Benedetto Croce and the Uses of Historicism* (Berkeley: University of California Press, 1987), 41–46.

5. Norberto Bobbio, *Ideological Profile of Twentieth-Century Italy* (Princeton, N.J.: Princeton University Press, 1995), 69–71.

6. Croce, *That Which Is Living and That Which Is Dead in the Philosophy of Hegel* (1907), trans. Douglas Ainslie (London: Macmillan, 1915).

7. Croce, *The Philosophy of Giambattista Vico,* trans. R. G. Collingwood (London: Howard Latimer, Limited, 1913).

8. Croce, *Estetica come scienza.*

9. Roberts, *Benedetto Croce,* 4, 15, 139–41, 270–71.

10. Roberts, *Benedetto Croce,* 6.

11. Croce, *Storia d'Italia dal 1871 al 1915* (Bari: Laterza, 1928).

12. Croce, *Storia d'Europa nel secolo decimonono* (Bari: Laterza, 1932).

13. Roberts, *Benedetto Croce,* 221–23, 261.

14. Massimo L. Salvadori, foreword to Norberto Bobbio, *Ideological Profile of Twentieth-Century Italy* (Princeton, N.J.: Princeton University Press, 1995), xxxiv.

15. Antonio Gramsci, *Quaderni del carcere* (Turin: Einaudi, 1948–51).

16. Ward, "Intellectuals, Culture and Power," 89.

17. Giame Pintor, "L'Ultima lettera" (November 28, 1943), quoted in *Ideological Profile of Twentieth-Century Italy,* by Norberto Bobbio (Princeton, N.J.: Princeton University Press, 1995), 166.

18. Roberts, *Benedetto Croce,* 253–65.

19. Robert S. C. Gordon, "*Impegno* and Modernity: 'High' Culture," in *Italy Since 1945,* ed. Patrick McCarthy (New York: Oxford University Press, 2000).

20. Ward, "Intellectuals, Culture and Power," 91–93.

21. Gordon, "*Impegno* and Modernity," 211.

22. Giovanna Borradori, ed., introduction to *Recoding Metaphysics: The New Italian Philosophy* (Evanston, Ill.: Northwestern University Press, 1988), 1–5.

23. Umberto Eco, "*Intentio Lectoris:* The State of the Art," in *Recoding Metaphysics,* ed. Giovanna Borradori (Evanston, Ill.: Northwestern University Press, 1988), 27–43; Eco, *The Role of the Reader: Explorations in the Semiotics of Texts (Advances in Semiotics)* (Bloomington, Ind.: Indiana University Press, 1979).

24. Emanuele Severino, "The Earth and the Essence of Man," in *Recoding Metaphysics,* ed. Giovanna Borradori (Evanston, Ill.: Northwestern University Press, 1988), 180–84.

25. Borradori, ed., introduction to *Recoding Metaphysics,* 25–26.

26. Renzo De Felice, *Mussolini,* 8 vols. (Turin: Einaudi, 1965–98).

27. Ann Fremantle, *The Papal Encyclicals in Their Historical Context* (New York: Mentor Books, 1956), 152.

28. Patrick McCarthy, ed., "The Church in Post-war Italy," in *Italy Since 1945,* (New York: Oxford University Press, 2000), 134–41.

29. McCarthy, ed., "The Church in Post-war Italy," 138–40.

30. Percy Allum, "Catholicism," in *The Cambridge Companion to Modern Italian Culture,* ed. Zygmunt Barański and Rebecca J. West (Cambridge: Cambridge University Press, 2001), 103–4.

31. Allum, "Catholicism," 106–7.

32. Martin Clark, *Modern Italy, 1871–1982* (London: Longman Group, Ltd., 1984), 371.

33. McCarthy, ed., "The Church in Post-war Italy," 148.

34. Enzo Pace, *L'unita dei cattolici in Italia* (Milan Editori Guerinie Associati, 1995), 139.

35. Peter Jan Margry, "Merchandising and Sanctity: The Invasive Cult of Padre Pio," *Journal of Modern Italian Studies* 7, no. 1 (Spring 2002): 89.

36. Margry, "Merchandising and Sanctity," 96–97; Paul Ginsborg, *Italy and Its Discontents* (New York: Palgrave Macmillan, 2003), 133.

37. "Pope Beatifies Monk Persecuted by Church," *The Independent* (London), May 3, 1999.

38. Franco Garelli, "Destra cattolica or cattolici di destra?," *Il Mulino* 44, no. 358 (March–April 1995): 252–65; "Who Will Follow Him?" *The Economist,* October 4, 2003.

39. "Pope Asks Jews for Forgiveness at Wailing Wall," *The Independent* (London), March 27, 2000.

40. McCarthy, ed., "The Church in Post-war Italy," 145–46.

41. "The Holy See," http://www.vatican.va/roman_curia/congregations/cfaith/documents/rc_con_cfaith_doc_20040731_collaboration_en.html.

42. Peter Hebbleth Waite, "John Paul on the Road Again," *National Catholic Reporter* 31, n. 5 (November 18, 1994) : 10.

43. "Pope Brings Anti-Mafia Message to Sicily," *Chicago Sun-Times,* November 23, 1995.

44. "John Paul Makes First Papal Address to Italy's Parliament," *The New York Times,* November 15, 2002.

45. Donald Sassoon, *Contemporary Italy: Economy, Society, and Politics Since 1945,* 2nd ed. (New York: Addison Wesley Longman, 1997), 159.

46. Jeffrey Fleishman, "Italians Fight U.S. Use of Death Penalty," *Philadelphia Inquirer,* August 20, 2000.

47. "The Doctrinal Weight of *Evangelium Vitae,*" *Theological Studies* 56 (1995): 560–65.

48. Lewis S. Mudge, "*Veritatis Splendor* and Today's Ecumenical Conversation," *The Ecumenical Review* 48, no. 2 (April 1996): 158–62.

49. "Saints before Soaps on Italian TV," http://news.bbc.co.uk/1/hi/world/europe/2814287.stm.

3

Marriage, Gender, and Family

EVEN IF ITALIANS LARGELY DISMISS VATICAN POLICY on such matters as birth control and divorce, there is little question that family traditions remain a dominant and cohesive force in Italian culture. This is not only the case with respect to the home, but, as historian Paul Ginsborg has argued, "familism" (defined as exclusive emphasis on family values and actions) retains its durable influence on Italian public life as well. This pull toward family considerations has strengthened with the recent prosperity of the family unit. Familism is particularly important, according to Ginsborg and others, because it weakens Italians' dedication to civic responsibility and their associations with civil society and the national government. It has been said that Italy is not so much a national state as it is a collection of millions of families.[1]

Consequently, while Italians trust their own families, they display a characteristic mistrust toward government, which, in turn, has impaired formal institutions and opened the door to a political system built largely on client-patron relationships ("clientelism"). As a result, in matters of local government and bureaucracy, Italians often cultivate personal relationships to manage such mundane matters as postal service, medical care, banking, and permits for remodeling or expanding houses. Others disagree with this assessment of the negative impact of familism, arguing instead the reverse: that it was an unworthy government that created mistrust and necessitated reliance on family and patronage. Whichever may be the case, few would argue the central significance of family in Italian life.

The Italian family—and in fact all of Italian society—has undergone sweeping and significant changes in the second half of the twentieth century,

Passeggiata. Family in Perugia on a Sunday. Courtesy of the author.

more dramatic in pace and magnitude than at any time in the history of the peninsula. As late as World War II, about half of Italians worked in agriculture, with the other half roughly split between the industrial and service sectors. Industrialization contributed to the Economic Miracle of the 1950s and 1960s, which in turn raised the standard of living substantially and created unprecedented prosperity. Italian per capita income rose at the highest rate in Europe during this era, exceeding 80 percent of British per capita income by 1970. For the first time, many Italian families were able to purchase such consumer durables as washing machines, refrigerators, televison sets, motor scooters, and automobiles, even moving beyond the popular, minuscule Fiat 500 (the famous *Cinquecento* or "Topolino") and 600 to larger, family-sized sedans. Such impressive gains in material life, however, did not mask the many thousands of families who lived in squalor, particularly in the hovels and high-rise apartments around most urban centers.

With the rapid expansion of the industrial sector in the postwar era, the number of industrial workers increased steadily until 1970, when about 40 percent of Italians (nearly 5 million) worked in industry as the farming sector shrank. However, by the 1990s, Italy had moved beyond industrialism into its postindustrial phase. Farmers now accounted for a mere five percent of the workforce, surpassed dramatically by service workers who now numbered well over half the working population.

As the twentieth century unfolded, these far-reaching economic changes reshaped Italian society. Members of farming families moved to cities in search of industrial and service jobs. This urbanization movement spurred the construction of sprawling, high-rise apartments and shanty towns that circled major cities from Rome to Milan. Most often the internal migrants were men, many of them southerners, either unmarried or moving in advance of their families. In the 1950s and 1960s, between 8 and 9 million Italians moved north and to cities. Their willingness to sacrifice for their families by taking low-paying jobs in fact contributed to economic expansion by keeping wages depressed in Italian industry.[2]

By the 1970s, many Italian families included several wage-earners. Often, not only did all the adult men and women in a family work, but each worked several jobs. Typically, each would hold a "day job" in civil service or business with generous vacation, healthcare, and retirement benefits, then supplement income by working a part-time job, often self-employed, which would avoid additional tax burden. Furthermore, Christian Democrat governments provided subsidies for family-owned shops. The result is that Italy had a much greater number of small retail stores, bars, restaurants, and artisan workshops—and fewer supermarkets—than any other European country. Even after layoffs at large industrial factories in the 1980s and 1990s, unemployment rates remain relatively low, the urban middle class has continued to grow, and Italy's "black economy" thrives. These untaxed ("off the books") earnings provide the family substantial additional wealth to invest in securities, purchase an automobile, a home, or even a vacation home. About 70 percent of Italians own their homes, representing a substantial increase over the past several decades.

Many Italians have recently favored the safe and lucrative government savings bonds (BOTs, treasury bonds have been particularly popular) and similar investment instruments. So enthusiastic were Italian investors that they saved an average of nearly 25 percent of income, ranking Italians second only to Japanese in savings habits. Families held a substantial portion of government debt, producing a higher ratio than in most countries, where banks tend to hold more government debt than in Italy. Furthermore, because high inflation kept interest rates, dividends, and bond yields high, the heavily invested Italian families "kept up with inflation," suffering relatively less from high inflation rates than did families in countries where investments were more meager. In fact, high returns on investments actually increased demand during a period of high inflation, providing Italian families more disposable income, and enabling them to make more discretionary, luxury purchases such as a seaside apartment or a second car. A recent survey ranked Italians with Germans in owning more cars per capita than other Europeans; however, these, like all Italian statistics, show strong regional variations such as a higher concentration of large and German-made cars in the North than in the South.

In the face of this surging prosperity, many Italians were excluded from the new affluence. In the mid-1980s, about seven percent of Italians lived below the poverty line. In the South, almost one in five were engulfed in poverty. As time has passed, several groups of Italians seem most vulnerable: urban youth, particularly those living in the dilapidated fringes, because of dire employment prospects; the growing number of elderly, because of inadequate services; and the burgeoning immigrant population, with many employed in the worst-paying jobs as an alienated underclass.

THE ITALIAN FAMILY IN THE TWENTY-FIRST CENTURY

In the context of the economic and social changes that have swept Italy in the past half century, the family unit remains particularly important. While large industry, both private and government-owned, has foundered and accounts for a declining portion of the domestic product, family-owned businesses remain dynamic and productive and account for much of Italy's prosperity over the past several decades. It has been estimated that four of five Italian businesses are family-owned and employ fewer than 50 persons.

The largest private company in Italy, the automotive conglomerate Fiat, has been in business for more than 100 years and is owned by the Agnelli family of Turin. Although the recent deaths of patriarch Gianni Agnelli and his younger brother Umberto, combined with a record $4.5 billion loss in 2002, jeopardizes the future of the company, it now rests in the capable hands of Luca Cordero di Montezemolo, who most recently headed up the successful Ferrari Formula 1 racing team.

All across the economic landscape are family-owned businesses, large and small, from the great fashion houses of Milan to the niche industries of the Veneto, to local artisans' shops and family-owned small retail stores in every village in the country. Their influence is so great that they have traditionally shaped legislation to favor their interests; and their skill at manipulating tax laws is so acute that they routinely operate "off the books," defrauding the government of massive revenues. The result is that salaried employees carry a disproportionate share of the tax burden, paying uncommonly high rates.

Many families—not just the famous industrialists—function as economic units, or "firms," geared to produce income for the benefit of the members. This phenomenon has been described as "local family capitalism."[3] While the father largely maintains his traditional role as patriarch, sociologists believe that he now functions less in the style of the arbitrary master of the first half of the century and more as manager of the family unit. In fact, it has been said that Italy's impressive prosperity is attributable, not so much to judicious government or even to a culture of shrewd corporate management, but to the collective efforts of Italian families, each acting to advance its own interests.

It must be remembered at the same time that this model of "family as firm," important as it is, largely ignores those families ensnared in poverty and hopelessness. Especially in the ramshackle suburbs of some cities (the southern cities of Naples and Palermo come to mind), families struggle mightily. Young men in particular are drawn to the "black economy," drug trade, criminal organizations, construction labor, and the poorest-paying jobs in the service sector, which often provide the best opportunities for employment. It was estimated in the 1980s that more than one-third of Palermo's population was trapped below the poverty line, with no evidence of improvement. Nonetheless, although such families may be unable to play the entrepreneurial role often attributed to the families of the middle class, poor families continue to furnish a sanctuary from the brutality and deadening absence of opportunity in the world outside.

Although the family continues to play an exceedingly important role in Italian life, the familiar Italian family, whose image was fixed in the rural villages of a bygone era, has changed dramatically. No longer is the nuclear family large (mother, father, and four or five children) and no longer are gender roles as rigidly delineated. Nor is a large family viewed as a financial asset that will improve family earnings; with changing values that have accompanied the decline of the agricultural and industrial sectors, the additional family members are more likely to be viewed as a financial strain. The stereotype of an Italian woman marrying early and bearing many children has been shattered by the reality that by 1980, the average Italian family included parents and one child. The American pattern of large numbers of young, single women rearing children while supported by government subsidies simply does not exist. An Italian woman aged 20 is one-tenth as likely to bear a child as an American of the same age.[4]

Furthermore, there is evidence that children and adult women have begun to break away from some traditional family constraints in favor of greater individual expression, particularly in spending free time with friends. No longer does all socializing revolve around the family. At the same time, there are indications that Italian fathers have become more involved in nurturing children, even while struggling somewhat to adjust to their new roles.

Some statistical trends help to explain the changes in the family. The number of marriages per thousand Italians dropped from 7.1 in 1950 to 5.4 in 1989, close to the European average. That means that, while more than 400,000 Italian marriages were performed just after World War II, the number had dropped to just over 300,000 50 years later. Despite the drop in total marriages, four of five couples still choose to take their vows in church. And although the number of common-law marriages has increased, it remains below the average for the rest of the continent. The same can be said for out-of-wedlock births: they increased from 2.4 percent of all births in 1961 to 7 percent in 1992, still one-fourth the rate in France. At the same time, the number of divorces increased until 1988, when they began to decline to a rate of 10 percent of marriages, about one-third the rate of France and one-fourth the rate of Britain. Italian civil marriages end in divorce at a significantly higher rate than religious marriages, so that religious influences are believed to be a factor inhibiting divorce. But because the Italian rate is also lower than the rate in other Catholic countries, other deterrents help explain the low rate: the requirement that couples must be legally separated for three years before qualifying for divorce; a backlog in the judicial process; substantial economic penalties for divorce, including employment and housing difficulties; and the fact that most European countries accommodated divorce for a century before Italy. As might be expected, regional differences persist, with the North reflecting the European averages, while the South retains larger families with fewer divorces and out-of-wedlock births. As for extramarital relationships, many Italian men persist in keeping mistresses, often involving long-term relationships. Particularly for politicians and successful businessmen, such relationships are almost expected, if not fully accepted.

The most dramatic change by far is found in the diminishing size of the family, most evident in the declining birth rate. In the "baby boom" years of the 1960s, Italian women bore more than 1 million babies per year, contributing to a growing population. Thirty years later, Italy had essentially reached zero population growth, with predictions that, in spite of increasing immigration, Italian population will decline by the second quarter of the twenty-first century. Italian women are producing fewer than 1.3 children, the lowest rate in Europe and among the lowest in the world. Southern regions came closest to reaching the rate (slightly more than two children per

Wedding in Cortona. Courtesy of the author.

family) required to sustain the population and actually showed some population growth (attributable to immigration); in contrast the North showed a
declining population, with the northern region of Liguria setting the record
with less than one child per family. Family size in the northern region of Piedmont numbers only 2.5 members. By 1994, deaths exceeded births throughout the peninsula, reinforcing the prospect of population decline.

   Although the family has decreased in size, in other ways it has proven resistant to change. For example, the percentage of nuclear families has remained
above 50 percent for the past half century, while the percentage of extended
families has fallen only gradually. The slight decline in the percentage of
extended families reflects a trend throughout Western Europe, while the percentage of extended families in Italy remains much higher than the European
average. Surprisingly, the extended family remains strongest in the Center
and weakest in the South and the islands (the very regions where family sizes
are largest). It has been suggested that both the extended family and the large

nuclear family reflect differing regional strategies to provide security and solidarity by similar means.[5]

Another striking feature of the Italian family is the elongated period during which Italian children remain at home, often into their thirties, and typically until marriage. This growing trend helps also to explain lower birth rates, since Italians now tend to postpone marriage until they have completed their education and reached some degree of financial independence from parents. Relatively few Italian students leave home to attend a university, especially because of the scarcity of university housing and the lack of scholarship and loan funds. The pattern is for Italian youth to attend a local university, with little importance attached to seeking a university with a superior reputation.[6] Even at the completion of a degree, Italian youth typically remain at home because parents and the family home exercise a strong attraction, and because of practical considerations such as the difficulty in finding adequate housing and jobs and the desire to save money. One recent study showed that half the male population and one-quarter of the females remained at home at age 29.

Recent research suggests that these trends are now so firmly established that they constitute new social structures. This extended stay in the home by young adults has created a new interval in the life cycle of Italians, one that has intervened between adolescence and full adulthood. As a result, an entirely new form of family relationship has emerged in which the family includes two adult generations cohabiting simultaneously. Consequently, the traditional assumptions by which adult children would provide support to parents has been replaced by an ongoing dependency of young adult children.[7]

These new social structures have produced ambiguous consequences. There are indications that prolonged coresidence has produced some negative impact by interfering with the abilities of young adults to fulfill their expectations for a more satisfactory life. At the same time, most results seem positive in contrast to similar patterns in Anglo-Saxon countries. Development among the younger generation of Italians does not seem to have been impeded and, in fact, may be encouraged by the prolonged stay. Neither is there evidence that young adults have lost freedom or the ability to make decisions. In fact, the personal autonomy that this generation of young adults enjoys while living in the home provides the best explanation for compatibility, especially when compared to the past, when such cohabitation was much more likely to have proven stifling. Other surveys suggest that young adults find comfort and general well-being in extending their residency and, in fact, that both parents and children find satisfaction in this arrangement. All agree on the primary importance of the young adults' "self-fulfillment," defined largely, but not exclusively, in terms of career. And all seem to agree as well on the benefits of postponing the realities of adult life, which is often seen as precarious and difficult.

Thus, in spite of the close proximity of parents and children, generational tensions are relatively mild and are outweighed by the benefits of prolonging the stay. Good relationships are often nurtured by a kind of informal "contract" among adult family members, so that young adults manage to exert greater social independence while living at home. The communication and support that are at the center of the parent-adult child relationship are typically provided by the mother, who is the essential component in maintaining a satisfactory quality of family life. And it is the quality of family life that young people view as the major factor influencing the worth of their prolonged stay. At the same time, fathers, who generally communicate better with sons than with daughters, play a less critical role in family communication. The greatest source of anxiety, particularly because parents often define their own well-being in terms of the success of their children, centers around the dire prospects for youth employment.

In all, Italian young adults still consider family their primary commitment, well ahead of social, religious, and political allegiances. Studies show a strong sharing of basic values across generations. Such close intergenerational relations, more amiable generally than in Anglo-Saxon countries and better than they were in Italy in the late 1960s, provide hope that Italian family ties may continue to compensate for the lack of adequate services to support an aging population.

The strongest domestic bond by far is the link between mother and son. The son's dependency on his mother is cultivated from birth as boys are pampered and forgiven their misdeeds. This well-known phenomenon has been labeled *mammismo* (excessive reliance on mothers' protection of adult males) and has become the source of widespread attention. Italians often refer to this relationship metaphorically as "Madonna and Child" and understand the reluctance of adult males to leave the nurturing environment of the matriarchal home. Some believe that the intensity of this relationship inhibits the development of autonomy and perpetuates dependency. Not only do Italian males tend to remain at home until age 30 or beyond, but they typically retain this special relationship throughout life, phoning their mothers regularly, treating them with special reverence, and showering them with attention, especially by delivering floral bouquets on special occasions. One study showed that well over half of Italian married men saw their mothers at least once per week, with one in three seeing them daily.[8]

Changes in the Italian family have paralleled changes in the identity and collective behavior of youth. Young people have both shaped their own place in

Italian life and, in turn, been influenced by changes in family. In contrast to the intergenerational solidarity that had characterized Italian families in the past, a "youth culture" has emerged in the past several decades, especially in response to improvements in standard of living and the resulting rise in expectations. In the years following the worldwide turbulence of 1968, young Italians demanded that the universities relax their admissions policies. And as youth unemployment remained high (more than 30 percent in the mid-1990s), Italians extended their time in the university as a sanctuary from the prospect of unemployment, thus lengthening the duration of their stay in parental homes. At the same time, a radical student movement developed, leading many young Italians to support left-wing parties and a wide range of radical factions. Thus many Italian youth redefined themselves as markedly different from older, more conventional generations, and a "generation gap" opened.

The long-term result of this emerging "generation gap" was not to alienate youth from older adults, but to reinforce the existence of a youth culture. Italy's new youth culture incorporates non-Italian tastes and behavior patterns, particularly American styles of clothing and music (including Italian rap) that now contribute to a distinctively youth-driven consumer demand. The new culture also features a more permissive sexual ethic, reinforced by surveys that indicate a growing acceptance of unmarried cohabitation among young Italians. As a result of embracing this youth culture, young Italians now identify more with peers and less with family than they did in the past. At the same time, changes in the traditional family may have contributed to

Young couple at cafe, San Casciano. Courtesy of the author.

emerging problems, particularly among the young, in the form of increasing rates of teen suicide, child neglect, and child abuse. And although the rates remain relatively low, there is concern that the diminishing of the traditional extended family may be contributing to a growing sense of loneliness and alienation among the young Italians.

In spite of such alarming signs, the most remarkable attribute of the Italian family is that, in the face of the changes that have assaulted traditional life in the peninsula during the postwar era, the family remains notably resilient. Grandparents are still actively engaged in providing care for children. While it is now more probable than ever that Italian children will have no siblings and will return home from school to find both parents at work, it is also likely that they will find grandparents at home. And even though the percentage of extended families has fallen in half to below 10 percent, some sociological studies indicate that a "modified" extended family remains in which two-thirds of close relatives live, if no longer in the same house, in the same city. Nearly 9 in 10 married Italians live within 40 miles of their mothers. With life expectancy improving, the Italian family is said to have grown "long and thin," with the traditional three generations often under the same roof, but with markedly fewer members.

At the same time, the trend toward smaller families does present challenges. The most ominous is to find the resources to support an aging population with adequate pensions and health care. In this respect, Italy faces the same dilemma that looms in the future of much of the industrialized world. Simi-

Addressing the world's problems, Cortona. Courtesy of the author.

larly, to keep pace with economic growth, Italy will need to replace workers, particularly skilled workers in the niche industries. Demographic patterns suggest that immigrants will have to fill many jobs, and that implies changes in what has been a homogeneous population reluctant to assimilate immigrants.

GENDER ISSUES AND SOCIAL MOVEMENTS

The many, far-reaching changes that have transformed the face of Italian society in the more than half century that has passed since World War II have dramatically influenced issues of gender. But just as the Italian family has weathered change, so traditional, male-dominated social and cultural conventions have proved resilient. The result is a kind of paradox. Although slow to adjust, Italy has undergone major changes in the status of women over the past several decades. At the same time, Italian homosexuals have begun to establish a presence in public life. Nonetheless, most observers would agree that Italy remains a male-dominated society in which women still face discrimination and homosexuals remain largely out-of-view, more "closeted" than in much of Europe and the United States.

As might be expected, changes in the Italian family have influenced the role of women. Traditionally Italian women were relegated to a domestic role that, even if venerated and exalted, left them with few rights, mired in an institutional and moral framework of inferiority. The roots of this condition run deep. In all regions, mothers still retain many of the characteristics of their traditional domestic, maternal roles, as might be expected. While fathers have begun to provide more nurturing, mothers continue to act as the primary caregivers, not only for children, but for husbands and grandparents as well. Scholars who have examined this important maternal role in the broadest historical context sometimes attribute it to the powerful model in the Catholic world of the Virgin Mary, the ideal not only of motherhood, but of virtue and modesty, and the essential force in Italian Catholicism. Others look to the Great Mother figure of the pre-Christian era and find cultural precedent in the idealization of the mother as a fertility symbol. Whatever the original source, the Italian mother holds an idealized role at the center of the family, reinforced for centuries by the Catholic Church. While the father may nominally head the Italian family, it is apparent that most Italian families function in a matriarchal fashion.

During the *Risorgimento*, some idealists had envisioned a new Italian nation that would free women from traditional oppression. However, their vision did not materialize. Instead the laws of the newly united Italian state restricted the rights of women to own property, or to control bank deposits or even their own children, subjugating them to men in each case. Italian mores imposed a suffocating double standard, by which women were largely deprived of the opportunity for higher education, while men enjoyed not only greater opportunity but a superior status in their personal conduct. For example, while male sexual offenses were widely ignored, women's adultery was promptly punished. Yet, at the same time that Italian women lived as second-class citizens, they contributed substantially to the Italian economy, particularly as underpaid workers in agriculture and textiles. It has been argued that women's contributions to Italian industrial development were indispensable.

Given the conservative social environment in which Italian women lived, it is not surprising that an organized women's movement developed only later in Italy than sister campaigns in Europe and the United States. Nonetheless, even before Italy was fully unified, several remarkable women began to publish feminist tracts. In the 1860s, the Milanese Anna Maria Mozzoni began to call for changes that would win her the reputation as the founder of the Italian women's movement. In 1864, at age 27, Mozzoni wrote a treatise advocating a revision of the traditional legal code, and in 1869 she translated into Italian John Stuart Mill's *Subjugation of Women.* That same year, Gualberta Alaide Beccari founded the journal *La Donna* (Woman), to which Mozzoni regularly contributed. And four years after that, Aurelia Cimino Folliero de Luna established *La Cornelia,* a journal that she dedicated to legal reform. In 1881, Mozzoni organized the Lega promotrice degli interessi femminili (League for the Promotion of the Interests of Women). At the same time the Parliamentarian Salvatore Morelli introduced a series of proposals to reform family law and extend civil rights to women, including the right to testify in civil proceedings, and (in 1878) the right to attain a divorce. In 1899, Sibilla Aleramo (born Rina Faccio) moved to Milan to direct the journal *L'Italia Femminile* (Women's Italy) in which she authored a series of articles on feminist topics. Aleramo emphasized women's qualities that she viewed as unique, especially spirituality, which she distinguished from men's. In 1906, she published her autobiography, *Una Donna* (A Woman), in which she detailed the frustrations of an unhappy marriage. The writings of Mozzoni, Folliero de Luna, and Aleramo helped to raise awareness of women's issues among the Italian middle class, including men, and anticipated contemporary feminist themes.

By the end of the nineteenth century, Italian women had begun to expand their campaign, calling for access to education and the male-dominated professions, while Mozzoni called for equal pay for women. At the same time, women factory workers became more politically aware as the Italian Socialist Party began to organize. Labor unions and the Socialist Party, particularly because of the efforts of Anna Kuliscioff of the PSI, for the first time opened the campaign for women's rights to women of the working class. The term "feminism" began to appear in the press, particularly in *La Donna,* while some degree of consensus developed to address the problems of prostitution and harsh working conditions.[9]

When it came to winning the right to vote, however, progress was severely delayed. Although Morelli had repeatedly introduced legislation to grant women the vote, first in 1867, the effort repeatedly misfired. Women simply failed to win the necessary support of major political parties, the Vatican, or the Liberal coalition of five-time Prime Minister Giovanni Giolitti. Ironically, women were trapped in a political paradox. The Socialists and other parties of the left feared that enfranchising women (particularly in the South) would fortify conservative and Catholic votes, while conservatives and Catholics opposed woman suffrage because of fear that it would destabilize the family and undercut conservative values. Thus when Giolitti sponsored a major expansion of the right to vote in 1912, he excluded women from the ranks of the 5.5 million new voters, partly because he was soliciting support from the Vatican, which was resolutely opposed to woman suffrage.

Having failed to win the vote in the years before World War I, Italian women found their campaign overwhelmed, first by World War I, then by the rise of Fascism. Although Futurists and others who supported the early Fascist movement campaigned against the conventions of middle-class society, they proved to be unsympathetic to the women's agenda. Worse, once Mussolini took power and began to consolidate his regime, the Fascist government began to reinforce traditional gender roles by celebrating the cults of domesticity and motherhood as part of the Fascist campaign to expand the population. Thus for more than three decades, in a period when women made significant gains in the United States, the United Kingdom, and elsewhere, Italian women remained virtually immobilized in a status of legal and political inferiority.[10]

It was not until the fall of Fascism that Italian women began to move into the political mainstream. The women's push for the right to vote in the constitution of the new Republic was supported by all major parties. The Christian Democrats, who would later oppose parts of the feminist agenda, supported the women's right to vote because they had a larger percentage of women members than the PCI, their major rivals. Two years after women achieved the right to vote in 1948, the DC government passed legislation that provided paid maternity leave and protected mothers on the job. Nonetheless, the PCI embraced much of the feminist agenda—which the DC rejected—and continued to count a higher percentage of women in leadership roles by a large margin.

Not only did the major political currents of the modern era shape the destiny of Italian women, but economic influences played a significant role as well. A number of changes in the family are products of economic forces that have made women more prominent fixtures in the workplace. Surprisingly, statistics suggest that women actually lost jobs during the years of the Economic Miracle of the late 1950s and early 1960s, when women represented a smaller percentage of the workforce in Italy than in any European country. As they left the workplace to marry or rear children they were replaced by migrant males from the South, never to return to work. At the same time, rising wages allowed men to support families and encouraged women to return to traditional domestic roles. In turn, Italians began in the 1960s to idealize this new domestic role of women, supplied with an array of new appliances and accompanied by images that suggested that the modern Italian woman would proudly manage a well-equipped household. The result was that industrialization had, in some ways, actually restricted the public life of Italian women. At the same time, more open discussions of women's sexuality and gender roles in the 1960s began to suggest that changing attitudes about women in society might be imminent.

The era of Italian heavy industrialism passed quickly as Italy moved into the postindustrial, service economy. Consequently, by 1970 Italian women began to move into the job market with impressive results, increasing their numbers by 50 percent over the next 15 years. However, it is important to note that any discussion of changing social conditions in Italy must take into account the emphatic regional differences that have survived the industrial era and persist into the new century. The trend that took women out of the idealized role as housewife and into the workforce was substantially more prevalent in the Center and North than in the South, where traditional gender roles remained more resistant to change.

As women moved more directly into the job market, their political agenda broadened and won greater public attention. By demanding and gaining a measure of equal treatment as employees, they opened the door to new opportunities and gained greater job experience. In turn, women's career expectations rose and their demands for full legal equality and expanded educational opportunities increased. At the same time, political experience and ideology drove other demands. Women had been active in politics during the Resistance and thus were drawn to leftist political movements that had played a prominent role in liberating the peninsula at the end of World War II.[11] The Resistance-era Gruppi di difesa della donna (Groups in Defense of Women) reorganized as the Unione Donne Italiane (Italian Women's Union, or UDI). Dominated by communist women, the UDI acted as the precursor of one of the most dynamic feminist movements in Europe.

Spurred by the student protests of 1968 and the workers' demonstrations that followed, the women's movement moved to organize a number of separate groups that paralleled the major political parties, while maintaining their independence. Women found that neither dominant culture, Catholic nor communist, would embrace their agenda, just as gay rights and environmental activists would later find. As a result, women went outside the boundaries of party to build a countercultural movement that allowed them to aggregate greater influence and create new forms of expression, including numerous feminist groups, call-in radio programs, publishing houses, and bookstores.[12]

By the 1970s feminists had succeeded in recruiting a mass following and in placing major issues before the public, press, and Parliament. Finally they succeeded in pushing Parliament into an era of reform in which major parts of their agenda were written into law. The Parliament legalized divorce (1970), produced a family law that decriminalized adultery, provided for legal separation, and extended rights to children born out of wedlock (1975); made discrimination based on gender illegal (1977); and, notably, legalized abortion over the determined opposition of the Vatican and the DC (1978). Legalized abortion provided Italian women a strong guarantee of the right to choose (*"L'utero è mio e lo gestico io"*; "I control my uterus"). The Movimento di Liberazione della Donna (Movement for the Liberation of Women, or MLD), allied with the small Radical Party and committed to full legal equality of the sexes, organized the petition that forced abortion rights onto the ballot, and pushed for contraception and free medical services. In doing so, the MLD established the Italian women's movement as a major force, not only by gaining publicity for the movement with large public demonstrations, but by bridging normal partisan and social gaps. By 1980, over opposition of the Vatican and the DC, the women's movement had overwhelmingly defeated the attempt to repeal the abortion law and had established itself as a force in Italian politics.

In spite of numerous gains, however, as recently as 1990 Italian women made up a smaller percentage of legislators (eight percent of the lower house) than all other European nations except Greece, France, the United Kingdom, and Portugal. In the election of 1994, Italians elected 96 women to the 630-seat Chamber of Deputies, the largest number of women ever; however, that number dropped by one-third two years later. Notable Italian women in politics were Nilde Jotti, President of the Chamber of Deputies from 1979–92; Irene Pavetti, who held the same position in 1994; and Susanna Agnelli, Foreign Minister in 1995–96. As indelible a mark as these high-profile women leaders made, Italian women have experienced some difficulty in translating their legislative success into institutional reform.

The demise of the PCI and the notable decline of the UDI amplify the difficulty encountered by Italian feminists in transcending their role as an interest group. As a result, the mass public rallies have been largely relegated to the past. Italian women have not been able to match their impressive victories in the campaigns for divorce and abortion rights, and now appear more pragmatic and complacent in their politics than in the ideologically-driven campaigns of the 1970s. One indication of the softening of the women's political campaign is their support for the conservative, patriarchal prime minister, Silvio Berlusconi. Berlusconi raised the ire of feminists when he told his audience at the New York Stock Exchange in September 2003 that a reason to invest in Italy was that "we have beautiful secretaries,...superb girls."[13]

Many of the changes of the 1970s, as well as many that have altered Italian family life in more recent years, have been generated by women. A good example is the declining birth rate. Sociologists regard this trend as a product of conscious choice by women who have begun to weigh such factors as career and cost when considering childbearing, something that many women of the previous generation, with fewer educational and employment opportunities, would not have done. The weakening of the extended family is a harbinger of change. Fewer relatives are available in the home to provide child care at a time when state-provided services are meager and living space is often confined. The women's movement has achieved maternity leave and has backed a nationwide plan for nurseries, both important steps in enabling working women to continue to nurture the family, which remains primarily their responsibility. One recent study showed that women with at least one child were working an average of more than five and a half hours per day on household chores, while men worked less than one hour. Other studies confirm that Italian women remain at the center of the household, providing the bulk of nurturing, household maintenance, and other services.

While women remain the families' major caregivers, as they have moved into employment in greater numbers, they have not only reshaped their positions in the job market, but have generally altered their roles in society. As a result, recent feminists (neofeminists) have begun to move away from the earlier goals of gender equity—in part because of success, in part to reject the norms of male-dominated society—and in the direction of defining a new feminism.

Many neofeminists consciously reject traditional, culture-laden, "objective" views of women in favor of a new awareness of women's unique experience and consciousness. One prominent idea that accompanied this effort to realign awareness of women was the theory that, in the lives of women, "the private is political"; in other words, feminist thinkers argued that women define their political sphere, differently than men, to include many issues that had generally been regarded as private, including abortion and domestic violence. Other examples of new feminist directions are the movements to create women's studies programs in the universities, the first women's studies journal, *Donnawomanfemme* (DWF), a women's history summer school, women's networks and cultural centers such as the well-known *Centro Culturale Virginia Woolf* in Rome, organizations to protect against violence to women, a wide-ranging women's literature, and various lesbian organizations.[14] However, in spite of new energy and new directions in the Italian women's movement, and in spite of changes in law, family, and gender roles, most observers would agree that Italy remains a male-dominated society and culture.

The predominantly patriarchal Italian culture that resisted the expansion of women's rights also slowed the emergence of a gay rights movement. At the same time, several factors contributed to the erosion of traditional taboos against public debate on issues related to homosexuality. The "sexual revolution" of the 1960s created an opportunity for exploration of wide-ranging topics of sexual practices. Furthermore, the ability of feminist scholars and activists to create a nationwide discussion of issues of gender broke ground for gay activists to make similar, if belated, strides.

Italy's first gay liberation movement (*Fuori, Fronte Unitario Omosessuale Rivoluzionario Italiano,* the United Italian Revolutionary Homosexual Front, or "Out") organized in Milan in May 1971 in an era of flourishing radical politics. *Fuori* shared with the feminist movement the conviction that "the personal is political" and similarly rejected much of bourgeois morality, viewing gay liberation within the broader context of human emancipation. The most widely recognized Italian treatise on homosexuality is Mario Mieli's *Elementi di critica omosessuale* (*Elements of the Homosexual Critique,* 1977). Although revolutionary in its earliest form, *Fuori* spurned the PCI in favor of the Radical Party, with which it affiliated in 1974. In 1976, *Fuori* moved into the mainstream of politics as its leader, Angelo Pezzana, won a seat in Parliament, becoming its only openly gay member. Pezzana's election caused a defection from the left wing of the gay movement, which then engaged in the student revolt of 1977 and launched its new magazine, *Lambda,* and its first national meeting in May 1978.

By the 1980s *Lambda* had failed and *Fuori*'s influence and organization had dissipated. *Fuori* was replaced by *Arcigay,* which took its name from the Italian Cultural and Recreational Association (ARCI) within which it originated. The Italian lesbian movement first organized in 1981 as the CLI (Collegamento Lesbiche Italiane, Italian Lesbian League), emphasizing a distinct identity from male homosexuals and from the feminist movement. The next year, Felix Cossolo and Ivan Teobaldelli launched *Babilonia,* which endures as Italy's only national gay and lesbian magazine. By the mid-1980s, the gay movement turned its attention toward AIDS treatment and prevention and finally won the support of the health ministry in 1988. At the same time, gay candidates made some progress in politics, most notably when Paolo Rutter won a seat as Milan's first gay city councilman.[15]

Domestic partnership became a major political focus by the 1990s, bolstered by the European Parliament's decision to support gay and lesbian rights in 1994. By then, the gay liberation movement had diversified with the formation of special interest groups such as gay parents and had begun to show signs of splintering, as exemplified by two competing gay pride parades in 1997.[16]

The gay literary tradition in Italy is often regarded separately in lesbian and male homosexual categories because of distinct strains of development. Mainstream Italian writers such as Alberto Moravia and Elsa Morante had incorporated male homosexual characters throughout the postwar era, usually presenting homosexuality in a negative light, as had gay writers such as Pier Paolo Pasolini. The corpus of literature addressing the lesbian experience began to develop in the 1980s, most notably with Dacia Maraini's *Lettere a Marina* (*Letters to Marina,* 1980), and with other, more theoretical works.[17]

One incident that illustrates the degree to which homosexuality remains, even today, largely closeted in Italy involves the story of Alberto Aquarone, a renowned scholar of modern Italian history. Aquarone published soul-searching poetry about his hidden life and his unrequited love for a young man, but did so only under the pseudonym Davide L. Mattia. The supreme irony is that his sexuality remained hidden from the public eye even in death. At a major retrospective on his work, numerous scholars gathered to pay tribute, many of whom knew about Aquarone's sexuality. All were generous in acknowledging his contributions to the study of history; not one mentioned that he was gay.

NOTES

1. Paul Ginsborg, *A History of Contemporary Italy: Society and Politics, 1943–1988* (London: Penguin Books, 1990), 2–3; Ginsborg, *Italy and its Discontents* (New York: Palgrave Macmillan, 2003), 97–100; Charles Richards, *The New Italians* (London: Penguin Books, 1995), 126.

2. Percy Allum, "Italian Society Transformed," in *Italy Since 1945,* ed. Patrick McCarthy (New York: Oxford University Press, 2000), 14–15.

3. Ginsborg, *History of Contemporary Italy,* 416.

4. Donald Sassoon, *Contemporary Italy,* 2nd ed. (New York: Addison Wesley Longman, 1997), 114, citing 1995 statistics.

5. Giovanni B. Sgritta, "The Italian Family: Tradition and Change," *Journal of Family Issues* 9, no. 3 (September 1988): 372–96.

6. Sassoon, *Contemporary Italy,* 114–15.

7. Eugenia Scabini and Vittorio Cigoli, "Young Adult Families," *Journal of Family Issues* 18, no. 6 (November 1997): 608–26.

8. ISTAT (Istituto Nazionale de Statistica). *Indagini multiscopo sulle famiglie anni 1993–94, Aspetti della vita quotidiana II,* Rome, 1996, in *Italy and its Discontents,* by Ginsborg (New York: Palgrave Macmillan, 2003), 79.

9. Sharon Wood and Joseph Farrell, "Other Voices: Contesting the Status Quo," in *The Cambridge Companion to Modern Italian Culture,* ed. Zygmunt Barański and Rebecca J. West (Cambridge: Cambridge University Press, 2001), 141–49; Lucia Chiavola Birnbaum, *Liberazione della donna, Feminism in Italy* (Middletown, Conn.: Wesleyan University Press, 1986), 19–21; Judith Jeffrey Howard, "The Civil Code of 1865 and the Origins of the Feminist Movement in Italy," in *The Italian Immigrant Woman in North America,* ed. Betty Boyd Caroli, Robert F. Harney, and Lydio F. Tomasi (Toronto: The Multicultural History Society of Ontario, 1977), 14–20.

10. Victoria De Grazia, *How Fascism Ruled Women: Italy, 1922–1945* (Berkeley: University of California Press, 1992); Perry R. Willson, *The Clockwork Factory: Women and Work in Fascist Italy* (Oxford: Clarendon Press, 1993); Silvana Patriarca, "Gender Trouble: Women and the Making of Italy's 'Active Population,' 1861–1936," *Journal of Modern Italian Studies* 3, no. 2 (Summer 1998): 144–63.

11. Jane Slaughter, *Women and the Italian Resistance, 1943–1945* (Denver, Colo.: Arden Press, 1997).

12. David Ward, "Intellectuals, Culture and Power in Modern Italy," in *The Cambridge Companion to Modern Italian Culture,* ed. Zygmunt Barański and Rebecca J. West (Cambridge: Cambridge University Press, 2001), 91–92.

13. Sassoon, *Contemporary Italy,* 118–23.

14. Wood and Farrell, "Other Voices," 148–49; Mary Gibson, "New Perspectives on Italian Women's History," *Journal of Women's History 8,* no. 2, (summer 2003),169–80.

15. Luisa Passerini, "Gender Relations," in *Italian Cultural Studies,* ed. David Forgacs and Robert Lumley (New York: Oxford University Press, 1996), 144–59.

16. Eugenio Giusti, "Gay Movement," in *Encyclopedia of Contemporary Italian Culture,* ed. Gino Moliterno (London: Routledge, 2000), 251–52; Mario Mieli, *Homosexuality and Liberation: Elements of a Gay Critique,* trans. David Fernbach (London: Gay Men's Press, 1980).

17. Stephen Riedel, "Gay Writing," in *Encyclopedia of Contemporary Italian Culture,* ed. Gino Moliterno (London: Routledge, 2000), 252–54.

4

Holidays, Saints' Days, Festivals, and Food

EMBLEMATIC OF ITALIAN CULTURE is the widespread celebration of religious and secular holidays, most of which are ritualized by festivals featuring distinctive foods. In fact, one facet of Italian public life that remains essentially unchanged, by virtue of its connection to religion, tradition, and town, is the celebration of Saints' days and feast days. Many feature religious processions during the extended Christmas or Lenten seasons. A notable Easter celebration is the *Scoppio del Carro,* the fireworks display in the Piazza del Duomo in Florence. Other festivals are distinctly local in origin, such as the race of the *ceri* (candles) in Gubbio; the *Festa de' Noantri* in Rome; and the famous *Festa di San Gennaro* of Naples, the gathering in the cathedral to witness the liquefaction of the Saints' blood. Outside the realm of religion, venerable holiday customs endure, such as the *Palio,* Siena's classic horse race; Florence's archaic soccer match known as the *Calcio Storico Fiorentino;* the Venetian *Carnevale* (carnival); and both the opera season at La Scala and music festivals such as *Maggio Musicale* (Musical May) in Florence.

As a highlight of festivals, but also as an important feature in the everyday lives of Italians, food maintains a central importance in Italian culture. In fact, the influence of food in Italy is as great as any other factor, including family, religion, architecture, music, and soccer. Not only does food afford employment for a significant minority of Italian workers in agriculture, processing, export, preparation, and service, but it provides a focus for family life, identifies Italian regions, and has created durable images of Italians in the eyes of much of the world. Even if stereotypes of Italian food—pasta or pizza served with a flask of Chianti on checkered tablecloths—are inaccurate, the association of Italians with food is important. Italian food and its preparation and consumption *(gastronomia)* have influenced diets of much of the world for centuries.

SAINTS' DAYS, PUBLIC HOLIDAYS, AND VACATIONS

Saints' days and *feste* (festivals) are part of the rich tradition of Italian holidays that constituted the main focus of traditional leisure activity in Italy. Having evolved from time-honored Christian traditions, they often include processions, pilgrimages, or sacred dramas. Some festivals, known as *sagre*, are rural in origin and derive from ancient, pagan rituals, usually surrounding the fertility of the harvest and analogous rhythms of the cycle of human life. The ancient *sagre* remain connected with the first harvest and thus are most often celebrated in the spring and summer seasons. Throughout Italy festivals celebrate the ripening of every imaginable fruit and vegetable, from artichokes to zucchini blossoms, and even herbs such as oregano and rosemary. In the fall, Italians harvest grapes and olives, perhaps the most widely treasured fruits of the earth, and thus the objects of numerous *sagre*. Another greatly anticipated autumn delight is the white truffle season, which provides its own festivals in central Italy. By December the youngest (and most desired) olive oils appear on shelves, green and peppery, pressed in irregularly shaped bottles, providing yet another occasion for celebration. Wheat, more essential in sustaining life, has been less widely exalted since the Fascist era when Benito Mussolini, shirtless, wielding a scythe, wherever a photograph could be arranged, publicized his "Battle of Grain."

Religious festivals and feasts are dedicated to saints, usually the patron saint of a town or city or a prominent saint honored in several locations around the peninsula. In many instances, the Roman Catholic Church has managed to superimpose Christian symbolism and themes on ancient, debauched, pagan festivals and *sagre* in the same way that the early Christian Church illustrated its defeat of paganism by constructing sacred buildings atop the foundations of pagan temples.

A third type of *feste*, dating from the late medieval and early Renaissance era when the city states bloomed, extols urban pride. These *feste* celebrate the virtues of various cities and occupy a focal point of great civic pride, related closely to the phenomenon of *campanilismo* (intense pride in the bell tower, or *campanile*, of one's town).

These three categories of Italian festivals—ancient *sagre*, religious Saints' days, and urban festivals—maintain some distinction, particularly in a historical sense. At the same time, there is also some ambiguity in these types, since civic *feste,* including pagan and Christian elements, are often celebrated on the holiday dedicated to the patron saint of the town. The most helpful way to understand the celebrations in the contemporary context might be to follow the calendar, since the sacred and secular often merge on days of celebration.[1]

Italian religious holidays, many survivors of the ancient world, dot the calendar year-round. A number had been imported into the Roman Republic from the Greek deities (such as the cult of Dionysus) and from the mystery cults of the East (such as Cybele and Mithra). Many survived the Roman and early Christian eras. For example, Romans adapted the Greek spring festival of Dionysus (named Bacchus by the Romans) to several spring celebrations. The Romans celebrated the Bacchanalia at night in a mood of abandon, with masked revelry, generous consumption of wine, and sexual indulgence, all accompanied by loud drumming. The Roman historian Livy wrote that the three-day spring orgy of the Bacchus cult exhibited "debaucheries of every kind," which led the Senate to legislate against the celebrations in AD 186. Following the banning of the Bacchanalia, the Liberalia emerged on March 16, a more restrained Bacchus festival in which priests and priestesses paraded through the streets making sacrifices to the god at various parts of the city. On February 15, Romans annually celebrated the Lupercalia, thought to be an ancient festival of shepherds, in honor of Lupercus, the god of fertility. Priests, called Luperci, sacrificed goats and young dogs before indulging in a ceremony of ritual purification, bathing in blood of the animals. Young men then engaged in fertility rites by racing through the streets naked, covered partly in goat skins, striking those they passed, especially women, with goat skin thongs. The Roman government added its own sacred festivals, including those dedicated to the emperors, so that about half the days on the Roman calendar were dedicated to religious festivals. Each festival sacrificed to at least one of the gods and featured the ever-present food and wine. In addition, Romans competed in various contests and staged dramatic ritual performances.

In the fourth century AD, when the practice of the Christian religion was legalized, the Catholic Church began the process of superimposing Christian symbols on pagan feast days, an important step in establishing the church's influence on the peninsula. The festivals maintained some of their original character but now were celebrated in the names of saints and, in many cases, the Virgin Mary. San Giorgio (St. George) replaced Perseus, the more ancient serpent-slayer; St. John the Baptist, bearer of the tradition of ritual immersion, now assumed a saintly presence at Rome's summer water festival; and the Virgin Mary replaced a number of Greek and Roman deities, including Athena, Cybele, and Diana. The spring rituals of the Bacchanalia, Liberalia, and Lupercalia would eventually be subsumed and partially tamed by the church in the pre-Lenten ceremonies that became part of *Carnevale*. In addition, the Christian Church contributed Christmas and Easter, the former replacing the pagan celebration of the origin of the sun, the latter substituting for the pre-Christian ceremony honoring the rebirth of Attis, the god of vegetation and mythological partner of the goddess Cybele.

Epifania (Epiphany, January 6) marks the first Italian Christian celebration of the New Year, an occasion for exchanging gifts and the conclusion of the month-long Christmas season. On the eve of Epiphany, Italian children hang stockings by the fireplace in anticipation of candies provided by *La Befana,* a tattered but benevolent witch. However, according to the traditional rendition of the Three Magi, naughty children will find that La Befana has deposited coals in their stockings. Numerous events celebrate Epiphany throughout Italy.

As winter turns to spring, in anticipation of the fasting and penitence of the Lenten season, *Carnevale* provides the most raucous and extravagant festival of the year. Costumes, masked balls, and parades abound as Italians indulge in sensual pleasures including feasts of great abundance. Although the food of *Carnevale* varies widely, most Italian towns offer generous portions of meat and sausages, followed by *frittelle,* fritters dusted with powdered sugar and filled with various fruits and creams. The highlight is *settimana grassa* (Fat Week), including *Domenica Grassa* (Fat Sunday) and Martedì Grasso (Mardi Gras or Fat Tuesday), the final day of *Carnevale.* Tradition held that *Carnevale* lasted for several months, particularly in Venice, and many towns launched the celebration between Christmas and Epiphany. The parades often became rowdy, as participants engaged in playful combat using oranges, eggs, and various other foods. Today in Viareggio, a resort town on the Tuscan coast, revelers do battle with plastic clubs, and in the town of Ivrea in the Valle d'Aosta, rival teams compete by hurling Sicilian blood oranges at each other while racing on horse-drawn carts.

Italy's most renowned *Carnevale* is found in Venice where the masked balls are legendary and mask-making a highly valued craft. Tradition holds that the Venetian *Carnevale* originated in the twelfth century and continued through the medieval and early modern eras, featuring dances, tightrope walkers, bull fights, cart races, and magical performances in the Piazza San Marco, and a host of costumed parties and parades throughout the city. Revelers ran through the streets with torches lighting up the night sky and met on the final evening at San Marco for the burning of a large effigy of the traditional costumed character *Pantalone,* much to the delight of a chanting crowd. The tradition of tightrope walking is said to have been originated by a sixteenth-century Turk who reputedly walked a rope from a boat moored in the canal to the top of the *campanile* (bell tower) of San Marco.

These customs remain very much alive. In contrast to other cities, Venice hosts masked balls with full orchestras in the *piazze* (town squares), and a spectacular floating procession of decorated boats and masked revelers along the Grand Canal, so that the entire celebration creates a panorama of public ceremony. Meanwhile, private parties, some of which trace their origins to the medieval era, dazzle in the city's great *palazzi* (palaces). One of the renowned balls was the charity ball at the famous opera house, La Fenice, suspended since the tragic fire of 1996. The costumes demonstrate a strong connection with a tradition of stylized costumes and masks deriving from the *commedia dell'arte*, the popular theater of the sixteenth and early seventeenth centuries. Among the best known are *I dottori* (the doctors), including *Il Medico della Peste* (the doctor of the plague), with the characteristic mask featuring a long beak; *Il notaio* (the notary public); *Arlecchio* (the Harlequin), outfitted in a colorful mix of diamond-shaped patches; *Pantalone* (the miserly Venetian merchant); the fun-loving and egg-throwing *Mattaccino;* costumed stilt-walkers; and the always popular, much-abused *Pulcinella* (the "Punch" character of the "Punch and Judy" puppet show), with hooked nose and sugar loaf hat. *Carnevale* provides a perfect opportunity for public flirtation, a long-standing convention. The stylized costumes and masks are supplemented with more modern creations, as large groups of Italian students now join in the revelry. The Venetian festival has become so overwhelmingly popular that city authorities have been forced to turn back buses of tourists. *Carnevale* concludes on *Martedì Grasso,* the final day before the beginning of the Lenten season.

On March 19, the bountiful *Festa di San Giuseppe* (St. Joseph's Festival) provides an interlude in the Lenten season of fasting. Traditionally a national holiday, the *Oggi di San Giuseppe* (St. Joseph's Day, now merely elective) is widely celebrated in villages and cities throughout the peninsula and in the islands, especially throughout Sicily. In most towns, the *Festa* includes both a dramatic performance and a meatless banquet, the latter presented either by the town or by individual families. The centerpiece is an improvised altar or table abundantly filled with traditional foods of the day, particularly a variety of specially decorated breads and pastries. (In addition to being patron saint of carpenters, families, orphans, the homeless, and others in need, San Giuseppe also serves as patron saint of pastry chefs.) In the informal drama, children (*virgineddi,* "little virgins") typically assume the roles of the Holy Family members, initiating the festivities by sampling the traditional ornamental breads and pastries and distributing samples to friends. What follows is a ritual dinner, the *cena di San Giuseppe.*

Palm Sunday is celebrated throughout Italy as the beginning of Easter week (Holy Week) in much the same fashion as in other countries. Churches are decorated with arrangements of gilded palm fronds and olive branches, blessed by the priest, and distributed to the congregation. Most spectacular is the celebration at St. Peter's Basilica in Rome where throngs await to receive a palm blessed by the Pope. Traditionally, Holy Week proceeded with the ancient ceremony of the blessing of the houses. After the house had been given its spring cleaning, a local priest sprinkled holy water in each room in symbolic renewal of baptism. Like many venerated practices, the blessing of the houses has greatly diminished.

Throughout the week, numerous solemn dramatizations and processions commemorate aspects of Christ's passion, varying by locality. On Good Friday in the southern region of the Basilicata a torchlight procession recreates Christ's path to crucifixion, while in Taormina in Sicily lantern-bearing, black-clad women parade through the streets to assist the Madonna in finding her son. Some form of this drama is repeated in countless Italian towns. In much of Sicily, ceremonies similarly focus on the suffering of the Virgin Mary and reflection on death. In Avellino in the Campania, members of a confraternity whose white hoods are crowned with thorns lead a procession while bearing crosses. In the Sicilian port city of Trapani, members of an ancient, hooded confraternity lead men representing the various trades who carry historic Easter sculptures on their shoulders from the church through the narrow streets at a slow, dramatic pace that carries them into the next morning. "The drama is reflected in the emotional intensity of the suffering Jesus," writes Carol Field, "in the eyes of the Roman soldiers that blaze with fury,...the wrought-up expression on Pilate's face, and the anxiety and grief of the Madonna."[2] Women dressed in black precede the Madonna sculpture, said to be searching in vain for her son, as the crowd falls into the procession, trailing the Madonna on her path to the church. Once she enters, the "mourners" disperse to enjoy dinner.

Italians celebrate Easter Sunday *(Pasqua)* with a great variety of colorful pageantry and celebration. Although general themes of resurrection and of the suffering and euphoria of the Virgin Mary dominate, the Easter celebration varies from city to city and village to village, as with other *festes*. Sicilian celebrations alone illustrate the many variations of the Easter theme. In Piana degli Albanesi near Palermo, women adorned in fifteenth-century costumes dispense decorated eggs, symbolizing fertility and resurrection. The residents of Adrano (province of Catania) celebrate Easter morning with a pageant called the *"diavolata."* In the main piazza, a stage is divided into sections representing "heaven" and "hell." As the ceremony begins, a red-clad Lucifer leads a band of devils in a ritualized battle against the forces of good, including an angel who ultimately prevails on Lucifer to pronounce "Viva Maria!" At the same time in Modica (province of Ragusa), a statue of the Madonna draped in black is carried to the Church of Santa Maria where she begins the search for her son. When she finds him in the main piazza, she embraces him. At that moment, her black cape falls, releasing a flight of blue-ribboned white doves. Similar in theme—but unique—is the Easter pageant in Lanciano (Chieti province) where figures representing Jesus, the Virgin Mary, and St. John are carried in a procession to the Piazza Plebiscito where, after great anticipation, they meet. To conclude the celebration, the statues are taken to the cathedral where they remain until members of the confraternities collect them.

The best known and most spectacular Easter celebration occurs at the Cathedral of Santa Maria dei Fiori (the Duomo) in Florence. The *Scoppio del Carro* (explosion of the cart) is said to have originated in the medieval era. On Easter morning, Florentines and tourists gather in the Piazza del Duomo to get a glimpse of the large and highly decorated cart, which is pulled into the piazza between the baptistery and the cathedral by brightly decorated oxen. At the appointed time, after bands of flag throwers and musicians have built anticipation, the crowd is alerted to the event by herald trumpeters. Inside the cathedral, the Bishop of Florence lights a small rocket in the shape of a dove attached to a wire, propelling the dove out the main entrance into the piazza to explode into fire inside the cart, lighting fireworks and creating a large plume of smoke to the delight of the crowd. Successful performance of the rocket traditionally was viewed as a good omen for the coming spring harvest.

Several spring holidays follow the Easter season, but none rival it in pageantry. *Pasquetta* (Little Easter or Easter Monday) is a widely celebrated secular holiday, providing recovery from the events of the previous week's celebrations. Italians typically travel to the countryside for a picnic or lunch at

Scoppio del Carro, Piazza del Duomo, Florence. Courtesy of the author.

an outdoor trattoria to welcome in the spring season. On April 21, Romans celebrate the founding of their city, set in tradition as 753 BC. Four days later, April 25, marks both Italy's national holiday, *Anniversario della Liberazione* (Liberation Day), and the *festa di San Marco* (festival of St. Mark), the patron saint of Venice. Liberation Day celebrates the beginning of the partisan, anti-Fascist insurrection in northern Italy against occupying German forces and the Fascist Republic of Salò in 1945. The uprising led to the capture and execution of Mussolini two days later and to the capitulation of the Germans the next month; thus the role of Italian resistance fighters in contributing to the victory of the Anglo-American allies remains a source of pride. Today, with revisionists discrediting the resistance movement, Liberation Day has become more controversial and less a unifying influence than in the immediate postwar era. The same day in Venice, the *festa di San Marco* is distinguished by the traditional procession to the piazza San Marco and by the more recent custom by which Venetian men present their beloved with red rosebuds (a blossom is a *boccolo*) lending to the festival its alternate name, the *Festa del Boccolo.*

May celebrations begin in Italy on *Calendimaggio,* or May Day eve, and continue through the next day. Assisi hosts a notable *Calendimaggio* festival that includes a lovesong contest and a torchlight procession through streets lined with silk banners. Maypoles still can be found in many villages, suspending *prosciutto,* sausages, cheeses, and money from the top as prizes for the first to climb the greased pole. A number of villages feature romantic serenades on May Day, complete with their own Queen of May.

May Day, or *primo maggio,* is an Italian national holiday that invokes a range of images. As the international workers' holiday *(festa del lavoro),* May Day marks a time when labor unions, crafts guilds, and the remnants of the Communist and Socialist parties sponsor parades and demonstrations in numerous cities to exalt the contributions of labor. At the same time, May Day recalls the primeval rites of spring that the Romans revived in a frolicking feast of flowers, fertility rites, drinking, dancing, food, risque songs, and sexual abandon—all done to honor the goddess Maia, inspiration for the Queen of May. In an effort to reform the bawdy Roman celebration, the Roman Catholic Church introduced *San Giuseppe* (St. Joseph) as the patron saint of workers and endorsed the celebration of Labor Day on May 1.

The extended Easter season concludes with several religious celebrations that usually fall in the month of May. Ascension Day is the fortieth day or the sixth Sunday after Easter, followed 10 and 11 days later by Pentecost and Corpus Christi. Ascension Day is an ancient Christian festival marking the "flight" of Christ to heaven and is marked by various representations of fowls, often consumed in an Ascension Day banquet. Many Romans place an egg by a lighted candle in a window to be blessed on Ascension Day by the Madonna. Florentines mark Ascension Day with *La Festa del Grillo* in recognition of the cricket's chirping that heralds the spring. Festivities center at the Cascine park, with crickets now readily available in specially decorated, tiny reed cages. It is said that the cricket will bring good luck if it sings—or if it is freed.

Pentecost, 10 days later, evolved from the Jewish festival ending Passover and usually incorporates a flight of birds or doves. The Umbrian hill town of Orvieto celebrates its Ascension Day with a Feast of the Dove on the steps of the glorious thirteenth-century Gothic-Romanesque cathedral. In a dramatization reminiscent of the *Scoppio del Carro* in Florence, firecrackers announce the firing of a "dove" toward the cathedral where it lights a fire, sending flames above the heads of sculptures of the Madonna and the Apostles. The next day features colorful Corpus Christi processions in many villages and cities. In Orvieto the procession leads to a reliquary in the cathedral, while in the town of Genzano outside Rome, the procession crosses the large floral mosaic laid out in elaborately designed patterns on the town's streets.[3]

The month of May provides the additional opportunity for a number of spring festivals, the most notable of which are two major cultural events, *Maggio Musicale* and the *Festival dei Due Mondi* (Festival of Two Worlds) in Spoleto. *Maggio Musicale* has provided a significant musical event for Florentines and visitors since 1933 and has hosted such guest luminaries as conductors Bruno Walter, Wilhelm Furtwängler, Zubin Mehta, Herbert von Karajan, and Riccardo Muti. Performed both by the local symphony and guest conductors and orchestras, *Maggio Musicale* is regarded, along with the festivals of Bayreuth and Salzburg, as among the most important European musical events. The Spoleto Festival follows in June and July. Initiated in 1956 by the Italian-American composer Gian Carlo Menotti, the festival originally was designed to provide young American artists the opportunity to perform in Europe. The festival premiered with a legendary performance of Verdi's "Macbeth" directed by Luchino Visconti. Two years later American choreographer Jerome Robbins presented his "Ballets USA." Since its debut, the festival has established its reputation by offering memorable performances by such notable artists as Placido Domingo, Luciano Pavarotti, Cecilia Bartoli, Jean-Yves Tibaudet, Rudolf Nureyev, and the Paul Taylor and Twyla Tharp dance companies.

Among Italy's traditional May festivals is the famous *Corsa dei Ceri* (candle race) in the Umbrian hill town of Gubbio. The evening before the event features preliminary parades, music, and lavish banquets. The next morning, drummers, trumpeters, and colorful processions announce the race, as the city's Piazza Grande fills with visitors in anticipation of the main event. The race features three towering wooden structures, resembling candles, each with a sculpture of a saint perched on top: San Giorgio, Sant'Antonio, and Sant'Ubaldo, Gubbio's patron saint, who always reigns triumphant. The *ceri* are carried up and down the narrow, steep streets by teams of men dressed in contrasting red, yellow, and black costumes, finishing with a climb from the central piazza up Monte Ingino to complete the race at the basilica. A torchlight procession follows as the signal to begin the post-race festivities.

The month of June leads into an active season of summer festivals. On June 2, Italians celebrate the founding of the Republic *(Anniversario della liberazione)*. On that day in 1946, voters abolished the monarchy and replaced it with a republic. The president of the republic presides over the annual military parade down the via dei Fori Imperiali in Rome, culminating in the laying of the wreath on the tomb of Italy's unknown soldier at the Piazza Venezia. The president then hosts a gala celebration at his residence in the Quirinale palace. Several weeks later, on June 13, Italians commemorate St. Anthony of Padua, patron saint of children, the poor, and animals, who before his death preached in Padua where the grand Saints' Basilica now stands. The Franciscan church in Rome dedicated to St. Anthony *(Sant'Antonio dei Portoghesi)* is the national church of the Portuguese (Anthony was born in Portugal) and to Brazilians as well. On St. Anthony's day in Rome, decorated horses and mules are blessed at the church in a colorful ceremony.

Corsa dei Ceri (candle race), Gubbio. Courtesy of the author.

June 24 is a day of the celebration of the *festa* of *San Giovanni Battista* (St. John the Baptist) in many cities and towns, including Florence, Genoa, Turin, Rome, and the Cinque Terre villages of Monterosso and Riomaggiore. Its proximity to the summer solstice lends a special connotation to the *feste,* a sense of embracing the summer season. Since the ancient period, Italian farmers have celebrated midsummer with torchlit processions and bonfires to dedicate the seasonal crops. Since midsummer also marked the traditional birth of St. John the Baptist, the Roman Church simply imposed its ceremony, as it did in so many instances, on the existing pagan festival.

In the Sicilian town of Acitrezza, near Catania, a band leads a procession of brightly dressed children through the main piazza to the church, where fireworks announce the beginning and the end of mass, when the crowd shouts: "*Evviva San Giovanni* (Praise be to St. John)!" Eventually the statue of St. John is brought from the altar to the steps of the church. At the end of the festivities, the faithful retire to the seashore to enjoy a final fireworks display. In Rome, the day is celebrated at the basilica of San Giovanni Laterano, where the Saints' skull is said to be buried and where today strands of brightly colored lights add a spirit of festivity to the surrounding streets. The Roman tradition is to dine on snails (*lumache,* a proverbial protection against witches) and to indulge in an evening of food and white wine that celebrates both the sacred and the secular occasions. In the town of Ossuccio on the shores of Lake Como, inhabitants float thousands of snail shells, the mollusk having been replaced with oil-burning wicks. The small town of Spilamberto (near Modena in the Po Valley) celebrates the *festa* with a contest to produce the best classic balsamic vinegar (*aceto balsamico,* aged at least 12 years).

San Giovanni Battista is patron saint of Florence, where he is remembered as a symbol of the economic success and good government that the city enjoyed in the medieval era (the destructive internal conflict is presumably not attributed to the saint and is conveniently forgotten on this day). The *festa* includes a parade in spectacular sixteenth-century costumes, which sets the tone for *Calcio Storico Fiorentino,* the historical football match, which resembles rugby more than soccer, and features teams from four quarters of the city: Santo Spirito (whites); Santa Croce (blues); Santa Maria Novella (reds); and San Giovanni (greens). The evening concludes with a fireworks display at the Piazzale Michelangelo or the Boboli Gardens.

At the end of June, Rome celebrates the religious *festa di Ss. Pietro e Paolo* (Sts. Peter and Paul), who, tradition holds, were martyred in Rome by the emperor Nero and whose relics were transferred to the catacombs of San Sebastian by Pope Sixtus V on this date in AD 258. This day is yet another example of the Church's campaign to "Christianize" pagan holidays, in this case the festival dedicated to Rome's mythical founders, Romulus and Remus.

The *festa di Ss. Pietro e Paolo* is one of Rome's most important holidays and provides the occasion for many Romans to embark on a brief escape to the countryside or the beach. Catholics celebrate the occasion with mass at three primary churches: St. Peter's Basilica, St. Paul's Outside the Walls, and the catacombs of San Sebastian that house the relics.

Just as the Florentines have imposed the *Calcio Storico* on a religious holiday, so the residents of Siena celebrate the *Palio delle Contrade* on the feast day of *Santa Maria Assunta* (the Assumption of the Virgin Mary). The *Palio* (literally, a banner featuring the image of Santa Maria Assunta) is one of Italy's most renowned and picturesque festivals. Dating from the thirteenth century, it is now celebrated on both July 2 and August 16 in the Piazza del Campo, the historical center of the city. The Palio begins with a procession in which the 17 *contrade* (or districts of the city) carry banners displaying their distinctive symbols, including the giraffe, the caterpillar, the owl, and the tortoise.

Piazza del Campo, Siena, site of the Palio. Courtesy of the author.

Preliminary festivities, lasting about four hours and including an elaborate medieval pageant, lead to the *Corsa di Palio,* the frantic horse race around the dirt-filled piazza, featuring horses decorated with the colors and symbols of the *contrade.* The workhorses, acquired by the *contrade* from local farmers, are ridden bareback by jockeys *(fantini),* who race three times around the oval to the thunderous cheers of the audience. The winner, predetermined on the eve of the race in a series of negotiations and bribes among the *fantini,* proudly displays the banner as the post-race, torchlit banquet fills the streets with merriment and celebration.

In the week beginning with the third Saturday in July, Romans celebrate the *Festa de' Noantri* ("our own festival") that features a carnival-like atmosphere in the streets and *piazze* of the ancient quarter of Trastevere, where booths offer every conceivable item of food, apparel, and other consumer goods. But like many Italian festivals, the *Festa de' Noantri* incorporates religious elements, including a procession on the first Saturday of the *Beata Vergine del Carmine* ("Madonna of Noantri"). The throngs walk behind a

Roast pig, Festa de' Noantri, Rome. Courtesy of the author.

statue of the Virgin Mary, accompanied by confraternities and a band and escorted by mounted police. The procession winds its way from the Church of S. Agata down the Via della Lungaretta and the Viale Trastevere and to the Piazza San Cosimatoto, where the crowd greets them with shouts of "Viva Maria!"

The most important summer holiday is *Ferragosto* ("August holiday"), celebrated in mid-month in conjunction with the Catholic holiday of the Assumption of the Virgin Mary. The celebration dates from the reign of the emperor Augustus, who named the month and the holiday in honor of himself, and now is best known as a time when Italians flee en masse from the cities to the shores and the mountains. *Ferragosto* provides yet another example of a holiday that the Roman Catholic Church appropriated from pagan ritual, converting the August 13 festival of the goddess Diana (queen of heaven) to a celebration of the ascension into heaven of the Virgin Mary. Italians in many towns still express reverence for the Virgin through elaborate parades. In Messina (Sicily), where the festival continues for two weeks, worshipers carry an ornamented, 60-foot pyramid *(La Vara)* arrayed with angels and a Christ figure, accompanied by *I Giganti* (the giants), two towering, papier-mâché figures representing the traditional founders of Messina, Zancleo and his queen. In Sassari (Sardegna), celebrants dance through the streets carrying the *Candelieri,* colossal, decorated columns of wood. Romans celebrate Assumption Day primarily at the church of Santa Maria Maggiore on the Esquiline hill.

One of the memorable fall festivals is *La Regata Storica* (the historic regatta) in Venice, celebrated the first Sunday of the month and dating from at least the thirteenth century. Against the backdrop of the great *palazzi* (palaces) of the Grand Canal, bedecked with colorful tapestries, a brilliant procession of elaborately carved, classic boats sets the tone for the day's festivities. Venetians and visitors aboard every imaginable type craft observe the day's festivities from the canals. Three categories of races (children's, women's, and six-man crews) initiate the competition, with the women's event tracing its origins to the seventeenth century and being dominated by Maria Boscola da Marina for 40 years in the eighteenth century. The preliminary contests build interest for the main event, a contest among brightly attired *gondolieri* (gondola captains) aboard gondolas specially equipped for racing. By the end of the day, the Grand Canal and the Piazza San Marco radiate light and merriment.

Ancient Italian traditions hold that the dead return to earth on the first two nights of November. Thus Halloween developed from the grotesque masks of the pagan debauchery designed to drive away the spirits. The next day, November 1, *Ognissanti* (*Tutti i Santi* or All Saints' Day) remains a national holiday. It originated in the pre-Christian traditions that celebrated the mysterious return to earth of witches and demons during this period of agricultural dormancy. The eighth-century pope Gregory III consecrated a chapel in St. Peter's basilica to all saints and established November 1 as the day of recognition. In subsequent centuries, the church Christianized the festival, turning it into *Ognissanti,* a day to honor all saints and to compensate for any failures to honor any of them during the preceding year. The following day, November 2, although not a national holiday, is recognized in Italy as *Il giorno dei morti* (the day of the dead). Some Italians celebrate the occasion with gifts for children, especially sweets, delivered during the night by the departed souls who have responded to the gift requests of the children. The holiday remains important in Sicily, where many families visit family burial plots after praying for the souls in purgatory.

December is a month with a number of traditional holidays, including the three to four weeks of Advent, the feasts of *San Nicolò* (St. Nicholas, December 6) and *Santa Lucia* (St. Lucy, December 13), followed by another 12 days of celebrations between Christmas and Epiphany when the *ceppo* (Yule log) is burned in the fireplace. However, only three of these days are now recognized as official holidays by the Italian Republic: *Immacolata concezione* (Immaculate Conception, December 8); *Natale* (Christmas); and December 26, the *Oggi di S. Stefano* (St. Stephen's Day, or Boxing Day). The feast of the Immaculate Conception is said to date from the reign of the Byzantine emperor Basil II early in the eleventh century. In Rome, the pope celebrates the feast by appearing at the Piazza di Spagna (the Spanish Steps) to drape a wreath of flowers on the monument of the Virgin Mary and thus to inaugurate the Christmas season.

Natale in Italy typically begins with the family's *cenone,* the Christmas eve fasting dinner based traditionally on fish (often including a serving of *anguilla,* eel), and concludes with midnight mass. The season is notably festive, with bands playing in the *piazze,* the aroma of roasting chestnuts in the air, and a *presepio* (crèche) or nativity scene seemingly on every street corner, shop window, schoolroom, and house. In the artistic tradition of the *presepio,* many provide elaborate depictions of shepherds, Mary, Joseph, and the baby Jesus *(Gesù Bambino)* in an Italian landscape. Italian children request Christmas or Epiphany gifts from *Gesù Bambino* (addressed to *paradiso,* heaven) who is said to make his rounds on a donkey, dropping off gifts as children sleep. *Babbo natale* (Santa Claus) has crept into the Italian Christmas season in spite of the Vatican's resistance. Holiday foods abound, including seasonal cheeses and nuts, *tartuffe* (truffles), *bottarga* (caviar), candied fruits, *dolci* (sweets), and various breads such as holiday versions of *pannetone* and *panforte.* The extravagant Christmas dinner, with a rich array of regional variations, provides the culmination of the seasonal feast.

As important as feasts remain in Italy today, they have declined drastically in number from the early nineteenth century when about one day of every two was officially designated a holiday, Saints' day, *sagra,* or *festa.* The change actually began to be noticed in the era of unification when Piedmontese prime minister Camillo di Cavour began to limit holidays—as part of his more general campaign to restrict the influence of the church—in an effort to raise economic productivity to the level of northern European states. The success of the Piedmontese in dominating Italian unification enabled them to impose much of their secular agenda on the new Italian kingdom, including their limitation of holidays. The trend continued into the twentieth century, so that the Italian republic has reduced the annual number of official holidays to 10, about the same as in the United States. Nonetheless, numerous *feste* and local Saints' days persist, and the tradition of festivals remains a vital part of Italian life.

ITALIAN COOKING (LA CUCINA ITALIANA AND GASTRONOMIA)

If it is true that you are what you eat, as is sometimes said, then Italians are a diverse people, because Italian cooking varies widely throughout the peninsula. Foreigners' perceptions of the Italian diet as one of pasta and pizza, tomatoes and garlic, while not entirely inaccurate, is at the same time deceiving. The most credible generalization about Italian cooking might be that it

Castello di Volpaia, a winery in the Chianti district. Courtesy of the author.

is based primarily on fresh ingredients grown or acquired locally and prepared and consumed in accordance with local and regional traditions of home cooking *(la cucina di casa,* or *la cucina casalinga).* For example, Piedmontese cooking differs from Tuscan cooking, just as Tuscan cooking may be distinguished from the fare served in Florence, the Tuscan capital. In fact, regional influences on the Italian diet are so strong that many argue against the existence of Italian national cooking. In the medieval and early modern periods, well before Italy unified, the aristocracy and the urban elites sustained a single "Italian" style of cooking, while rural populations ate what was locally affordable. This discrepancy persisted well into the twentieth century as widespread malnutrition persisted. With the spread of prosperity in the postwar era, malnutrition largely vanished, and previously deprived rural populations adapted themselves to various aspects of urban culture, including food preparation and consumption. Thus an Italian model of cooking spread, but avoided the kind of standardization of diet that frozen, ready-to-eat, and "fast" foods brought to the United States.[4] Instead, food and wine achieved a kind of cult status and in the 1990s a "slow food" movement spread to counter the incursion of chain restaurants such as McDonald's. Even at the beginning of the twenty-first century it has been estimated that fewer than three percent of Italians patronize fast-food restaurants. At the same time, regional pride reinforced local styles and tastes, and the outside world became acquainted with such styles as "Bolognese" and "Tuscan."

It is also important to note that, in spite of the existence of world-class restaurants and aristocratic traditions, it would be a mistake to identify a *alta cucina* (gourmet cooking) as important in contemporary Italy. In spite of the opening of restaurants that feature a kind of continental fare, the best of Italian food is prepared in the homemade style to meet the highest standards. Furthermore, not only is the preparation of food of great significance, but so is its consumption. It has been said that Italians regularly practice the art of eating as part of the tradition of "making art out of life."[5]

As we move into the age of pervasive globalization, the regional identities of Italian cooking are being accentuated as never before. Such regional variations in food developed from the geography and topography of the peninsula and from the varied cultural and historical roots and political identities of its inhabitants. Since the Italian peninsula was fragmented into various political units until the unification of the Kingdom of Italy was completed in 1870, deep traces of varied, even ancient cultural influences can still be identified in the gastronomy of the peninsula, from the Etruscans and the Greeks of the eighth century BC, through Roman, Byzantine, French, Germanic, Spanish, and, more recently, the immigrant populations from the Balkans (especially Albanians) and the former African colonial territories (especially Ethiopians).

Latin writers such as Horace, Cato, and Pliny provide strong evidence of an "Italian" culinary taste in the Roman era. They wrote of such favorite Roman foods as wild boar from Tuscany, bass from the Tiber River, radishes from the Alban hills, onions and cabbages from Pompeii, asparagus from Ravenna, leeks from Ostia, semola wheat from Campania, and bread and wine from Piceno. Romans shared with Greeks the view that diet centered on bread, wine, and olive oil, and with the spread of Roman imperial culture, those elements constituted the basis of a Mediterranean diet. Romans initially regarded the Germanic diet of beer, meat, and butter as "barbaric," a view that modified after the Germanic tribes immigrated in large numbers and Germanic kings began to rule the peninsula. Eventually, diets on the peninsula incorporated products from both cultures, and Roman dietary customs persisted on the peninsula well into the modern age.[6]

In the medieval era, Christian traditions imposed the alternation of "fat" and "lean" foods, and the Crusades introduced Oriental spices to the peninsula, although such exotic embellishments eluded the tables of the poor. At the same time, southern Italian port cities incorporated Arab culinary influences (including Mesopotamian and Persian) that began to distinguish southern fare from northern styles of cooking and eating. Experts on food trace recipe collections back to thirteenth-, fourteenth-, and fifteenth-century Naples, Siena, and Rome where they find recipes for Roman cabbage and macaroni, Florentine eggs, Parmesan and Bolognese torta, and Genoese spinach pie. The recipes were circulated throughout the peninsula, indicating an awareness of "Italian" cooking that featured local specialties.

The craving for spices persisted in Italy through the Renaissance era, as did the tendency to mix flavors in a single dish. Such Roman concepts as "sweet" (honey) and "sour" (vinegar) endured as well, although Arabs had brought citrus fruits and cane sugar to the peninsula in the late middle ages to replace honey and vinegar.[7] One of the most often repeated narratives of Italian Renaissance food is that Catherine de'Medici introduced Italian gastronomy to France in the sixteenth century and thus enabled French cooks to develop their own distinctive Parisian mode of cooking. Included in the tradition was the gift of the fork, which Catherine provided to the cruder French who were still eating with their hands. It is true that in 1533 the 14-year-old Catherine took her forks and her chefs, along with a sizable retinue, to Marseilles to be married to Henri de Valois, son of the French king. At court, her chefs began to prepare artichokes, broccoli, savoy cabbage, veal, beef tournedos, truffles, melons, zabaglione, ice cream, and iced aperitifs, and she entertained lavishly in the style of her great-grandfather, Lorenzo the Magnificent.[8] A number of observers gave her credit. However, whether Catherine's influence deserves the status it has been afforded is questionable, because the reciprocal exchange of culinary influences between Italy and France had existed for two centuries before Catherine's arrival. Nonetheless, the Italians' use of vegetables and certain Roman traditions contributed to the French diet, and French cooks even criticized their Italian counterparts for being excessively serious about their work.[9]

The Renaissance gave birth to the most complete cookbook since the Roman era and the first modern cooking school, founded in Florence, the recognized culinary leader of the period. Apart from Medici extravagance, Florentines generally dined simply on lamb, fowl, veal, trout, bean soup, and homemade pasta, much as they do today. The Renaissance saw the first commercial production of pasta in Naples, where dried pasta still prevails, and the introduction of coffee from the East.

By the end of the Renaissance, foods from the Americas had entered the Italian diet, especially tomatoes, green beans, and corn. Regionalism now prevailed in Italy as recipes made explicit references to towns and regions. French cooking had now won international renown, surpassing the reputation of Italy, and French influence spread through Piedmont into the peninsula, raising the question of whether this did not simply mark the return of Italian cooking in modified form.

In the nineteenth century, before unification of the peninsula, regional identities of Italian cooking became more firmly entrenched. However, with political unification in 1860 came efforts to establish a degree of culinary unity. In 1891, the Florentine Pellegrino Artusi published a gastronomic map of Italy, focusing primarily on Florence and Bologna. Italy's entry into World War I in 1915 further contributed to the creation of a national diet when the military decided on a series of menus used to prepare meals for a disparate assortment of soldiers from every region of the nation. With the consolidation of Fascist power in the next decade, Mussolini's regime promoted nationalism and tourism through a series of maps, books, fairs, and festivals identifying regional specialties and an "Italian style" of gastronomy. Some maps even reflected imperialistic ambitions by placing symbols of Italian food beyond Italy's borders.[10]

Many of these historical influences on Italian gastronomy persist. And while it might be possible to identify "Italian cooking" from afar, it remains considerably more difficult to do so from within the peninsula where differences often seem to outweigh uniformity. The reason for the internal differences in gastronomic habits is that the historical factors that produced the idea of a national cooking are usually outweighed by geographical disparities, notably climate. Although the greatest contrasts are to be found between northern and southern cooking, others persist.

The Alpine regions to the far north incorporate the French styles of the French-speaking Valle d'Aosta and the Austrian diets of the Alto Adige, where

German is often the language of choice. French influences remain strong in the Piedmont and its capital, Turin, where French was in the nineteenth century the court language of the House of Savoy, the Italian monarchy. Particularly in the cities and lowlands of Piedmont, French influences and studied, sophisticated preparation derived from the Savoy court produce a delicacy not often matched elsewhere. The combination of the refined Turinese cooking *(la cucina Torinese)* with the more robust approach of the mountainous provinces of Piedmont can be superb. An example is *fonduta,* which combines the rich, yellow, aged *fontina* cheese with the prized white truffle *(tartufo bianco).* Typical of Piedmont, *fonduta* is distinguished from Swiss fondue by the thin topping of truffles and the absence of white wine and kirsch. Also distinctive of the region are the "big" red wines made from the prized *nebbiolo* grape, most notably Barbaresco and Barolo, perhaps the most noble of the Italian wines.[11]

At the base of the Alpine ranges is Italy's only wide plain, the Po River valley, running westward from Venice and the Veneto through Lombardy into Piedmont. The well-watered plain of the Po, Italy's "bread basket," is home to Italy's major dairies and grain producers. As a result, the Piedmontese rely on butter for cooking fat, rice for *risotto,* and corn for *polenta,* staples in the Piedmontese diet and hallmarks that often are viewed as characterizing "northern" cooking. It is said that workers from the south, drawn north by the prospect of industrial jobs, introduced dried pasta to Piedmont and Lombardy in the nineteenth century.[12] Milan, the Lombard capital, is home to a distinctive style that traditionally featured slow cooking over wood-burning stoves. Among the most distinctive Lombard dishes are *risotto alla milanese,* rice with saffron slowly simmered with butter, onions, wine, and stock; and *osso bucco,* a veal shin bone with the marrow inside, cooked slowly in wine, stock, onions, and tomatoes and served on rice. The leading Lombard wine, made from the *nebbiolo* grape, is Valtellina.

In Venice and the northeastern regions, a variety of traditional fares distinguishes the cooking. Aside from the Austrian style of Trentino-Alto Adige and the Slavic influences found in Friuli-Venezia Giulia, the Veneto features its own distinctive varieties. Traditional Venetian food is sometimes obscured from visitors because the tourist trade has demanded a "typical Italian" menu in many popular restaurants. However, even restaurants catering to tourists tend to provide offerings from the sea, most notably scampi, such Mediterranean fish as orata, *anguilla* (eel), various shellfish, and *baccalà* (dried cod), often accompanied by rice. *Risi e bisi* (rice and peas) is a Venetian favorite, braised with butter, *pancetta* or *prosciutto,* and onions, and topped with Parmesan cheese. The Veneto is a prolific wine-producing region. Whites prevail, most notably Soave, but such favorite reds as Valpolicella, Merlot, and Cabernet abound.

Just south of Piedmont, Lombardy, and the Veneto lie two regions widely renowned for their gastronomy, Liguria and Emila-Romagna. Liguria and its capital, Genoa, are known for consuming the fruits of the sea, especially mussels, clams, eels, and lobster, embellished by herbs grown on the local hillsides. Liguria is home to the Italian Academy of Cooking in Savona and claims credit for originating two staples of the Italian diet, *ravioli* and the hearty vegetable soup known as *minestrone*. Also typical of the region is the *pesto* sauce made from basil leaves, parsley, garlic, pine nuts, and *Pecorino Romano* and *Parmesan* cheeses.

Of all Italy's regions, none exceeds Emilia-Romagna in reputation for rich and elaborately prepared meals and highly valued food products. Its plains are home to wheat, corn, and sugar beet fields, its cattle are much sought, and Italy's best tomatoes and asparagus are said to be harvested here. Local products have achieved worldwide renown, especially aged pork products and cheeses. The most prized sausage is *mortadella,* the most famous ham, the cured *prosciutto di Parma,* and the most sought-after cheese, the buttery *Parmigiano Reggiano.* The herb-perfumed, aged *aceto balsamico* (Balsamic vinegar) from Modena is revered as both a seasoning and a topping for desserts. The region's capital has earned such a reputation for gastronomy that it is known as Bologna *"la grassa"* (the fat). It is famous for its pastas, including lasagne, tagliatelle, cappelletti (often prepared with a meat sauce known as ragù), and tortellini (served in broth), and for such meat dishes as *involtini alla cacciatora* (rolled veal scallops stuffed with chicken liver and *prosciutto*) and *zampone* (stuffed pig's feet).

Although separated from Bologna by a mere 65 miles of road, Florence could hardly provide a greater contrast in dietary customs. While the Bolognese prepare extravagant, rich dishes with great flare, Tuscans take pride in simplicity, shunning sauces and spices in favor of fresh, seasonal beef, game, beans, and other vegetables prepared simply with local herbs. This unadorned style of simple elegance has produced memorable results. As is the case in Venice, tourism has driven many Florentine restaurants to specialize in pastas, but traditional Tuscan cooking features *arista di maile* (roast pork), pierced with rosemary, sage, and garlic, prepared on a spit over an open flame; *zuppa di fagioli* (bean soup); and the most celebrated Tuscan fare, *bistecca alla Fiorentina* or *costatta* (rib steak) *alla Fiorentina,* cut from the prized Chianina cattle and prepared with olive oil, salt, and pepper over a wood fire. Tuscan wines abound, the reds having won greatest attention. Among the best are Brunello, Vino Nobile di Montepulciano, and Chianti Classico, the more carefully controlled "big brother" of the flask of Tuscan table wine best known to tourists.

While they certainly could be given individual treatment, the regions around Rome, Le Marche, Umbria, and Lazio supply the capital with the

Casoncelli, a dish typical of Bergamo. Courtesy of Katrina Reiners.

Generous selection of cheeses, Campo de' Fiori, Rome. Courtesy of the author.

abundant variety of food and wine that characterize the Eternal City. As is the case in Florence and Venice, tourist demands tend to obscure local dietary traditions in many high-profile restaurants. But in Rome's many simple *trattorie* and *osterie,* Roman fare is served, often in outdoor gardens, especially in Trastevere and in residential neighborhoods. Among Romans' favorite dishes are *porchetta,* spit-roasted, stuffed suckling pig; *abbacchio,* suckling lamb roasted with rosemary; *fettucine al burro,* ribbon-shaped egg pasta in butter; *gnocchi* made from flour (as opposed to potatoes, which is the custom elsewhere); *spaghetti alla carbonara* (with *guanciale* pork, eggs, and cheese) and *spaghetti all'Amatriciana* (*guanciale,* tomatoes, peppers, and onions); and two styles of artichokes, *carciofi all Giudia* (small, young artichokes fried in olive oil) and *carciofi alla romana* (stuffed and baked). Favorites from the surrounding regions are the *tartufo nero* (black truffle) and sausages from Umbria and fish from the coastal Marche. Lazio is best known for its white wines, among which Frascati stands out, while Umbria features whites from Orvieto and the Torgiano reds.

Southern Italy is so enormously varied in culture (in spite of stereotypes to the contrary) as to preclude detailed descriptions of the many culinary traditions. Nonetheless, in the same way that Rome serves as a focus for the food and wine of the central regions, so Naples is the gastronomic center of the South. Naples is internationally known for its pizza, so much so that it was recreated and popularized in response to tourist demand. Neapolitan pizza is traditionally simple and fresh, with tomato sauce, mozzarella cheese, and herbs adorning a moderately thin, oiled crust. From the pizza is derived the

Chianti vineyards. Courtesy of the author.

salsa pizzaiola, which is used to prepare beef, pork, clams, and other main courses.

Much of the South is mountainous, and thus traditionally its agricultural population has struggled to support itself, particularly in the interior. Of the six southern regions, Campania (of which Naples is the capital) and Apulia afford the best climate and soil, and both provide an abundance of seafood, which, in addition to vegetables, provides the South with its staple. Pasta in its various forms is a pervasive food in the South, much of it manufactured and dried in tubular form as spaghetti, *maccheroni* (macaroni), or one of the seemingly infinite shapes, and usually topped with a robust sauce. The pasta dishes often incorporate vegetables such as eggplant, tomatoes, and peppers. Bread is another southern staple, much of it still made in the home. Along the coastal South, the fruits of the sea are consumed in great quantity, particularly swordfish, lobsters, oysters, squid, prawns, and sea urchins. Fish soups are popular, including *zuppa di vongole* (clams), a *brodetto* in the Abruzzi, and the Neapolitan *zuppa di pesce alla marinara,* fish soup prepared in tomatoes and garlic and served over bread. A great quantity of wine is produced in the southern regions, but much is not exported and thus is not well-known. Among the best are the red wines of Apulia.

Sicily is acclaimed for its pastries and confections, said to have been introduced to the island by Arabs in the ninth century. The best known are *cannnoli,* cylindrical pastries filled with *ricotta* cheese, and *cassata,* a layered pound cake with *ricotta,* cream, chocolate, and orange-flavored liqueur. Citrus fruits, vegetables, and olives influence the Sicilian menu and breads abound, as do pastas such as *pasta con sarde* (sardines) and *spaghetti al nero di seppi,* pasta that has absorbed the black "ink" of the cuttlefish. *Caponata,* a marinated eggplant and tomato dish, is a popular accompaniment to a main course such as swordfish, tuna, or sausage. Second only to Apulia as a southern wine-producing region, Sicily is known for its Marsala and such whites as Corvo.[13]

Although Italy's islands are often historically grouped with the South, Sardinia does not fit that category as comfortably as does Sicily. Sardinian cuisine is distinctive, a product of a geography that has split the island markedly between its forbidding inland mountains and its cosmopolitan coasts, some of which have recently developed as world-class resorts. The inland herding of sheep and goats has dominated the diets of Sards, producing cheeses such as *pecorino sardo, casu marzu,* and *fiore sardo,* and an ample supply of lamb and goat. Other Sard favorites are pork, wild boar, fowl, and beef, often roasted on a spit over an open fire of olive and juniper woods, and a mullet caviar known as *bottarga.* Like other Italians, Sards eat their share of pastas and breads, including the paper-thin *pane carasau.* The most sought-after Sardinian wines are the red Cannonau and the white Vernaccia di Oristano.

Memorable as are the local specialties and distinctive as are the regional differences in Italian gastronomy, some credible generalizations have been made. It is clear that internal migration spread regional tastes around the peninsula, particularly from South to North. Tourism has reinforced this standardization by introducing demands based on stereotypical renditions of the Italian meal. Even if an Italian national cooking cannot be accurately defined, a number of traditional elements survive throughout the country. Tomatoes are widely used, and starches (bread and either pasta, rice, or polenta) accompany most major meals, whether consumed at midday or in the evening. Those meals are still eaten in courses, *antipasto* followed by *pasta*, then a *seconda* of meat or fish, finished by a dessert of fruit and/or cheese. Wine is ubiquitous at mealtime, accompanied by sparkling water. Clearly food remains a very important component of family life. One observer noted that "the amount of time spent in the daily rituals related to the preparation and consumption of food, as well as the cleaning up afterwards, is impressive, and the priestess of this cult of food is the mother."[14]

Many Italians begin their days with an *espresso* on the way to their shops or offices, usually at a favorite bar where the *barista* (bartender or barmaid) hails them by name and seldom needs to ask for an order. These same bars usually provide an appealing array of freshly baked pastries and orange juice *(spremuta d'arancia)*, squeezed on request, as well as a supply of daily newspapers and a range of other coffees and juices. Dogs are not an uncommon sight in bars, often admired and called by name by customers and employees alike. By the afternoon, many bars become havens for old men and their card games, readily abandoned on weekends in favor of a televised soccer game or bicycle race. In the spring, outdoor tables, tablecloths, and umbrellas appear at bars and restaurants, usually on the same day throughout the town, as harbingers of the season. Once the tables appear, locals and tourists populate them, seeking a ray of warming sun, reading, smoking, and conversing for extended periods. In the fall, on the same day, in the same manner in which they appeared months earlier, outdoor tables and umbrellas are whisked away for storage until the following spring.

Morning also is the time for shopping for the daily meals. Traditionally, women shop daily for fresh cheeses, meats, fish, and seasonal fruits and vegetables, usually in a series of small, specialized, neighborhood shops such as a *forno* (bakery) or a *macellaio* (butcher shop), or at one of the many open-air or enclosed farmers' markets. This daily shopping venture is truly a participatory sport, with shopper and shopkeeper engaging in a dialogue about the

meal and cooking method, during which the shopkeeper selects the best spec-
imens from the bins to fill the requests so that the fruits and vegetables have
not been handled by shoppers. It would not be unusual, for example, to
request a fresh green salad for four, then watch as the shopkeeper filled the
request. Italy's many skilled butchers routinely perform the most delicate
operations (such as boning a rabbit) with great flair.

Midday marks the large meal, often enjoyed at home with family during the
"siesta" break when most shops and many offices close (although large retail
stores and other offices in some cities now remain open). Those who opt for
restaurants (men often gather at noon; families and couples for the evening
meal) will be able to choose a pizzeria, a *tavola calda* (a kind of cafeteria), a
trattoria, or a *ristorante* (restaurant), most family-owned and operated. Waiters
are often skilled, proud, and service-oriented, and it is not uncommon for the
cook to circulate among customers, especially in the many neighborhood
restaurants. The only chain restaurants that are found widely are those on the
autostrada, usually operated by the AGIP petroleum company and Autogrill
S.p.A. (including licenses to retail food outlets such as Spizzico, Ciao, and

Tresoldi panificio (baker's shop), Bergamo. Courtesy of Katrina Reiniers.

American companies such as Burger King and Starbucks), although the golden arches of McDonald's stores have now appeared in many cities.

In January 2005, Italy's comprehensive new law banning smoking in bars, restaurants, and other public places went into effect. The law provides for heavy fines (up to $350) for smokers—doubled if in the presence of a child or a pregnant woman—and heavier fines (up to $3,000) for bar and restaurant proprietors who fail to enforce the law. Many are skeptical about its effectiveness and public opinion is divided in a nation in which about one-quarter of the population reportedly smoke.[15]

At the same time, change has come to Italian food preparation and consumption. The movement of women into the workforce has limited their preparation time and created additional demand for prepared foods. Although most Italians still prefer small specialty shops, supermarkets featuring prepared foods have spread, appealing to the needs of a busier population. Aesthetic standards have changed. No longer is bulk universally considered a sign of well-being. With the new popularity of gymnasiums and workout facilities, more Italians are limiting consumption. "The pot belly and the double chin, badge of honor of the early gourmets, now seemed not only implausible but ridiculous," observed one recent writer. "Worse yet, the lively new body turned its back on its own history, opposing the dietary and gastronomic models that had once weighed it down."[16]

NOTES

1. Carol Field, *Celebrating Italy* (New York: HarperCollins Publishers, 1997).

2. Field, *Celebrating Italy,* 409–10.

3. Helen Barolini, *Festa* (New York: Harcourt Brace Jovanovich, 1988), 214.

4. Alberto Capatti and Massimo Montanari, *Italian Cuisine: A Cultural History,* trans. Aine O'Healy (New York: Columbia University Press, 1999), xiv–xv.

5. Marcella Hazan, *The Classic Italian Cookbook* (New York: Alfred A. Knopf, 1980), 5.

6. Capatti and Montanari, *Italian Cuisine,* 1–89.

7. Capatti and Montanari, *Italian Cuisine,* 90.

8. Peter D'Epiro and Mary Desmond Pinkowish, *Sprezzatura* (New York: Random House, Inc., 2001), 226–31.

9. Capatti and Montanari, *Italian Cuisine,* 110.

10. Capatti and Montanari, *Italian Cuisine,* 6–31.

11. Waverley Root, *The Cooking of Italy* (New York: Vintage Books, 1968), 149–59.

12. Hazan, *The Classic Italian Cookbook,* 3–5.

13. Root, *The Cooking of Italy,* 183–87; Roy Domenico, *The Regions of Italy* (Westport, Conn.: Greenwood Press, 2002), 270.

14. Donald Pitkin, *The House That Giacomo Built* (Cambridge: Cambridge University Press, 1985), quoted in Paul Ginsborg, *Italy and its Discontents* (New York: Palgrave Macmillan, 2003), 77.

15. Frances D'Emilio, "Italy's new smoking law one of Europe's toughest," *The Washington Times,* http://washingtontimes.com/business/20050110-122435-9767r.htm.

16. Capatti and Montanari, *Italian Cuisine,* 298.

5

Leisure Activities and Sport

ONE OF THE MORE REVEALING ASPECTS OF ANY CULTURE is the manner in which the population spends its leisure time. Italians exude great enthusiasm for sporting competition of many varieties. In fact, the fervor of Italian fans for soccer, auto racing, and cycling is world renowned, as anyone will attest who has witnessed the *tifosi* (feverish fans) spill onto the track, waving their colors after a victory by team Ferrari at a *Grand Prix* race. Moreover, Italians traditionally have spent leisure time in conversation, in a culture that values verbal exchange. This custom can be witnessed any day in the animated conversations among small groups of friends exchanging views in the piazzas; the erudite and lengthy lectures of university professors; the intense, regularly televised dialogues on politics and sport; the evening *passeggiata* (in the South, *lo struscio*) that brings a virtual parade of well-dressed friends and families, often arm-in-arm, up-and-down the town's most popular pedestrian boulevard, frequently interrupted by a stop at a *gelateria* (ice cream shop) or at a bar for an *aperitivo* (apertif); groups of teens, gathered around tables in a neighborhood *pizzeria*, talking over the music while consuming large portions of pizza, pasta, and the ever-popular French fries; and perhaps most recognizably to tourists in the use of hand gestures to emphasize a point. It should be noted, however, that although this tradition of public conversation may appear to the observer to indicate a pervasive openness, such appearances may be deceiving, for Italians often prefer to engage in a more formal, reserved, and reluctant manner among strangers than do many Americans.

This culture of conversation can be seen as a product of a variety of influences: an educational system that requires oral examinations and thereby cultivates verbal skills; a culture that instills social values, views conversation as an aspect of community, respects knowledge, and expects openness and gregariousness among friends; a climate that encourages gathering in public places; and a tradition that can be traced at least to the Romans.

In spite of such strong traditions, several important modernizing trends have significantly altered Italian sport and leisure in the past generation, including the convergence of corporate business and politics with the sporting world. That imposing combination of political power and revenues—from broadcast, cable, and pay-per-view television, corporate sponsorship, and merchandising—has converted much of Italian sport into spectacle, although perhaps to no greater extent than in the rest of the Western world. Olivetti, Ferruzzi-Montedison, and Benetton are examples of companies whose investment in sport provided them at least enhanced visibility.

At the same time, leisure activities and sport in Italy have changed markedly over the past century, reflecting fundamental changes in society. In particular, the prosperity that accompanied the Economic Miracle has yielded the necessary time and money to accommodate more elaborate vacations and to expand and popularize a number of diversions, both active and passive. More recently, the advent of televised sporting contests has propelled certain sectors of Italian sport—most notably soccer (known as *calcio*, or football) and Formula 1 (*Grand Prix*) racing—firmly into the realm of big business. As a result of expanded coverage on television and in the press, intense commercial support, widespread wagering, and success in international competition, mass followings have emerged, with millions of viewers to be found huddled around television sets on any given Sunday. The publicity has inspired the spread of youth sporting leagues, particularly in soccer and basketball. And the advent of prosperity has enabled Italians to attend musical and theatrical performances in unprecedented numbers and has enabled adults to devote time to physical exercise in a wide array of colorfully attired cycling clubs or one of the new and widely available gyms.

Boosted by corporate sponsorship and marketing, *calcio* surpassed cycling in popularity as a spectator sport, while professional basketball surged in public enthusiasm, and volleyball and water polo remained popular. A 1991 poll on televised sport indicated that 58 percent of Italians preferred soccer, followed by auto racing and cycling.[1] Related to the commercialization of Italian sport is the success of Italian companies in producing and marketing sports equipment and the importance of the Italian market. In the early 1990s, Italy was the fourth-ranking market for sports equipment at more than $5 billion in purchases.[2]

The Early History of Sport in Italy

In the years before Italian unification, sport in Italy, as in the rest of Europe, was largely confined to the upper, leisure class who engaged in such activities as hunting, Alpine skiing, fencing, horseback riding, tennis, and mountain climbing. In contrast to other European countries, however, sport was being organized at the same time that the nation state was emerging in Italy. Sport thus reflected the values of the dominant northern urban elites, which in turn tended to idealize the British and northern European models of government and economics as well as sport, and hence introduced physical education into Italian schools in 1878.[3] Understandably, by the 1890s, the new socialist movement took a position against sport as elitist or "bourgeois." Then as the values of competitive individualism, performance, and teamwork accompanied the simultaneous advent of both English industrialism and soccer into Italy, the Roman Catholic Church countered these modernist (and English Protestant) characteristics of sport—as it countered other forms of modernism—with its own program, in this case regimented calisthenics, a kind of corporeal catechism. Seldom in Italian history would the forces of socialism and Catholicism be so harmonious. Taking the initiative to gain some influence over the burgeoning interest in sport, the Church organized the Federation of Italian Catholic Sporting Associations in 1906.

By the 1890s, Italians had already begun to organize soccer clubs, including the Genoa football club (1893), which won the first Italian championship in 1898; Juventus, begun by former students of Turin's *Liceo D'Azeglio* (c. 1897); and two clubs in Milan, the Milan Cricket and Football Club (1899) and Inter (1908). The latter three remain staples of today's Italian *Serie A* (A Division) soccer, while Genoa was relegated to *Serie B* (B Division). Italian soccer clubs originally were amateur and the sport was viewed as a "people's game," since it was played most avidly in the northern industrial towns by factory workers. It has been noted that the rise of soccer not only accompanied industrialization, but thrived because of corporate support even in the early days, with Pirelli subsidizing Milan and Fiat's Agnelli family purchasing Juventus in 1925.[4] The Agnelli purchase provided the model for a second phase of Italian football when many of the clubs were acquired and closely held by prominent northern families. Only in 1942, when AS Roma prevailed, did a team south of Bologna win the national championship.

Whereas soccer aroused support in the industrial cities of the North, cycling developed strong support all through the peninsula, particularly in the poorer and less industrialized South, even though the racing champions usually hailed from the North. For the first half of the century, cycling inspired greater following in Italy than any other sport, and Italians excelled in world competition. In 1909, Luigi Ganna won the first *Giro d'Italia*, which later achieved importance second only to the *Tour de France*. Alfredo Binda was a celebrated three-time world champion (1927, 1930, and 1932), and a five-time champion of the *Giro*, winning a total of 41 stages. However, no Italian succeeded in winning the Tour de France until the legendary Fausto Coppi achieved the goal two decades later.

FASCISM AND SPORT

When Benito Mussolini consolidated his power in the late 1920s, his regime began to manipulate recreation and sport in the pursuit of several goals. One was to control and expand existing recreational organizations and physical education programs in schools for the purpose of engaging the masses. To do this, the Fascists created the *Opera Nazionale Balilla* (ONB), the children's group, and the *Opera Nazionale Dopolavoro* (OND) workers' group. By 1938, the number of instructors of physical education and sport working for the Fascist government soared to 140,000 and the participants in ONB to nearly 4 million. However, despite the growth, equipment and facilities remained spotty, and the regime always favored boys over girls. By the late 1930s, physical education had begun to resemble military training, incorporating marching, shooting, and bomb-throwing.[5]

A second goal of the regime was to emphasize sport as a symbol of Fascist virility. The Fascists expanded Italian sporting facilities, focused on international competition, and converted the Italian Olympic Committee and the soccer and gymnastics federations into Fascist agencies. By the 1930s, the Fascists basked in the international success of Italian athletes, both teams and individual champions. In the 1932 Los Angeles Olympics, after a Fascist march, the Italian team finished second to the United States with 12 gold medals. The Italian soccer team won back-to-back victories in the 1934 and 1938 World Cups. In boxing, the Italian-American immigrant Primo Carnera won the world heavyweight title—the first Italian to do so—by defeating Jack Sharkey in New York in 1933. While briefly basking in glory, Carnera made a triumphant trip to Rome, put on a black shirt, and paid his respects to Fascism. In 1935, after Carnera had been battered by Max Baer and then Joe Louis, race driver Tazio Nuvolari, "the Flying Mantuan," achieved perhaps his greatest victory in the German *Grand Prix* at Nurburgring. When he drove his Alfa Romeo past a Mercedes to cross the finish line before a bevy of Nazi officials, Nuvolari supposedly demonstrated Mussolini's success in exceeding German engineering, although racing experts attributed the victory to the Italian's brilliance and fearlessness. Like other nations, Italy used such success in sporting contests as nationalist propaganda. In the case of Nuvolari, victory carried with it the additional impression of Italian progress in technology and design. The legendary *Mille Miglia,* the 1,000-mile auto race initiated by the Fascists in 1927 and won by Nuvolari in 1930, showed off new Italian roads and chauvinistically traversed newly acquired territories near the Austrian and Yugoslav borders. Ironically, as if to demonstrate both the superiority of German technology and Italo-German collaboration, Nuvolari left Alfa to accept Dr. Ferdinand Porsche's offer and drove a Porsche to victory at the Italian *Grand Prix* at Monza in 1938.

Aviation, even more exhilarating than auto racing, became Mussolini's sport of choice in demonstrating the heroism of the "new Fascist man." Illustrating this heroism, Minister of the Air Force Italo Balbo landed his aerial flotilla of 24 Savoia Marchetti SM.55X flying boats on Lake Michigan at the Chicago World's Fair in 1933 after an intrepid crossing of the Atlantic. Meanwhile, like the Nazis, the Italian government approved the testing of the performance-enhancing capacity of stimulants and hormones. In 1935, the Fascists mounted a sports display in the *Palazzo d'Arte* in Milan and trumpeted the success of Carnera, Nuvolari, Balbo, and others as heroes and goodwill ambassadors, thus exploiting sport for propaganda.[6]

However, the celebrated success of both Nazis and Americans at the 1936 Olympics (when Italy slid to fourth place) may have encouraged the Fascists to redirect their efforts and to emphasize recreation in an effort to use sport as a unifying force in building a consensus. At the same time, as the depression lingered, Fascists turned sport, especially soccer, into a spectacle that would provide mass entertainment and escape from the realities of a dismal economy. Throughout the 1930s, Italians gathered around radios in bars, cafes, and clubs to listen to sporting events. In the cities and rural villages, the *Dopolavoro* led the initiative to spread recreational activities, especially those that stressed the favored "moral values" of teamwork and discipline.[7]

POSTWAR SPORTS

Cycling

In the immediate aftermath of World War II, the new Catholic, Socialist, and Communist parties all vied for control of sporting organizations in the wake of Fascism's fall. In the midst of heated Cold War political rivalry emerged a series of remarkable confrontations between two cyclists, Fausto Coppi (Communist) and Gino Bartali (Christian Democrat). The respective newspapers built the rivalry to mythological proportions, describing the younger Coppi as the "wave of the future" when he challenged "God's cyclist" Bartali, whom the Catholic press called "the perfect Christian athlete," virtuous and prayerful. Among the most memorable events in Italian sporting history were Bartali's 1948 and Coppi's 1949 victories in the Tour de France.

Cycling remained the dominant Italian sport in the immediate postwar era, and its popularity proved infectious. Italian professional teams could be seen practicing on back roads, and the color and accessibility of the sport inspired ordinary Italians to participate enthusiastically, especially on weekends. The Milan–San Remo race opens the season in March, while the *Giro d'Italia* commands a huge following on the roadsides, television stations, and newspapers as it winds through more than 3,000 kilometers in about three weeks' time. Like most Italian sports, the *Giro* has become heavily commercialized. It is launched with a caravan of vehicles (in 2003 there were 66), each designed to resemble the sponsor's product, samples of which are tossed to the large crowds. In 2003, the *Giro* raked in over $8 million in sponsors' fees and sold Italian television broadcast rights for about $12 million, while the towns that hosted a stage of the race paid a total of $2.4 million for the privilege.[8]

Italian cyclists have attained notable success in international competition and have inspired ardent support. By compiling multiple victories in the

Bicycle race, Civitavecchia. Courtesy of the author.

Giro, the Milan–San Remo, and the Tour de France, often in head-to-head competition, Bartali and Coppi dominated the scene as sporting heroes. In 1973, Felice Gimondi claimed the world championship, the first Italian to win the three major races (the French, Spanish, and Italian). Francesco Moser prevailed as World Champion in 1977, then seven years later won both the *Giro* and the Milan–San Remo races. In all, Italians have captured the World Championship 15 times, most recently Gianni Bugno in 1992 and Mario Cipollini in 2002. Women entered Italian sports competition after World War II, and by the 1980s, women's cycling won widespread interest. At the 1996 Olympic games in Atlanta, Paola Pezzo and Antonella Bellutti took home gold medals in women's mountain biking and velodrome, respectively, while Imelda Chiappa took the silver medal in the road race.

Italy's most recent cycling hero was Marco Pantani who, in winning the 1998 *Tour de France,* became the first Italian to do so since Gimondi in 1965 and only the seventh rider to win both the *Giro d'Italia* and *Tour de France* in the same year. Pantani's reputation was quickly sullied, however, when in 1999, with a huge lead in the *Giro,* he failed a drug test, was disqualified, and never fully returned to form. However, many Italians continued to define cycling largely in terms of Pantani and believed his protestations of innocence. In June 2003, he entered treatment for depression and drug addiction and in October was acquitted of sports fraud in the doping charges stemming from the 1999 *Giro* because Italy's sports fraud law was not in place in 1999. Tragically, in March 2004, Pantani was discovered dead in a hotel room in Rimini after extended cocaine abuse.[9]

More recently, Paolo Bettini won the World Cups of 2002 and 2003, while Gilberto Simoni prevailed in the 2001 and 2003 *Giro.* At the end of 2003, 7 Italians ranked in the world's top 15 cyclists, including Bettini, Simoni, Alessandro Petacchi, Davide Rebellin, Danilo Di Luca, Michele Bartoli, and Dario Frigo. In the 2004 *Tour de France,* Ivan Basso finished third and Pietro Caucchioli eleventh.

Soccer

Even as cycling sustained interest among Italians, soccer began to gain in popularity. There are several explanations. Although Italian cycling remained strong, Italians were challenged internationally, so that many of the most successful and most highly publicized cyclists were non-Italian, such as the Frenchmen Bernard Hinault and Jacques Anquetil, the Belgian Eddie Merckx, and the Spaniard Miguel Indurain. At the end of the twentieth century, Coppi was named Italy's greatest athlete. And at the same time as Italian cyclists were meeting stiff competition, Italian soccer was emerging. Just behind Coppi in the poll was Giuseppe (Peppino) Meazza, the captain of Italy's 1934 and 1938 World Cup soccer champions.

The reasons for the rise of Italian soccer are apparent. In 1948, each first division *(Serie A)* team was permitted to import three foreign players, and in response, Italian clubs immediately dipped into the talent-rich South American market to recruit top players, particularly those of Italian ancestry. They soon moved into the Western European market, and by the 1990s had reached into Eastern Europe and Africa. By then EU labor standards had eliminated all barriers to recruiting within the continent. This brought an immediate elevation in "star quality" as familiar names from world competition flocked to the Italian league. Among the best were the Welshman John Charles; the Brazilians Paulo Roberto Falcao, Zico, and Ronaldo; and the Argentinians Diego Maradona and Gabriel Batistuta. At the same time, the foreign players also brought a faster, more exciting style to Italian soccer, which had formerly favored a defensive strategy.

After recovering from an embarrassing showing in the 1966 World Cup (ousted by North Korea), the Italian national team played well in international competition, accelerating the sport's popularity. The *"Azzuri"* as they are called (with reference to their blue uniforms) defeated Germany to advance to the final match in 1970, only to be beaten 4–1 by Brazil. By 1970, attendance had grown to an average of 30,000 per *Serie A* match and soccer had clearly outstripped cycling as the favored sport of Italians. The national team remained competitive, and in 1982, the *Azzuri* swept through Argentina, Brazil, and Germany on the way to their third World Cup championship, largely on the play of striker Paolo Rossi. In the 1990s, with midfielder Roberto Baggio leading the way, the Italians managed to reach the semifinals and finals before losing. The popularity of soccer was greatly enhanced by both the media (especially such sports publications as *La Gazzetta dello Sport* and *Tuttosport*) and betting schemes such as Totocalcio and Totogol, the receipts of which are contributed to the national Olympic committee. The Italian teams consistently used the strategy of defense and counterattack *(catenaccio e contropiede),* which most identify as "Italian football."[10]

The addition of top-notch, world-class players added a dimension of glamour that attracted media attention along with big salaries, contributing in turn to the commercialization of the game. As Italian soccer grew in popularity, more Italian businessmen financed teams, and by the 1980s the league became more dependent on corporate money. Hollywood film producer Vittorio Cecchi Gori, for example, spent millions of dollars to recruit the striker Batistuta ("*Batigol*") to his La Fiorentina club, elevating the team to the level of serious competitor for the *Serie A* championship and, at the same time, making it dependent on Cecchi Gori's fortune. The Agnelli family of Fiat still

controls Juventus, which holds more national championships (25) than any
Italian club. Prime minister, media baron, and Italy's richest man, Silvio
Berlusconi, owns AC Milan, the second most successful club in history with
13 championships. In fact, Berlusconi's presence has further transformed the
world of Italian sport by immersing it more deeply into the realms of business, television, and politics, a phenomenon that has been labeled "unprecedented hybridization."[11]

SOCCER, CORPORATE BUSINESS, AND POLITICS: A POTENT MIX

Berlusconi acquired the Milan Football Club in February 1986 when the
organization was facing serious problems. Within a decade the tycoon took
the proud but troubled club to worldwide prominence. By applying the
entrepreneurial, marketing, and management strategies that had enabled his
Fininvest empire to soar to enormous success as a maverick holding company,
Berlusconi reinforced the myth of his own genius in the process. In effect,
Fininvest simply added the football club to its construction, television, and
public relations empire, then utilized all its resources to transform a team into
a marketing and media colossus. Berlusconi's timing was impeccable. The

Atalanta Bergamasca soccer game. Courtesy of Katrina Reiniers.

Italian team had put on a brilliant and inspired performance in defeating
Spain in the 1982 World Cup, creating great enthusiasm as well as an
expanded televison audience. Meanwhile, the European Championship
promised the opportunity to broaden interest well beyond previous levels,
while Parliament passed a law enabling football clubs to offer shares on the
stock market.

Berlusconi seized the moment. He reorganized the operation, finding
numerous new sources of revenue, remodeling the stadium, aggressively
signing new international players, advertising extensively, maximizing television revenues, and vastly expanding fan support and season ticket sales
while bringing hooligans (known in Italy as *ultràs*) under greater control.
The results were extraordinary. Within six years, AC Milan had won four
Italian *Serie A* championships, three European championships, and numerous other international titles. And as the Berlusconi model gained notoriety,
the remaking of AC Milan transformed the whole of Italian football. Revenues grew by geometric proportions. Televison revenues alone grew from
$2 million in 1982 to more than $500 million in 1998, much of it now generated by pay TV and by the seemingly endless hours of commentary.[12]
Since Berlusconi acquired AC Milan, ticket sales as a percentage of revenues
have dropped from 92 percent to 13 percent, while television now produces
about two-thirds of revenue.[13] Italian football produces more than $5 billion
in revenues and looms just outside the top 10 most profitable Italian industries. One menacing issue that leaves the best Italian teams financially vulnerable—despite marketing reforms and lucrative televison contracts—is
the enormous capital investment in players. In 1999, Parma topped the list
with $147 million in contracts, ahead of Milan ($139 million) and Lazio
($108 million).[14]

It has been argued that Berlusconi's motive was never simply to pursue
profit for AC Milan—although Fininvest and all its components were very
aggressive in pursuit of profit—but also to establish his image as a man of
vision and an intrepid entrepreneur, always with an eye on self-promotion and
politics.[15] Berlusconi used AC Milan as a paradigm of the new Italy he visual-
ized. The other football clubs such as Fiat's Juventus, like the government of
the republic itself, were bogged down in a stifling familial and corporate culture that inhibited innovation, modernization, and entrepreneurship. In contrast, Berlusconi positioned himself as the deft miracle worker who could
apply his genius to Italian sport in the same way that he had transformed Italian media—even if it meant, as his critics pointed out, manipulating, violat-
ing, or changing the laws. In the process, he enhanced a reputation that would
enable him to claim that he was the one man who could lead Italy out of its
own political morass.

It has also been argued that when Berlusconi brought Gianfranco Fini into his first cabinet, he legitimized Fini's *Alleanza Nazionale,* heir to the neo-Fascist MSI, and in doing so, gave public authenticity to right-wing extremists and their racist and anti-Semitic tirades. Whether it is accurate to attribute this rise to Berlusconi—there was a similar rise in much of Europe—political extremism was accompanied by unprecedented racist violence and xenophobic demonstrations by *ultràs* at football games. In January 2005, Lazio captain Paolo Di Canio gave a much-publicized Fascist salute to his team's fans after scoring a goal.[16]

Berlusconi's maverick approach to AC Milan, based on his Fininvest business strategy, was not the final word in the economics of Italian football. The Lazio club, part of a global food conglomerate, was the first football team to list on the stock market and tended to focus primarily on stock value. The Parmalat corporation took advantage of its international brand recognition and distribution and advertising networks to purchase international teams and recruit their players to advertise its milk products worldwide.

Once he committed to electoral campaigning, Berlusconi made extensive use of the symbolism of sport. He began by naming his political movement (consciously not a party) *Forza Italia!* (Go Italy!), fashioned after the cheer for the *Azzuri,* and adopting the national team's recognizable colors. He mobilized AC Milan's fan clubs to recruit party supporters, imposed a "friend-enemy" duality in his campaigns that demonized the opposition, and touted his own success as an entrepreneur of sport. Berlusconi was quoted as remarking derisively about one of his electoral opponents: "How many championship cups has he won?"[17] Once in power, Berlusconi manipulated the laws to create even greater opportunities, not only for his publishing and television empire, but for his football team as well.

Italian soccer has become a major industry, in line with similar developments in the rest of Europe, and particularly in step with the English system in which virtually all the teams are listed on the stock market. Currently two Italian clubs are listed on the Milan market in addition to Lazio: Inter Milan, and AS Roma (Berlusconi says that he sees no advantage in listing AC Milan). In fact, the entire *Lega Calcio* (Italian soccer league) is deeply entrenched in Italian finances, and especially in the economics of the television market. The *Lega Calcio* distributes the enormous income from televised soccer (the 1988 figure was $60 million) primarily among *Serie A* clubs. On the one hand, media giants have acquired soccer clubs, as in the case of Berlusconi's AC Milan and Cecchi Gori's Fiorentina; on the other, many clubs have launched television channels and interactive Internet operations while hauling in the revenues. Clearly, the old myth of Italian soccer as a "poor man's game" has been permanently deflated.[18]

The major force escalating costs is the rise in player salaries. In the 1997 and 1998 seasons, as competition for top players intensified, spiraling player salaries (more than 60 percent of total expenditures) consumed the appreciable increase in revenues over the same years. The competition for players escalated with the 1995 European Court of Justice ruling that allowed teams in EU-member states to own an unlimited number of players from other EU-member states and enabled a player to leave his team at the completion of a contract without compensation to the team. As a result, Italian teams have aggressively recruited the world's best, to the point that in a recent European Champions League match, only 5 of AC Milan's 11 starting players were Italian. By the end of the century, personnel costs had surged to new levels. Inter Milan paid Lazio $45 million to acquire forward Christian Vieri, then paid Vieri $4 million per year, while Juventus paid forward Alessandro Del Piero $5 million per year.[19]

Mounting debt from player contracts and construction of facilities—combined with stagnating revenues—has pushed five of the top six Italian soccer clubs into debt and several to the verge of bankruptcy. As recently as 2002, Juventus was valued at $241 million, second only in value to Manchester United of England among publicly traded soccer clubs. Lazio and Roma ranked fifth and sixth at $111 and $96 million, respectively. But values have dropped precipitously in the face of mounting debt and plummeting television revenues. In 2002, Italy's 18 *Serie A* clubs reported an operating loss of $764 million and debt of $3 billion. Many also owe back taxes and fees to the players' pension fund. Cecchi Gori's Fiorentina was forced into bankruptcy in June 2001, unable to meet debts of $22 million, and others face similarly dire circumstances.[20] The predicament was so severe that in early 2003 the Italian Parliament passed the *salva calcio* (save soccer) law that allowed the Italian clubs an accounting method for deferring more than $1.15 million in losses over 10 years. The *salva calcio* law then triggered a Europe-wide crisis when the EU ruled that the law violated European standards, which require such losses to be recorded immediately. The EU held that postponing the debt gives the Italian teams an unfair advantage in bidding for players and competing for the European Champions League. Although the resolution is in doubt, there is no question that the Italian soccer business will be faced with difficult financial decisions in the years ahead.[21]

Today, in spite of scandals involving fixed games, drug use, bankruptcy, and allegations that clubs provided call girls for players and that referees favor the dominant teams, more than 20 million Italians consider themselves soccer fans, one-half of whom sometimes watch the *Azzuri* matches and one-fourth of whom read the sports newspapers on a daily basis. Groups of fans traditionally maintained identities that reflected regional and ideological elements within the political culture, so that AC Milan attracted industrial workers from the unions and left-wing groups, while Inter Milan appealed to the right-wing and the middle class and the Bologna club drew from the communists of "red" Romagna. Observers have noted contrasts in the ritualized songs and other behaviors of the "structured mobs" that dominate the stadium culture. They note, for example, that the fans of Juventus project an elitist image fitting the historical role of the city of Turin, while the supporters of the Napoli club express an ironic sense of victimization at the hands of the wealthier and more powerful North.[22]

Changes in fan behavior began to surface in the late 1960s with the rise of the *ultrà* groups, partly in imitation of English hooligans, but uniquely Italian. The *ultràs* began as colorful but loosely organized efforts to provide spectacle at the stadium—the Inter Boys, the *Fossa dei Leoni* (Lion's Den) of AC Milan, and the Red and Blue Commandos of Bologna. But in the wake of the radicalism of 1968, the *ultrà* groups became politicized and aggressive, exerting some influence over the clubs and the stadiums and claiming control of the *curva* (the curved portions of the stadiums). The *ultràs* then began to take control of some portion of ticket distribution and the sale of merchandise so as to finance the groups. By the mid-1970s, the *ultràs* became more centrally structured, more violent in confronting others, more extreme in their rhetoric and imagery, and even more likely to use weapons. By 1990, the *ultràs* adopted more overtly political and regional identities, as, for example, northern *ultrà* groups rallied behind the northern autonomy movement of the Lombard League and the Lazio *ultràs* held up posters of Mussolini and shouted racist and xenophobic slogans and chants. The Salerno *ultràs* set fire to a train. Fan violence has even caused the cancellation of matches, as happened in a Turin–AC Milan match in the spring of 2003. And while Italian soccer fans have not yet formed a nationwide organization as English fans have, it was reported that the president of the Lazio team feared to attend a home game because of the intensity of the protest by the team's fans against the introduction of pay television to restrict the broadcast of Lazio matches. Although the Italian clubs have kept many more inexpensive seats in their stadiums than the English teams, the thought is that Italian fans may well emulate the English fans in forming their own coalition if economic trends continue.[23]

FORMULA ONE RACING: SCUDERIA FERRARI AND THE *TIFOSI*

The zeal exhibited by Italian fans at Formula One auto races provides ample evidence that the passion of Italians is not limited to soccer alone. The zeal for racing is aroused almost exclusively by *Scuderia Ferrari* (team Ferrari) and its

Ferrari F310, driven by Michael Schumacher in the 1996 Formula One season.
Courtesy of Leah Ammerman.

signature scarlet racing machines. Ferrari is the singular product of the legendary Enzo Ferrari (1898–1988). Ferrari created his racing team in 1929 and
achieved notable success managing Alfa Romeo's efforts until 1938. After leaving Alfa in a bitter dispute, he began to design racing cars, first at Modena, then
at Maranello. By the end of World War II, he had settled on a V-12 engine
design that Ferrari would utilize successfully until 1995. Franco Cortese drove
the Ferrari to its first *Grand Prix* victory in Rome in 1947. Subsequently, Luigi
Chinetti and the Englishman Lord Selsdon (Peter Mitchell-Thompson) drove
a Ferrari 166MM to victory in the famed 24 hours of Le Mans, the beginning
of a brilliant two-decade run. Enzo Ferrari, the irascible *"Commendatore"* (the
honorary title of distinguished citizen by which he was known), never missed a
racing season after the World Championship was inaugurated in 1950, and
always took great pride that his was the only team that built engine, chassis, and
gearbox, in contrast to other constructors. He drove his team and his drivers
relentlessly, and when *"Il Commendatore"* died, Scuderia Ferrari had accumu-
lated more *Grand Prix* victories and more World Championship points than
any other team, a tradition that Ferrari carries on admirably. Eight drivers have
won World Championships at the wheel of a Ferrari: Alberto Ascari (1952 and
1953); Juan Manuel Fangio (1956); Mike Hawthorn (1958); Phil Hill (1961);
John Surtees (1964); Niki Lauda (1975 and 1977); Jody Scheckter (1979); and
Michael Schumacher (2000, 2001, 2002, 2003, and 2004).

   In fact the phenomenal popularity of Michael Schumacher ("Schumi," as
Italians affectionately call him) rivals and perhaps exceeds that of all other Ital-

ian athletes, in spite of his German nationality. The seven-time World Champion—he won in 1994 and 1995 driving for Benetton—is perhaps the greatest in the long line of Ferrari drivers. The Ferrari team consists of chief of racing operations Jean Todt, technical director Ross Brawn, and Ferrari chief executive Luca di Montezemolo. Ferrari continues to excel, in spite of numerous Formula One rule changes designed to increase competition, and in spite of continuing corporate problems in Ferrari's parent, Fiat, and lingering questions about whether shareholder Mediobanca would float Ferrari on the stock market.

YACHTING, SKIING, AND BASKETBALL

In addition to soccer, cycling, and Formula One racing, Italians continue to show great enthusiasm for a range of spectator sports, particularly yachting, skiing, and basketball. Yachting has provided Italians great entertainment. As the Italian postwar economy expanded, wealthy Italian businessmen and corporations subsidized world-class yacht racing so that Italian teams have acquired the technology and financial resources to become competitive. Italy has challenged for the America's Cup since 1983, and has twice won the prestigious Louis Vuitton Cup, first in 1992 with the late billionaire Raul Gardini's *Il Moro di Venezia.* That same year, the *America3* edged out *Il Moro di Venezia* by 52 seconds in the closest America's Cup race in history. In 2002 in New Zealand, the *Luna Rossa* of the Italian team Prada, led by Patrizio Bertelli and skipper Francesco de Angelis, was eliminated in the quarter finals of the America's Cup by the American yacht *OneWorld.*

Skiing has traditionally been popular in Italy, but Alberto Tomba (known as "*la bomba,*" "the bomb") made it the rage when in 1988 he doubled in the Winter Olympics with gold medals in the slalom and giant slalom. When the handsome 22-year old Carabinieri noncommissioned officer from Bologna doubled again in 1992, he became the first Alpine skier to win gold medals in consecutive Winter games. Tomba's success, achieved with great flair, captured the nation's imagination, providing an Italian icon in a sport in which even the Italian skiers had traditionally been German speakers from the Tirol-Alto Adige region. "*Tomba la bomba*" was afforded rock-star status, and when he retired, his 50 World Cup victories placed him second all-time to the legendary Ingemar Stenmark of Sweden. Women's Olympic and World Cup champion Deborah Campagnoli has rivaled Tomba as both athlete and celebrity, having signed lucrative advertising deals with Benetton and other Italian companies. Italians have competed successfully in a wide range of other Olympic events, including fencing, target-shooting, wrestling, weightlifting, and various boating races. Over the history of the modern Olympic games, Italians have fared well, standing sixth (behind Britain and France) in total medals.

A 1990 survey indicated that about 22 percent of the Italian population over three years old participates in a sport (31 percent of males and 14 percent of females). Volleyball has enjoyed a particular boost in popularity, partly as a result of the three consecutive world championships won by the Italian men's team (1990, 1994, and 1998), European championships in 1989 and 1993, the World Grand Championship in 1993, a World Cup victory in 1995, a record number of eight World League championships between 1990 and 2001, and the women's world championship in 2002. In 1990, about 600,000 Italians were reportedly playing volleyball, more than 60 percent of them women.

Basketball gained popularity in Italy in the 1960s when American players were allowed to compete in Italian leagues. Among Italy's prominent professional teams are former European champions Pallacanestro Olympia Milano and Pallacanestro Varese. In the 1980 Olympics, the Italian team won the silver medal behind Dino Meneghin, considered Italy's all-time best player. As a result of this growing interest, more than 300,000 Italians were playing basketball in 1991. Gymnastics, competitive dance, tennis, baseball, rugby, and water polo also have grown, while such traditional games as *bocce* and *pallone elastico* (a four-on-four game played with an elastic ball) hold their own. In contrast, it has been reported that winter sports, hunting, and fishing have experienced a substantial drop.[24]

RECREATIONAL SPORT

A recent phenomenon in Italian life is the fitness club. Studies suggest that more than 4 million Italians exercise regularly at a gym. This new enthusiasm for "working out" (*"andare in palestra,"* to go to the gym) marks a distinct change in the use of leisure time. During the Fascist era, the regime employed organized physical activity to reinforce their ideology and build a consensus, but with Mussolini's fall, the emphasis shifted to exercising for personal reasons. Once the government had largely abandoned the direct sponsorship of fitness, commercial gyms began to appear, charging fees for the use of their facilities. In the 1980s, fitness clubs began to multiply, shifting the emphasis in their advertising from physical discipline to the pleasure derived from working out. In contemporary Italian culture, the appeal of working out incorporates the ideals of both function and form: One will be able to live more productively while developing a more attractive body. According to one observer, the aesthetic has changed, particularly with respect to the ideal woman's body, from the soft curves of the 1960s and the "cult of thinness" of the 1970s to a "new muscular femininity."[25] The most popular varieties of exercise in Italian gyms now combine dance, aerobics, and weight training in widely advertised, attractive facilities. Thus physical fitness, like many other forms of leisure activities and sport, have synthesized the commercial and the physical to claim an ever-larger place in Italian life.

NOTES

1. Nicola Porro, "Italian Sports: Between Government and Society," in *National Sports Policies,* ed. Laurence Chalip, Arthur Johnson, and Lisa Stachura (Westport, Conn.: Greenwood Press, 1996), 261.

2. Patrick McCarthy, "Sport and Society in Italy Today," *Journal of Modern Italian Studies* 5, no. 3 (Fall 2000): 322–23; Porro, "Italian Sports," 267.

3. Porro, "Italian Sports," 255.

4. McCarthy, "Sport and Society," 325.

5. Patrizia Dogliani, "Sport and Fascism," *Journal of Modern Italian Studies* 5, no. 3 (Fall 2000): 327–43.

6. Dogliani, "Sport and Fascism," 327–43.

7. Dogliani, "Sport and Fascism," 335–41.

8. Eric Sylvers, "Breaking Away, with a Sponsor," *The New York Times,* June 3, 2003.

9. Matt Rendell, "The Long, Lonely Road to Oblivion," *The Observer,* March 7, 2004; "Marco Pantani," *The Economist,* February 28, 2004.

10. Gerry P. T. Finn and Richard Giulianotti, *Football Culture* (London: Frank Cass, 2000), 156.

11. Nicola Porro and Pippo Russo, "Berlusconi and Other Matters: The Era of Football-Politics," *Journal of Modern Italian Studies* 5, no. 3 (Fall 2000): 348.

12. Porro and Russo, "Berlusconi and Other Matters," 355.

13. Emanuela Poli, "Italian Media and Telecommunications Authority," *Journal of Modern Italian Studies* 5, no. 3 (Fall 2000): 376.

14. Porro and Russo, "Berlusconi and Other Matters," 355.

15. Porro and Russo, "Berlusconi and Other Matters," 353; Patrick McCarthy, "*Forza Italia:* Old Problems Linger On," in *Italian Politics,* ed. Roberto D'Alimonte and David Nelkan (Boulder, Colo.: Westview Press, 1997), 51–64.

16. Porro and Russo, "Berlusconi and Other Matters," 367; "Di Canio Claims innocence in row," BBC SPORT http://news.bbc.co.uk/sport1/hi/football/europe/4163979.stm.

17. Porro and Russo, "Berlusconi and Other Matters," 365.

18. Poli, "Italian Media and Telecommunications Authority," 371–93.

19. Poli, "Italian Media and Telecommunications Authority," 374.

20. Richard Heller, "Big Kick," *Forbes,* July 8, 2002; Kate Noble, "No Money, No Kickoff," *Time* (Europe), September 2, 2002, p. 104.

21. Eric Sylvers, "Grudge Match: Italy vs. the Bean Counters," *The New York Times,* November 11, 2003.

22. Rocco de Biasi, review of *La partita di calcio,* by Christian Bromberger, *Journal of Modern Italian Studies* 5, no. 3 (Fall 2000): 415–17.

23. Adam Brown and Andy Walsh, "Football Supporters' Relations with Their Clubs: A European Perspective," *Soccer & Society* 1, no. 3 (Autumn 2000): 88–94; C. Podiliri and C. Balestri, "The *Ultras,* Racism and Football Culture in Italy," in *Fanatics!,* ed. Adam Brown (London: Routledge, 1998).

24. Porro, "Italian Sports," 260. The Italian team won the World League in 1990, 1991, 1992, 1994, 1995, 1997, 1999, and 2000.

25. Roberta Sassatelli, "The Commercialization of Discipline: Keep-Fit Culture and its Values," *Journal of Modern Italian Studies* 5, no. 3 (Fall 2000): 396–411.

6

Literature

The Extraordinary Tradition of Italian Literature

The Italian literary legacy is so masterful that it challenges contemporary writers to meet historical standards of international excellence. The culture that produced Dante, Boccaccio, Petrarca, Carducci, Pirandello, and so many other brilliant novelists, poets, and essayists has continued to excel in the postwar era. Such Italian writers as Ignazio Silone, Alberto Moravia, Pier Paolo Pasolini, Leonardo Sciascia, Salvatore Quasimodo, Eugenio Montale, Italo Calvino, Natalia Ginzburg, and Umberto Eco have gained universal acclaim and have won a number of Nobel prizes.

Scholars trace the origins of Italian literature (as distinguished from Roman, Latin, or the medieval French or Provencal literature that medieval Italians read) to a localized tradition of poetry written in the vernacular languages of Umbria, Tuscany, and especially Sicily at the thirteenth-century court of Frederick II Hohenstaufen.[1] However, the foundation of a literature composed in a distinctly Italian language is attributed to three Tuscan masters known as *trecentisti* (men of the fourteenth century): the Florentine poets Dante Alighieri, Giovanni Boccaccio, and Francesco Petrarca.

Educated in the standard Latin curriculum and influenced by a circle of Florentine writers, Dante composed his *Vita Nuova* in the 1290s and his *Commedia (Divine Comedy)* in the following decade. In his *Vita Nuova* Dante wove poetry through a prose framework, exhibiting the influence of the troubadours of Provence and the love poetry of the Sicilian court, while engaging in both autobiographical and spiritual reflection. The autobiographical dimension includes the celebration of his unrequited love for "blessed Beatrice"—perhaps one of several Florentine women, possibly only an ethereal vision—who brought him both euphoria and agony.

The *Commedia* is Dante's great epic poem. He wrote his allegory in three parts that he called the *Inferno* (Hell), the *Purgatorio* (Purgatory), and the *Paradiso* (Heaven). In each part, Dante engages in a dreamlike odyssey wherein he encounters a series of figures, historical and mythological, virtuous or vile, each of whom has been rewarded or punished to illustrate Dante's multilayered social, political, and religious message. The Roman poet Virgil guides him through hell and purgatory, his beloved Beatrice through heaven. Dante wrote the poem in three-stanza rhyme (known as *terza rima*) in Italian for readers of his generation, and its numerous editions contributed to the spread of a standard Italian (Tuscan) language and to the establishment of the work as a true classic, studied acutely almost 700 years after its appearance. In addition to his major works, Dante composed other poems, works of philosophy, and a political treatise.

Giovanni Boccaccio and Francesco Petrarca (Petrarch) were Florentine friends and literary giants. After a stint as an accountant in Naples, Boccaccio began to compose lyric poetry under the influence of the work of Dante, about whom he lectured and wrote in later life. Boccaccio composed his masterpiece, *Il Decamerone* (*Decameron*, or "Ten Days' Work") between 1348 and 1353. It was a series of 100 lively stories set in a villa outside Florence among a group of 10 friends who retreated to the hills to escape the plague (which had struck Florence in 1348) and the resulting physical and moral decay of the city. Filled with rustic humor, *Il Decamerone* has been lauded for its craftsmanship, skillful character analysis, and poetry. Each day ends in a *canzone* (a short lyric poem) for which the writer became famous. Boccaccio's other works include *Il Corbaccio (The Old Crow)*, two romances, *Il filocolo* and *L'amorosa Fiammetta (Amorous Fiammetta)*, and a number of scholarly works, including *De Claris Mulieribus (Concerning Famous Women)*.

Of the three masters of fourteenth-century Italian literature, Petrarca is sometimes considered the most important in setting literary standards of the European Renaissance. Born in Arezzo, Petrarca traveled widely for the church and the Visconti family of Milan before returning to Tuscany in 1350. Forsaking the practice of law and diplomacy, he pursued the study of humanism and wrote in many genres in both Latin and the Italian vernacular, thus invigorating both languages. But his crowning achievement was his *Canzoniere (Songbook,* known originally as *Rime in vita e morte di Madonna Laura,* Rhymes in the Life and Death of Madonna Laura), a book of 366 amorous sonnets, ballads, and madrigals dedicated to his passionate love for

Laura, including *Una donna più bella assai che il sole* ("A woman more beautiful by far than the sun"). The *Canzoniere* is admired both for its technical brilliance and its contribution to the development of a literary tradition in the Italian language.[2]

Overlapping the work of the *trecentisti* were the Italian humanist writers, most notably Coluccio Salutati, Leonardo Bruni, and Lorenzo Valla. The humanists celebrated the political traditions of their various cities, whether "democratic," as in the case of Florence, or the more openly autocratic traditions of Milan and Venice. In Rome, Valla devoted much of his life to translating ancient manuscripts while serving in the papal secretariat under Pope Nicholas V. Despite individual loyalties, these humanist writers shared a perspective that celebrated intellect, achievement, and active participation in the political life of the city as a great virtue. Their ideals circulated from city to city, dispersing a new intellectual culture throughout the peninsula. Among their principles was a strong commitment to education, based on the belief that the aristocratic youth had to prepare themselves to rule.

Three Italian writers excelled as sixteenth- and seventeenth-century successors to the humanists: Ludovico Ariosto, Torquato Tasso, and Galileo Galilei. All were exceptional contributors to the literary tradition of the Italian Renaissance. Born in Reggio Emilia, Ariosto wrote sonnets and comedies and is best remembered for his epic poem *Orlando Furioso,* which earned him the reputation as the "Italian Homer." Tasso, regarded as the premier poet of the Italian Renaissance, completed his famous epic poem of the First Crusade, *Gerusalemme liberata (Jerusalem Delivered)* in 1581. Although known primarily as the founder of modern science for his scientific discoveries and treatises, Galileo Galilei also wrote poetry and critical analysis of Dante, Petrarca, Ariosto, and Tasso. Not surprisingly, it is not his poetry but his lucid prose writing, especially his scientific essays, that rank Galilei as a major literary figure.

As the movement to unify the Italian peninsula spread, Italian writers of the romantic school expressed renewed enthusiasm for Italian nationalism, at least in a romanticized, abstract form. Among the best known of these Italian romanticists were Ugo Foscolo, Alessandro Manzoni, and Giacomo Leopardi. Foscolo generated interest in Italy's past in his most famous works, *Dei Sepolcri (Of Sepulchres)* and *Le ultime lettere di Jacopo Ortis (The Final Letters of Jacopo Ortis).* Such artistic expression kept alive, at least among a small elite, the ideals on which more realistic forms of nationalism would later build. Manzoni published his famous romantic, historical novel *I Promessi Sposi (The Betrothed)* in 1840.[3] In describing the lives of Milanese lovers living under Spanish rule in the seventeenth century, Manzoni provided a metaphor for ordinary Italians who relied on their Catholic faith to protect them against alien forces of oppression. Leopardi, often considered the finest lyric poet of his day, published ardently patriotic poems among his less-celebrated works, including *All'Italia* ("To Italy") in 1818, and other minor poems in which he sympathized with the fate of Italians, while condemning Austria and France.

EARLY TWENTIETH-CENTURY WRITERS

With the success of unification, the era of romanticism in Italian literature gave way to the realities of the modern world. In the era preceding World War I, Italian writers wrote in a variety of genres. Two writers who anticipated the modern traditions wrote in the latter part of the nineteenth century: Giovanni Verga and Giosuè Carducci. The Sicilian novelist and playwright Verga developed the influential school known as *verismo,* or realism, in which he depicted the lives of Sicilian peasants in stark detail. Among his best known works are *Cavalleria Rusticana,* the source of Mascagni's opera, and *I malavoglia,* from which filmmaker Luchino Visconti would derive his 1948 movie *La Terra Trema.* Poetry thrived as well. The Tuscan Carducci became the first Italian to win the Nobel Prize for literature (1906) based primarily on his earlier works, *Rime nuove (New Rhymes), Odi barbare (Pagan Odes),* and *Rime e ritmi (Lyrics and Rhythms).*

Italy's transition to twentieth-century culture is emphatically marked by two writers: Gabriele D'Annunzio and Luigi Pirandello. D'Annunzio, born in the Abruzzi and educated in Florence and Rome, wrote extravagant poetry and prose. In his lifestyle as well as his writing, D'Annunzio conducted a one-man assault on conventional mores and aesthetic standards. He worked in a wide variety of media, including poetry (e.g., *Canto novo,* "New Song"), fiction (*Il Piacere,* "Pleasure" and *La Gloria,* "Glory"), and drama (*Il Fuoco,* "The Flame of Life"). By 1910, the poet had moved into politics, becoming first a socialist, then a member of Parliament, then an ardent nationalist. In many ways, D'Annunzio's elaborate iconoclasm reflected, in exaggerated form, the new generation's excesses, its impatience with the *status quo,* and its inclination to seek extreme alternatives to the conventions of bourgeois life. Also representative of changing values at the advent of the new century was the Sicilian dramatist Pirandello, who introduced highly original elements into his plays, most notably *Sei personaggi in cerca d'autore* (*Six Characters in Search of an Author,* 1921). In staging six unfinished characters, Pirandello raises questions of relativistic morals and subjective reality, anticipating the pessimism and existentialism that would influence much of modern literature.

Just as fiction writers used modern themes, so Italian poets of the twentieth century reflected an awareness of modernization and rapid acceleration of change, making a conscious statement that their generation had broken dramatically with the classical and romantic traditions of Italy's past. No group of these avant-garde poets embraced change more enthusiastically than the Futurists. Beginning with Filippo Tommaso Marinetti's *Futurist Manifesto* of 1909, Italian Futurist writers forcefully rejected tradition, especially humanist values, while exalting the aesthetic of the machine and glorifying conflict and combat. Italy's foremost Futurist poet was Ardegno Soffici, who combined visual and auditory imagery to simulate motion. Another group of poets, known as the *crepuscolari* (those who viewed life with ironic melancholy), answered modernization differently. The best known *crepuscolari* were Guido Gozzano, Marino Moretti, and Sergio Corazzini, who took shelter in the commonplace themes of everyday life, often finding only a drab and meaningless existence.

The Futurist movement produced no narrative equivalent to their poetry, since they viewed the novel as a tradition-laden and static form of literature. In fact, it has been argued that the production of early twentieth-century Italian novelists was relatively weak, both in terms of what had preceded it—most notably Manzoni and Verga—and what French and English novelists were producing. The most respected of the pre-Fascist Italian novelists are Italo Svevo, Giuseppe Antonio Borgese, and Federico Tozzi. Svevo, who was born Ettore Schmitz in Trieste, viewed writing as a pursuit of contemplation and self-examination. *Una vita* (*A Life,* 1892) serves to analyze the drabness of capitalist society through the eyes of an intellectual-turned-banker who ultimately commits suicide. In *La coscienza di Zeno* (*Confessions of Zeno,* 1923), a businessman from Trieste provides a narrative of his life of self-deception through his sessions with a psychoanalyst. Svevo found in his writing a source of self-analysis, thus utilizing the novel to explore the intimate, personal sphere, a radical departure from most Italian novelists. Borgese, literary critic and professor at the universities of Turin, Rome, and Milan, wrote the novel *Rubé* in 1921 before fleeing Fascism to teach at universities in the United States. The novel is the story of a man, Filippo Rubé, searching for his own identity while he attempts to adjust from the exhilaration of combat in World War I to a drab, postwar existence. Ultimately Rubé is crushed in a socialist demonstration. Borgese's novel is valued especially for the author's insight into Italian middle-class culture in the postwar era.

Federico Tozzi added significantly to the literature of the early century by completing a series of novels just before his death in 1920. Tozzi used expressionism—especially fragmented language that creates images of a discordant existence—to portray the dissonance between the traditional Italian rural life and the increasingly powerful urban bourgeoisie. Tozzi's masterpiece is *Con gli occhi chiusi* (*With Eyes Closed*), published in 1919.

Fascism, War, and the Immediate Postwar Era

Mussolini's Fascist regime imposed strict censorship that, although not by any means air tight, managed to chill the creative climate and discourage the production of original literature. Thus, with the exception of Benedetto Croce's *La Critica* (see Chapter 2), periodicals that provided independent social and economic commentary were virtually nonexistent, and few memorable novels emerged. Poetry, in contrast, seems to have suffered less from Fascist censorship because its messages were both more personal than overtly political and stated in less direct language. Among poets who published in the Fascist era were Umberto Saba (born Umberto Poli), Giuseppe Ungaretti, Salvatore Quasimodo, and Eugenio Montale. Saba, much like Italo Svevo before him, regarded poetry as a vehicle for self-examination. Saba dedicated his life to assembling a poetic autobiographical study, published posthumously in 1961 as *Canzoniere (Songbook)*. Included are poems that reflect the innocence of youth, a tribute to the suffering and spirituality of animals, and *Trieste e una donna (Trieste and a Woman)*, a love song to his wife.

Like Svevo and Saba, Giuseppe Ungaretti wrote self-analytical poetry, but was much more sweeping in his pursuit of redemption. Through language and sound, Ungaretti attempted to recapture the freedom, individualism, self-fulfillment, and lost innocence that he believed modernization had stolen from humankind. This theme of deliverance propels such poems as *L'Allegria* ("Joy"), *Il dolore* ("Grief"), and *Sentimento del tempo* ("Feeling of Time"). *Sentimento del tempo* was written during the Fascist era, but like much of Ungaretti's work, it was so romantic in his use of time, his dwelling on absolute values, and his mystical pursuit of God, that Fascist censors could hardly find fault with the work.

Salvatore Quasimodo produced a dense and imposing body of poetry that often emphasized sound and color more than subject matter and departed from reality to explore the depths of a natural world viewed through myth and history and expressed in lyrical passages. His most famous work, *Ed è subito sera (And Suddenly It's Evening)*, includes a large collection of compositions that delve into the natural mysteries and the enigmatic past of Sicily. Quasimodo was one Italian poet who survived a number of conflicts with the Fascist regime, having been denounced as an anti-Fascist and harassed by a blackshirt squad. Nonetheless, he managed to be appointed Professor of Italian Literature at the Giuseppe Verdi Conservatory of Music in Milan where he taught until his retirement. In 1959 Quasimodo was awarded the Nobel Prize in literature.

Eugenio Montale, another Nobel Laureate in literature (1975), is regarded as one of Italy's great modern poets. He published his first collection of poetry, *Ossi di seppia* ("Cuttlefish bones") in 1925 before moving from Liguria to Florence where he directed a major publishing company until removed from the position for his refusal to join the Fascist Party. Montale moved to Milan in 1948 where he wrote for *Il Corriere della sera,* Italy's leading national newspaper. His profound pessimism—that poetry was incapable of making a positive contribution to life—distinguished him from the other major Italian poets of his day. "We can only tell you today, / what we are *not,* what we do *not* want," Montale wrote in the introduction to *Ossi di seppia,* evidencing his pervasive negativity. Like Saba, Montale examines nature as a source of renewal but finds only anguish and alienation. In part, Montale's negativism is explained by the context in which he wrote: the rise of Fascism and Nazism, Italy's invasion of Ethiopia, and the Spanish Civil War all assaulted his humanistic values. The barbarity and inhumanity of the world around him drove Montale to seek a new reality in his 1939 collection called *Le occasioni* ("The Occasions") and in *La bufera e altro* ("The Storm and Other Poems"), begun in 1940 and continued through World War II and into the Cold War. In *La bufera,* Montale expresses his disillusionment with the vulgar and strident postwar materialism that shattered his hope that an ideal world would emerge from the ashes of war. Anchored in wartime Florence, *La bufera* addresses life, death, and the tragedy of the age. Writing from a solemn, philosophical perspective, Montale uses a variety of rhyming patterns and structures, featuring both worldly and other-worldly figures.[4]

Italian novelists of the 1920s moved away from the naturalism of their predecessors in several new directions. Among the more important novelists of the day was Massimo Bontempelli who founded a review called *900* and led a movement called *stracittà* (ultra urban). These writers rejected existing myths that idealized rural Italy; instead they focused on the urban masses of the industrialized economy.[5] Bontempelli joined the Fascist Party and served for two years as secretary of the Fascist Union of Writers.

By 1930, Alberto Moravia's *Gli indifferenti (The Time of Indifference)* marked the emergence of a more successful period of Italian fiction. Moravia's novel, set in a middle-class Roman family during the Fascist era, utilized a kind of psychological realism to represent the alienation, emptiness, and "indifference" of bourgeois society. Although well received by critics and readers, *Gli indifferenti* was denounced by the Fascist government for undermining conventional morality. Moravia enjoyed great success with short stories and subsequent novels, including *Il conformista (The Conformist)* and *La ciociara (Two Women),* both of which were made into superb movies.

Some consider Carlo Emilio Gadda to be Italy's most original and greatest twentieth-century novelist.[6] Gadda's work is particularly celebrated for its unique use of language and its insight into the modern forces that drive humans to alienation and depression. Gadda enjoyed a long and productive career in which he published collections of short stories (*La Madonna dei filosofi, The Madonna of the Philosophers*), technical articles, and essays. An autobiographical novel (*La cognizione del dolore, Acquainted with Grief,* 1970) stands as his most important work along with a novel, *Quer pasticciaccio brutto de via Merulana* (*That Awful Mess on Via Merulana,* 1957). Critics have praised Gadda's work as a revelation of the depravity of ordinary life during the Fascist era.[7]

Gadda was a regular contributor to the literary journal *Solaria,* which provided a point of convergence of the works of numerous writers during the Fascist era, including Ungaretti, Saba, Montale, and Elio Vittorini. Vittorini's first novel, *Il gorafano rosso* (*The Red Carnation,* 1933), brought the wrath of Fascist censors for alleged excessive sex and violence. In his masterpiece, *Conversazione in Sicilia* (*Conversations in Sicily,* 1938), Vittorini used the first person to embark on a travel in time and space in search of lost wisdom. After traveling on a train to Sicily, the protagonist engages in a number of dialogues with historical and mythical characters about eternal truths, only to be jolted back to reality by news of his brother's death in battle. Vittorini's use of language and his lyrical style reinforced the timelessness of the novel and fixed its reputation as a classic.

NEOREALISM AND POSTWAR POETRY

The fall of Fascism, which began with the removal of Mussolini from power (July 1943) and continued through Italy's surrender to the Allies (September 1943) and Mussolini's assassination (April 1945), liberated Italian writers from censorship and unleashed two decades of pent-up creativity. The burst of artistic energy produced a genre known as *neorealismo* (neorealism), defining itself by referring to an earlier realist tradition in Italian literature found in the works of Giovanni Verga and others. Neorealist literature, heavily influenced by filmmakers such as Luchino Visconti and Roberto Rossellini (see also Chapter 9), is best described not as a "school," but as a body of works that brought common experience to the task of writing while demonstrating parallel approaches to similar subjects. The Italian neorealists reflected on the *ventennio* (the 20 years of the Fascist regime), the Nazi occupation, the heroic role of ordinary Italians in liberating the country from Fascists and Nazis, the brutality and inhumanity of the war and the concentration camps, and Italy's struggles to deliver on the promise of the new republic. The postwar writers used memoirs, historical fiction, and other forms to create a kind of epic documentary style, often driven as well by the ideological forces of the late Italian Marxist Antonio Gramsci and the Communist Party's attempt to establish hegemony over postwar culture.

Among the more important varieties of neorealist literature were the peasant novel, best represented by Carlo Levi's *Cristo si è fermato a Eboli* (*Christ Stopped at Eboli*, 1945), the works of Ignazio Silone (born Secondo Tranquilli), and the fictional "memoirs" and "chronicles" of the Fascist era such as Cesare Pavese's *La luna e i falò* (*The Moon and the Bonfires*, 1950). Pavese, who had been imprisoned for conspiring with the communist underground movement, wrote one of the first neorealist novels, *Paesi tuoi* (*Your People*, 1941), and a number of works with strong political implications, including *Il compagno* (*The Comrade*, 1947) and *La casa in collina* (*The House on the Hill*, 1948), which confronts the dilemma of an intellectual during the Resistance era and is often considered his best novel. Silone's work has become emblematic of the period, both because of the genre and his own experiences as an exiled anti-Fascist (although that role has recently been challenged on the basis of secret police files that implicate Silone as a double agent). While his work became enormously popular outside Italy, few Italians read it during the Fascist era. Among his successes were *Fontamara*, *Pane e vino* (*Bread and Wine*, 1936), and *La scuola dei dittatori* (*The School for Dictators*, 1938). The prevailing themes of Silone's work are his condemnation of Fascist misgovernment and of the suffocating poverty of the peasants of the Abruzzi region where his novels are set. His *Una manciata di more* (*A Handful of Blackberries*, 1952), written after the fall of Fascism, indicts his former Communist Party for their attempt to seize control of the peasant movement.[8]

Vittorini was a major literary force in the postwar era, a neorealist who bridged the gap to experimentalism. His *Uomini e no* (*Men and Not Men*, 1945) masterfully confronts the dilemma of the intellectual weighing political action against a more passive role during the height of the Resistance. Of equal importance in establishing his reputation was his editing of the influential journal *Il Politecnico*, which challenged the communist orthodoxy on the issue of the intellectual's role in politics.

Like Vittorini, Primo Levi employed a humanistic viewpoint, never engaging in direct political analysis. A chemist who was held in Auschwitz for more than a year, Levi brought the horrors of genocide to the Italian public in his *Se questo è un uomo* (*Survival in Auschwitz*, 1947), using a meticulous, straightforward style to analyze Nazi death camp experiments.

Women writers contributed significantly to neorealist literature as well, often introducing a fresh perspective that drew on the feminist maxim that "the personal is political." Natalia Ginzburg and Alba De Céspedes are among the important figures in this group. Ginzburg, who befriended a number of anti-Fascists in Turin and whose husband, Leone Ginzburg, died in a Fascist prison, wrote fiction in which the characters struggle with troublesome family situations. *Ti ho sposato per allegria* (*I Married You for Fun*, 1966) is a play dealing with newlyweds struggling to find meaning in marriage, while her memoir, *Lessico famigliare* (*Family Sayings*, 1963), recounts in quasi-fictional style Ginzburg's coming of age in interwar Turin. In *Tutti i nostri ieri* (*All Our Yesterdays*, 1952), Ginzburg moved beyond the confines of neorealism to a broader inquiry into middle-class life.

De Céspedes first gained notoriety with the appearance of her 1938 novel *Nessuno torna indietro* (*There is No Turning Back*). Ten years later, she published *Dalle parte di lei* (*The Best of Husbands*), set in the Resistance era, which challenged a number of social and familial customs, including the inequality of marriage. In the postwar era, De Céspedes gained recognition as a leader in presenting a woman's agenda to her readers.

Although neorealism dominated Italian literature in the immediate postwar era, a number of writers operated successfully outside that genre. Among them were two who employed religious viewpoints. Luigi Santucci's later works such as *Orfeo in paradiso* (*Orpheus in Paradise*, 1967) explore Christian and secular values, while Diego Fabbri's drama *Processo a Gesú* (*The Trial of Jesus*, 1954) places the audience as jury. However, such sacred themes in the postwar period were far outweighed by the secular.

Most notable among those who moved beyond neorealism were Alberto Moravia and Italo Calvino, who is regarded by many as the foremost Italian fiction writer of the latter half of the twentieth century. Calvino fought in the Resistance movement and escaped Fascist prison to become an active Communist and then a major contributor to the renowned publishing house of Luigi Einaudi, along with Vittorini, Pavese, and others. A contributor to a number of literary journals, most notably *Il Politecnico* and *Il menabò*, Calvino produced his first novel in 1947. *Il sentiero dei nidi di ragno* (*The Path to the Nest of Spiders*) features a young Genoese street urchin who conveys as a childlike fantasy the real events of the Resistance era. Thus, while Calvino conformed to some parts of the neorealist aesthetic, he pushed his novel beyond the bounds of the genre to approach realistic topics through fantasy. By doing so, he distinguished himself and produced a highly original collection of works. Among the most highly regarded are short stories such as *Ultimo viene il corvo* ("The Crow Comes Last"), collections such as *Gli amori difficili* (*Difficult Loves*) and *I nostri antenati* (*Our Ancestors*), and *Fiabe italiane* (*Italian Folk Tales*). The last two, published in the late 1950s, took Calvino away from realism to explore fable and fantasy. *Se una notte d'inverno un viaggiatore* (*If on a Winter's Night a Traveler*), published in 1979 near the end of his career, established Calvino's reputation as a writer of international renown.

Just as novelists provided a realistic memory of the trauma of war and Resistance, so Italian poets reflected multiple dimensions of the same reality in highly imaginative language and form. Although much of neorealist poetry is dismissed as overwrought and excessively heroic, the best poets of the era rose to the task of responding to events with subtlety and sensitivity that enabled them to confront great tragedy without succumbing to the simplest forms of balladry and romanticism.

Many of the postwar poets had managed to establish themselves in the Fascist era—including Eugenio Montale, Giuseppe Ungaretti, Salvatore Quasimodo, and Pier Paolo Pasolini—and reflected in their work their survival of repression and war. Montale collected his most notable postwar poetry in *La bufera (The Storm)*. Ungaretti's most important postwar works were *Il dolore* (*Grief,* 1947) and *La vita d'un uomo* (*The Life of a Man,* 1969), both autobiographical, evoking the horrors of Nazism, Fascism, and war at an intensely personal level as he confronts the losses of his own brother and son. Quasimodo's best wartime and postwar poetry includes *Giorno dopo giorno* ("Day after Day," 1947), a reflection on the Nazi air raids and occupation of Milan, and *La vita non è sogno* ("Life Is Not a Dream," 1949) in which the poet confronts the horrors of the battle of Stalingrad and the death camp at Buchenwald. The postwar poetry of Pasolini featured a variety of styles and subjects that was sometimes composed in dialect. Among his notable works were a collection of poems, *L'usignolo della Chiesa Cattolica* (*The Nightingale of the Catholic Church,* 1948), and the long poetic homage *"Le ceneri di Gramsci"* ("Gramsci's Ashes," 1954). In the latter, Pasolini speaks to the Italian Marxist icon, acknowledging Italy's failure to achieve Gramsci's vision of a heroic revolution of the working class. Pasolini's poetry, along with his adventures in narrative and dialect, in editing his journal *Officina,* and in boldly addressing such taboo subjects as homoeroticism, signaled a transition in Italian literature from neorealism to a more experimental, personal, avant-garde approach in which he would play a leading role.

THE CONTEMPORARY ERA: NEO-AVANT-GARDE AND EXPERIMENTALISM

By the mid-1950s, a number of changes had influenced Italian literature to the point that writers moved noticeably away from the themes of Fascism, war, and Resistance that had dominated the first decade of the postwar era. The transformation in literature largely reflected fundamental political and economic changes in Italian society. Events in the Soviet Union in 1956—particularly Nikita Khrushchev's "leaked" condemnation of Josef Stalin com-

bined with the Soviet invasions of Hungary and Poland—disillusioned many
left-leaning Italian intellectuals and began to erode their dominance of Italian
culture. At the same time, Italy's surging recovery known as the Economic
Miracle ("*il* boom") afforded greater capital investment for publishing houses
that, in turn, provided expanded opportunities for writers. A new generation
of writers now reached maturity. Most had not fought in the Resistance and
did not consider Fascism and war among their defining life experiences.
Instead, they looked ahead to issues that would emerge to dominate the next
decades: industrialization, immigration and internal migration, alienation,
mass culture, gender, globalization, and the threat of nuclear annihilation. At
the same time, women writers emerged in greater numbers and importance
than before, providing a surge of feminist works while joining the general
experimentation in form and language (including dialect). The contemporary
era can truly be said to have begun.[9]

Nonetheless, the break was not always sharp. Italian writers continued to
incorporate memory into fictional form, but with greater subtlety and a less
overtly political message, often addressing political events through the filter
of family. Among the best of this transitional genre are works by Natalia
Ginzburg, Carlo Cassola, Giorgio Bassani, and Giuseppe Tomasi di Lampedusa. Although Cassola fought in the Resistance, his writings rejected the
heroic themes of neorealism in favor of a more introspective and skeptical
rendition that runs through two novels, *Fausto e Anna* (*Fausto and Anna,*
1952) and *La ragazza di Bube* (*Bebo's Girl,* 1959). Bassani set his novels in
Ferrara, his hometown, where profound global events evolve in the context of
the provincial city's insular stability and customary calm. Best known are *Il
giardino dei Finzi-Contini* (*The Garden of the Finzi-Continis,* 1962) and
Cinque storie ferraresi (*A Prospect of Ferrara,* 1956). Bassani contributed
directly to Lampedusa's success. While serving as an editor at the great Fel-
trinelli publishing house, Bassani accepted for publication a manuscript from
the unknown Sicilian Lampedusa. *Il gattopardo* (*The Leopard,* 1958) became
a surprise bestseller and is considered one of the great Italian literary successes
of the century. Set in Lampedusa's beloved Sicily at the time of Italian unification, *Il gattopardo* provides a social and moral analysis of unification
through several generations of a poignant family narrative. Lampedusa's tone
of deep pessimism—that the change brought by unification will somehow
leave everything the same—resonated with Italian readers.[10]

A sharper break with the past came in what might be called the "industrial
novels." Italo Calvino was a well-known Italian writer before pioneering this
genre. By the end of the 1950s, Calvino had begun to explore the spoliation
produced by industrialization in such works as *La speculazione edilizia
(Plunge Into Real Estate)* and *La nuvola di smog (Smog).* Other examples of the

industrial literature of the 1950s and 1960s point to the prevailing maladies of the factory workers' existence. Luciano Bianciardi documented the emptiness and anxiety of the workers' world in *La vita agra* (*It's a Hard Life,* 1962), as did Goffredo Parise in *Il Padrone* (*The Boss,* 1965), which levels a fierce attack on industrial management as well as the popular culture of the era, and Paolo Volponi in *La macchina mondiale* (*The Worldwide Machine,* 1965), an indictment against the standardization of workers.

Luciano Anceschi's founding of the influential review *Il Verri* in Milan in 1956 marked the advent of an experimental movement in Italian literature known as the *neoavanguardia* (neo-avant-garde). The name derived from a recognition that these writers self-consciously defined themselves as experimental, both sympathetic to and separate from the literary avant-gardes of the earlier twentieth century. Most were poets, including those published in the anthology called *I novissimi* in 1961 and those who gathered in Palermo in October 1963 to form the *Gruppo 63* (which included experimental musicians and painters as well). Generally committed to a radical critique of society, the neo-avant-garde poets began by experimenting with language and structure.

Gruppo 63 included a number of university professors and well-connected editors who were enabled by their positions to maintain a presence in Italian culture and to agree on the political necessity of their work. Best known of *Gruppo 63* was Umberto Eco (see also Chapter 2), whose *Opera aperta (Open Work)* called for a new aesthetic, one that was unfinished and open to interpretation by the reader. In his introduction to *I novissimi,* Alfredo Giuliani, editor of *Il Verri,* states an important tenet of the neo-avant-garde poets: poetry is a means by which the poet leads the reader not to escape, but to confront reality, to abandon the self in order to cut through appearances. The most successful poet of the neo-avant-garde was Antonio Porta, whose percussive rhythms addressed a range of challenging subjects from personal relations (*I rapporti,* "Relations"), violence against women (*Brevi lettere,* "Brief letters"), and sadism in the concentration camps (*Come se fosse un ritmo,* "As if it were a rhythm").

Although poetry dominated the neo-avant-garde movement, Italian writers contributed experimental novels as well, often leading to controversy. Many of the *novissimi* and *Gruppo 63* experimented in prose, including Nanni Balestrini, whose *Tristano* makes use of "found languages" (excerpts from existing works) and Edoardo Sanguineti, whose *Il giuoco del'oca (Goose Game)* experiments with languages and dreams. Among other influential novelists of the 1960s were Anna Maria Ortese *(L'iguana, The Iguana)* and Luigi Malerba *(Il pianeta azzurro, The Blue Planet; Il fuoco greco, Greek Fire).* Particularly in their experimentation with language and the role of the reader, these writers clearly were moving toward what became known as postmodernism.

Changes in Italian literature also were sparked by political turmoil. The protests that began in the Italian universities in 1967 spilled into the streets and *piazze* to create a continuing sense of revolutionary fervor and violence that culminated in the spreading factory strikes of "hot autumn" 1969. This radical insurgency that spread through European cities and to the United States transformed much of Italian literature into overtly political diatribes. A number of literary journals lost their identity in the headlong rush to or away from politics in what Umberto Eco called the "suicide" of 1960s literary experimentation. The result was the emergence of a more personal literary trend that tended to focus on everyday, private life, with a new emphasis on the psychological. At the same time, women writers began to embrace "the personal as political" as they made a place for themselves in what had been a largely male-dominated tradition.[11]

Eugenio Montale set the tone for this transition. Italy's poet laureate, Montale moved beyond his previous work to focus on everyday life. Examples are *Diario* (*Diary*, 1973), *Quaderno di quattro anni* (*Notebook of Four Years*, 1977) and *Satura* (1971), which features poems dedicated to the memory of his wife. Among those who produced similarly introspective poetry in the 1970s were Nelo Risi *(Amica mia nemica, My Friend My Enemy)* Giorgio Orelli *(L'ora del tempo, Time's Hour)*, and Luciano Erba, all considered part of the *Linea lombarda* ("Lombard Line") of poets.

THE CONTEMPORARY ERA: FEMINIST AND REGIONAL WRITERS

Another product of the surge of late-1960s political radicalism was the emergence in the 1970s of a feminist tradition, often centered around women's cultural centers, such as the Centro Virginia Woolf in Rome, and feminist publishing houses such as Edizioni delle Donne and La Tartaruga. Among the leading Italian feminist writers of this period was the versatile Dacia Maraini, whose works address a range of women's concerns, including abortion, sexual violence, and prostitution. Her works include *Memorie di una ladra* (*Memoirs of a Female Thief*, 1972), *Donna in guerra* (*Woman at War*, 1975), and *Dolce per se* (*Sweet On Its Own*, 1997).

Elsa Morante had achieved success with her first two novels, *Menzogna e sortilegio* (*The House of Liars*, 1948) and *L'isola di Arturo* (*Arturo's Island*, 1957), when she published *La Storia* (*History: A Novel*) in 1974, a powerful indictment against history for its cruel treatment of society's weakest members. Like her other works, *La Storia* pictured family relationships through the eyes of a child. Although criticized by some feminists for her portrayal of the mother, *La Storia* was a popular success. Other women writers whose work made an impact in the 1970s were Anna Banti *(Un grido lacerante, A*

Scream), Gianna Manzini, *(Ritratto in piedi, Full-Length Portrait),* and Lalla Romano, *(L'ospite, The Guest).*

By 1980, several other women writers had begun to break through to enjoy success. Among them were Francesca Sanvitale, Rosetta Loy, and Giuliana Morandini. Most of Sanvitale's novels (for example *Il cuore borghese, The Bourgeois Heart* and *Madre e figlia, Mother and Daughter)* feature female protagonists set in her own lifetime, while *Il figlio dell'Impero (The Son of the Empire)* utilizes the setting of nineteenth-century France. Just as Sanvitale employs the feminist mother-daughter relationship theme, so does Loy, particularly in *Sogni d'inverno (Winter Dreams).* Morandini's work has reflected her roots in Trieste *(Caffè Specchi, Mirror Café),* while she has explored such topics as female madness and the impact of the Cold War on another city *(Angelo a Berlino, Angel in Berlin).*

In the same way that Morandini reflected a regional perspective, so did a number of Italian writers of the late twentieth century, particularly the Sicilian writers, of whom Leonardo Sciascia is the best known. Sciascia often wove an autobiographical thread through fictional narrative in the form of a detective story in which justice seldom prevailed. His first two novels, *Il giorno della civetta (The Day of the Owl,* 1961) and *A ciascuno il suo (To Each his Own,* 1966) dealt with the *mafia* and Sicilian society. More recently, Sciascia utilized the detective story to address capital punishment, which he opposed *(Porte aperte, Open Doors,* 1987), and to reflect on life and death *(Il cavaliere e la morte, The Knight and Death,* 1988).[12]

Sciascia's pessimism about Sicily is shared by a long line of Sicilian writers down through the end of the century. Among them are Giuseppe Bonaviri, Vincenzo Consolo, and Gesualdo Bufalino. Bonaviri moved beyond neorealism to produce narratives that interwove science and fantasy: *Il fiume di pietra (The Stone River,* 1964), *La divina foresta (The Divine Forest,* 1969), and *Notti sull'altura (Nights in the Hills,* 1971). Consolo, who practiced law in Milan, was known for the meticulous research that went into such novels as *Il sorriso dell'ignoto marinaio (The Smile of the Unknown Mariner,* 1976) and *Nottetempo, casa per casa (Night Time, House By House,* 1992), and in the sociological essay *Il barocco in Sicilia (The Baroque in Sicily,* 1991). Bufalino combined a tragic outlook with literary language to produce some notable works, including *Argo il cieco (Blind Argus), Le menzogne della notte (Night's Lies),* and collections of short stories set in Sicily, such as *Museo d'ombre (Museum of Shadows).* And although the Sicilians constitute the most self-conscious of regional writers, other regions produced their own voices. Giuseppe Dessí *(Paese d'ombre, Land of Shadows)* and Salvatore Satta *(Il giorno del giudizio, The Day of Judgment)* created Sardinian narratives, while Michele Prisco *(I cieli della sera, The Evening Skies),* Domenico Rea *(Gesú fate*

luce, Jesus, Make Light), and Carlo Bernari *(Tre operai, Three Workers)* contributed to a Neapolitan school. Other regional fiction came from Vicenza,
including Luigi Meneghello *(Libera nos a malo, Deliver Us from Evil)* and
Goffredo Parise *(Solitudes, Short Stories);* Friuli (Carlo Sgorlon, *Il trono di
legno, The Wooden Throne*), and Istria (Fulvio Tomizza, *Materada*).

By far the greatest Italian literary voice of the 1980s was Umberto Eco,
whose first novel, *Il nome della rosa,* emerged as a worldwide bestseller and set
the tone for a new decade of distinction in Italian literature. Eco applied his
experience as an experimental writer in *Gruppo 63* and professor of semiotics
(see also Chapter 2) to the narrative task with great skill. Thus the triumph of
The Name of the Rose (1980) is largely attributable to his success in making
the improbable connections between medieval and modern, and religious
and sexual, all in the framework of a detective novel that hangs on the significance of words as signs and codes. As a result, Eco is credited with contributing to postmodernist writing, not only in his literary theories, but in his
subsequent novels, *Il pendolo di Foucault* (*Foucault's Pendulum,* 1988) and
L'isola del giorno prima (*The Island of the Day Before,* 1994).[13]

Eco's commercial success reflected a broadening of the audience for Italian
literature, as Italian publishers consolidated assets and pursued a global market. At the same time, a new generation of Italian fiction writers took advan-

Umberto Eco, the influential professor of semiotics and author of best-selling novel
Il nome della rosa (The Name of the Rose). © David Lees/CORBIS.

tage of improving opportunities. Among them were veteran authors such as Bufalino, Pasolini, and the poet-essayist Andrea Zanzotto. An original member of *Gruppo 63* and a renowned poet, Zanzotto began to explore the use of Venetian dialect and vernacular language in his collections, *Filò* and *Galateo di bosco (A Forest Book of Etiquette)*. Others successfully used dialect poetry, including the Veneto poet Biagio Marin and the Lucanian Albino Pierro.

In ironic contrast to the localized focus on regional dialect and vernacular language, contemporary Italian writing has at the same time become increasingly global in its emphasis. Among the best examples of this international influence and appeal are the novels of Daniele Del Giudice, considered among the most promising of the newest generation of Italian writers. Written in characteristically sparse prose, Del Giudice's work includes *Lo stadio di Wimbledon (Centre Court,* 1983), *Atlante occidentale (Lines of Light,* 1985), and *Nel museo di Reims (In the Reims Museum,* 1988). Other recent trends in Italian writing feature "serious" writers utilizing such "popular" genres as the detective story, the Gothic novel, and science fiction, following the lead of such luminaries as Eco, Gadda, and Sciascia. Among the younger writers who have successfully employed the popular forms are Stefano Benni *(Comici spaventati guerrieri, Funny Frightened Warriors)*, Gianfranco Manfredi *(Uccelli da gabbia e da voliera, Caged Birds)*, Aldo Busi *(La delfina bizantina, The Byzantine Dauphine)*, Paola Capriolo *(Vissi d'amore, I Lived for Love)*, and Laura Manicelli *(Il fantasma di Mozart, Mozart's Ghost)*.

NOTES

1. Jonathon Usher, "Origins and Duecento," in *The Cambridge History of Italian Literature,* ed. Peter Brand and Lino Pertile (Cambridge: Cambridge University Press, 1999), 3–36.

2. John Took, "Petrarch," in *The Cambridge History of Italian Literature,* ed. Peter Brand and Lino Pertile (Cambridge: Cambridge University Press, 1999), 89.

3. Manzoni entitled an earlier (1827) version *Sposi Promessi,* but the 1840 version is standard.

4. Ernesto Livorni, "Montale," in *Encyclopedia of Contemporary Italian Culture,* ed. Gino Moliterno (London: Routledge, 2000), 375–77; Robert Dombroski, "The Rise and Fall of Fascism (1910–45)," in *The Cambridge History of Italian Literature,* ed. Peter Brand and Lino Pertile (Cambridge: Cambridge University Press, 1999), 505–8.

5. The writers who romanticized the moral superiority of rural Italy were part of what was called the *strapaese* movement.

6. Dombroski, "The Rise and Fall of Fascism," 527.

7. Francesca Parmeggianni, "Gadda," in *Encyclopedia of Contemporary Italian Culture,* ed. Gino Moliterno (London: Routledge, 2000), 249–50; Dombroski, "The Rise and Fall of Fascism," 530.

8. John Gatt-Rutter, "The Aftermath of the Second World War (1945–56)," in *The Cambridge History of Italian Literature,* ed. Peter Brand and Lino Pertile (Cambridge: Cambridge University Press, 1999), 538–47.

9. Michael Caesar, "Contemporary Italy (since 1956)," in *The Cambridge History of Italian Literature,* ed. Peter Brand and Lino Pertile (Cambridge: Cambridge University Press, 1999), 561.

10. Caesar, "Contemporary Italy," 563–65.

11. Caesar, "Contemporary Italy," 580–81.

12. Joseph Farrell, *Leonardo Sciascia* (Edinburgh: Edinburgh University Press, 1995).

13. Peter Bondanella, *Umberto Eco and the Open Text* (Cambridge: Cambridge University Press, 1997).

7

The Performing Arts

THE RICH LEGACY

AS IN THE LITERARY AND ARTISTIC TRADITION, Italians have made significant historical contributions to the performing arts. This is notably true in three genres: *commedia dell'arte,* classical tragedy, and lyric opera. *Commedia dell'arte* emerged in sixteenth-century Italy as unscripted, popular theater that used masked, stylized characters (Pantaleone, i Dottori, Arlecchino, Pulcinella, and others; see also Chapter 4) who provided humorous performances, often utilizing dialect. *Commedia dell'arte* played to all classes and spread throughout Europe when Italian professional acting troupes toured in the late sixteenth century. However, by the mid-seventeenth century, its popularity waned as the performances degenerated into slapstick routines that were all too predictable and distasteful humor that brought criticism from the church. The Venetian dramatist Carlo Goldoni provided an alternative to the improvisational *commedia dell'arte* with his carefully crafted comedies, modeled after the works of Molière and grounded in a satirical treatment of life in eighteenth-century Italy.[1]

At about the same time that *commedia dell'arte* emerged, classical tragedy enjoyed a rebirth. Renaissance Italy produced a substantial number of tragedies, including Gian Giorgio Trissino's *Sofonisba,* Giovanni Rucellai's *Rosmunda,* Sperone Speroni's *Canace,* and Pietro Aretino's *Orazio,* although only a small number of the tragedies were actually performed. Because audiences did not display great enthusiasm for full tragedies, the hybrid form of tragic-comedy emerged along with early opera, both of which fused serious and amusing elements.[2]

By 1600, the first of a brilliant array of Italian operas were performed, introducing a new art form that would dominate the Italian stage for three centuries. Among the first operas were Claudio Monteverdi's *Arianna* and *Orfeo,* with text written by the dominant librettist of the earliest period, poet Ottavio Rinuccini. From the courts at Mantua and Florence, opera spread to Rome and to the public stages and the *Carnevale* in Venice where it flourished. While the operatic performances in Mantua featured choruses, Venetian opera began to develop around the solo aria, and the classic style became the *opera seria,* a composition that linked a series of often flamboyant arias to a historical or mythological thread. Among the best composers of *opera seria* were Francesco Provenzale and Alessandro Scarlatti *(La Griselda).* By 1700, Italian opera had begun to dominate the European capitals and courts.

The work of Alessandro Scarlatti illustrates the connection between lyric opera and emerging new instrumental forms. Among Italy's great instrumental composers of the seventeenth and eighteenth centuries were the Bolognese Arcangelo Corelli, the Venetian Antonio Vivaldi, and the Scarlattis of Naples. Corelli's work linked the two centuries that he spanned and featured carefully calculated balance and precision, including sonatas for church and private performance. Most memorable are his 12 *concerti grossi,* a new orchestral form of extended works of three or four movements that Corelli perfected. Although Vivaldi wrote more than 40 operas and oratorios, he is remembered primarily for his more than 500 instrumental works. In addition to his symphonic compositions, Vivaldi is recognized for his development of the solo concerto. Although Neapolitan musicians were known largely for their theatrical compositions, Alessandro Scarlatti moved from opera to create an early form of the classical symphony, joining the strings to the flute, oboe, and trumpet in a three-movement form. His son Domenico composed 17 symphonies and was recognized throughout Europe for his innovations with the harpsichord, which he played masterfully, and for his bold harmonies.

The eighteenth century brought some important adjustments to Italian opera, which continued to thrive, often performed by celebrated *castrati,* eunuch singers who had been castrated before puberty to preserve their soprano voices. The poet Apostolo Zeno introduced *dramma per musica* (drama for music), a new system that favored serious dramatic elements at the expense of the comical and musical. Zeno's system separated the comedy so that it was performed between acts *(intermezzo).* The popularity of the *intermezzi* was so great—and *opera seria* was becoming so pretentious—that acting troupes began to compile the *intermezzi* into a repertoire and perform them widely. These performances were often called *opera buffa* (comic opera), a light, humorous form in which the spoken word was interspersed with song. Among the most successful composers of eighteenth-century *opera buffa* were Giovanni Battista Pergolesi, Baldassare Galuppi, and Giovanni Paisiello.

With the emergence of the *opera buffa,* several librettists won recognition. The prolific poet and melodramatist Pietro Metastasio contributed a number of influences to the emerging art, especially the repeated use of metaphor in arias, while Goldoni provided the *libretti* (texts) for a number of the *opera buffa* compositions of Galuppi. By the end of the eighteenth century, the *opera buffa* had begun to lose some of its appeal, and the Italian operatic tradition of relying simply on vocal displays was being criticized for lack of originality.

At the very time in the early nineteenth century that the reputation of Italian opera was in danger of decline, a brilliant array of Italian composers won notice. Widely recognized for their achievement, Paisiello and Gasparo Spontini were called to the court of Napoleon Bonaparte. Among the new generation of composers were Gioacchino Rossini, Gaetano Donizetti, Vicenzo Bellini, and Giuseppe Verdi, perhaps as illustrious as any group of operatic composers that ever appeared anywhere in a single period. A devotee of German music as a young man, Rossini premiered his first opera in Venice in 1810, then began a prolific production of sparkling and entertaining operas, known for historical romance, including his *Barber of Seville, William Tell,* and *Otello,* the first Italian Shakespearean opera. Even more productive than Rossini was Donizetti *(Lucia di Lammermoor, The Daughter of the Regiment, Don Pasquale),* who also directed productions and taught at the Naples Conservatory. Bellini mastered the melodic Italian vocal style known as *bel canto,* capturing a passionate lyricism suggestive of popular song that characterized Italian opera of the nineteenth century. His best known works are *Norma, La Sonnambula,* and *I Puritani (The Puritans),* set in the English Civil War. Bellini's premature death deprived Italy of one of its great musical talents.

Verdi grew up near Parma. Though rejected at the Milan Conservatory, he premiered his first opera at La Scala at age 26. His first great success was his third work, *Nabucco,* which Italians still remember for its thinly-veiled cry for Italian independence from Austrian rule. Verdi incorporated all the elements of Italian romanticism—especially historical references, boldness, and imagination—while compiling an extensive corpus of what has been called "social music" because of its popular appeal and its invocation of important social topics. Verdi's reputation as one of Europe's great musical geniuses developed from his many memorable operas: *Rigoletto, Il trovatore, La traviata, I vespri Siciliani (The Sicilian Vespers), Simon Boccanegra, Forza del destino, Don Carlos, Aïda, Otello, Falstaff,* and many more. So popular were the operas of the mid-nineteenth century that they have been described as a type of "folk music" that could be heard at parties and in the streets. Never had opera occupied a more important place in Italian life than in this era of national unification.[3]

Although he is better known for his performances than his compositions, Niccolò Paganini gained legendary status as a nineteenth-century musician, captivating audiences throughout Europe with his virtuoso accomplishments on violin and guitar. Paganini penned numerous instrumental compositions, including sonatas, concerti, and quartets.

While Italian lyric opera reached its greatest heights during the *Risorgimento* era, the next generation of Italian composers began to move away from the grand, romantic style of Verdi toward the realism *(verismo)* evidenced in the literary works of Giovanni Verga (see also Chapter 6). The writers and composers were called *scapigliati,* a self-styled group of Bohemians working in Milan who addressed the dark psychological and gritty sociological issues of modern urban life. One of the first of this school was Arrigo Boito *(Mefistofele, Mephistopheles)* who had worked as a librettist for Verdi. A better known example of *verismo* in opera is Pietro Mascagni's *Cavalleria rusticana,* based on a Verga story. Mascagni focused on the setting and idealized the peasant life, as did Ruggiero Leoncavallo in *I pagliacci.* The most successful of this school is Giacomo Puccini, who combined often brutally realistic stories with brilliant music and drama in *La Bohème, Tosca, Madama Butterfly,* and *Turandot.*

By the turn of the century, a number of Italian composers were departing markedly from the tradition of lyric opera. Among them was Ferruccio Busoni, who rejected the romantic tradition while boldly developing a new theory of music, including new scales and new instruments. Busoni wrote piano arrangements of Bach's works and composed his own *Fantasia contrapuntistica (Contrapuntal Fantasy)* and the opera *Doktor Faust.* By far more iconoclastic than Busoni were the Futurists, whose musical composers paralleled the dynamics of the Futurist literary and artistic movement. Foremost among the Futurist composers was Luigi Russolo, who introduced noise as an element in his compositions. One example was his *The Meeting of Automobile and Aeroplane,* which produced a riot when performed in Milan in 1913. Russolo and the Futurists anticipated later incorporation of various sounds by contemporary composers such as John Cage, and Futurist iconoclasm, in its audacious rejection of middle-class standards, is often viewed as a predecessor to early Fascism.[4]

CONTEMPORARY CONCERT MUSIC AND OPERA

Among the important transitional figures in twentieth-century Italian music were Ottorino Respighi and Alfredo Casella. Respighi's works won international acclaim, especially his tone poems *Fountains of Rome* and *Roman Pines,* his orchestral suite *The Birds,* nine operas, and several violin concerti. Casella was determined to create an Italian style equal to the European standards of the new century. He founded the Italian Society for Modern Music, conducted orchestras around the world, and incorporated influences from Stravinsky and Schoenberg. Among Casella's compositions are his *Concerto romano* and *Missa Solemnis "pro pace,"* both written and conducted during the Fascist era.

The Fascist regime's censorship of music was generally not heavy-handed, and thus some composers such as Luigi Dallapiccola thrived. Dallapiccola, who studied and taught in Florence at the Luigi Cherubini conservatory, established a reputation for lyrical 12-tone compositions, especially his opera *Volo di notte (Night Flight)* and *I Canti di prigionia (Prison Songs).* Influenced by Arnold Schoenberg, he nonetheless developed an original approach, often employing voice in pursuit of the theme of human freedom, for example in *Canti de liberazione (Songs of Liberation),* composed in 1954.

For Italian composers, as for other artists, the end of Fascism and war led to experimentation. Among the avant-garde composers of the postwar era were Luciano Berio, Bruno Maderna, and Luigi Nono, all committed to creating a post-Fascist musical culture in Italy. Generally regarded as Italy's preeminent postwar composer, Berio studied composition and conducting at the Milan Conservatory, then studied, taught, and conducted around the world. His compositions use texts from writers such as Umberto Eco and musical quotations from other composers. His *Sinfonia,* written for the New York Philharmonic in 1967–68, remains a milestone of twentieth-century composition. Maderna studied in Milan, Rome, Venice, and Darmstadt and taught internationally, while experimenting in electronic music with Berio. Nono studied under Maderna in Venice. A veteran Resistance fighter and committed communist, Nono created socially conscious compositions such as *Il canto sospeso (The Suspended Song)* and the controversial suite *Intolleranza (Intolerance).*

The Economic Miracle boosted serious music just as it influenced most of Italian life. Subsidies flowed to opera houses and municipal festivals, music publishers thrived, and serious music could be heard on the radio over *Radio Audizioni Italia* (RAI) and the cable radio network *filodiffusione.* As a result, enough Italian modernist composers won attention in Italy and abroad to merit consideration as a kind of "school," even though their approach was quite diverse and their reputations uneven. Among these avant-garde composers were Berio, Franco Donatoni, Sylvano Bussotti, and Salvatore Sciarrino. A student of Maderna and the Milan Conservatory, Donatoni continued to experiment with original concepts and complex structures, as in *Puppenspiel.* Bussotti is a visual and multimedia artist as well as one of Italy's most controversial composers, incorporating violent and erotic references in his highly theatrical works, such as *La passion selon Sade (Passion According to Sade)*. A precocious performer, Sciarrino moved to the electronic music of the avant-garde as reflected in his *Alto II,* a work for spoken word, three trumpets, and percussion. Aldo Clementi, studying with Maderna and others, pursued 12-tone technique, then experimented with painters and gravitated toward electronics in the 1960s and 1970s. His *Collage 3* imposed an electronic transformation on Beatles' music, while *Blitz* echoed the moves of chess players.

More recently, music programming has diminished, many of the radio symphonies have disbanded, and Italian record companies have been hesitant to take risks with serious, innovative music. However, several music festivals continue—including the prestigious Venice Festival of Contemporary Music—and a new generation of composers promises to carry on the tradition. The most notable of the newest composers are Adriano Guarnieri, Fabio Vacchi, and Luca Francesconi. Guarnieri directed the Florentine orchestra il Nuovo Ensemble "Bruno Maderna." Known especially for his harmonies, Guarnieri composed *Medea,* an opera-film derived from Pasolini's poetry *Il Trionfo della notte* ("The Triumph of the Night") and *Resistenza '95* ("Resistance '95") for amplified voices. Vacchi's music reflects elements of both neoromantic and avant-garde composition, and political and artistic inspiration. Among Vacchi's best-known works are *Due canti della sera* ("Two Evening Songs") for instrumental ensemble and his theatrical work *Il viaggio* ("The Voyage"). After studying piano and composition in Milan, Boston, and Rome and assisting Luciano Berio, Francesconi pursued wide-ranging interests, from jazz to cinema, television, and electronic music. Among his most interesting compositions are *Respiro* for trombones, *Dùolon* for violins, *Plot II* for saxophones, and a two-act opera, *Scene.*

Postwar Italian opera continues to follow the modern concept that, more than a simple showcase for voice, opera is a source of expression of artistic vision. In that tradition, several Italian composers, including Ildebrando Pizzetti and Gian Franco Malpiero, worked to create a modern Italian style of opera. Both rejected the atonality that was in vogue internationally in favor of Italian baroque and folk traditions. Pizzetti's *Assassinio nella cattedrale (Murder in the Cathedral)* and *Lo straniero (The Stranger)* integrate drama into a musical framework with familiar references, while the more eclectic Malpiero moved away from the classical tradition toward fantasy and surrealism with *Mondi celesti e infernali (The Worlds of Heaven and Hell)* and other theatrical and orchestral compositions.

Giancarlo Menotti enjoyed great success in the postwar era, especially by founding the Spoleto *Festival dei Due Mondi* in 1958 and composing a number of comic *(The Old Maid and the Thief)* and serious operas *(The Saint of Bleecker Street, Goya)*, while working actively in other media, including film. Menotti was instrumental in writing and presenting operas to a wide audience, preferring to open *The Medium* on Broadway, where it enjoyed great success. Always provocative, Menotti inspired both adulation and disdain from audiences and critics alike. Another composer who thrived in both classical and popular modes is Nino Rota, who not only wrote myriad works of modern music under the influence of Stravinsky, but penned notable soundtracks for movies by Visconti, Zeffirelli, Coppola *(The Godfather)*, and Fellini *(La Strada, La dolce vita, 8 1/2, and Amarcord)*.

Italy has recently produced its share of experimental opera, particularly from Nono, Goffredo Petrassi, Bruno Maderna, Lorenzo Ferrero, Paolo Arcà, and Salvatore Sciarrino. Ferrero has experimented with multimedia and tonality in his operas, especially *Marilyn*. Arcà combines strong theatricality with traditional references and accessible style of composition to produce such operas as *Angelica e la luna (Angelica and the Moon)* and *Il Carillon del Gesuita (The Jesuit's Carillon)*. Sciarrino also has integrated traditional references into his experimental compositions, as illustrated in his operas *Vanitas* and *Lohengrin*.

In the prewar tradition of Arturo Toscanini, Tulio Serafin, and Victor De Sabata, postwar Italian conductors have distinguished themselves as well, particularly Gianandrea Gavazzeni, Carlo Maria Giulini, Claudio Abbado, Riccardo Muti, and Riccardo Chailly. Gavazzeni lived a life of music, as a scholar, critic, composer, and conductor. In 1948, at age 39, Gavazzeni began to conduct at La Scala where he served as artistic director from 1966–68. He made his New York Metropolitan Opera debut in 1976, conducting *Il Trovatore*. Among his publications are *Donizetti* (1937) and *I nemici della musica (The Enemies of Music,* 1965). Giulini established his reputation by conducting a fiery rendition of Verdi's *Don Carlo* at Covent Garden in 1958 (a performance given credit for rekindling interest in the work), then by specializing in inspired recordings of Mozart, especially *Don Giovanni* and *Le nozze di Figaro*.

Claudio Abbado, a careful reader of musical scores whose directing sometimes is said to overshadow vocal soloists and instrumentalists, made his mark in 1965 at age 32 when Herbert von Karajan introduced him at the Salzburg Easter Festival to conduct Mahler's *Second Symphony*. After 12 years at Milan's Teatro alla Scala, Abbado left in 1965 to lead the Vienna Philharmonic, returning three years later to become opera conductor at La Scala where he remained until 1980. Not content to rely only on the classics, Abbado ventured into modern works of Berio, Pierre Boulez, and others. After performing around the globe, Abbado organized the European Community Youth Orchestra and conducted the Chamber Orchestra of Europe.

Like Abbado, Riccardo Muti has provided a consistent record of "literal" renditions. In his long and distinguished career, Muti has studiously avoided embellishments and particularly high notes that had been added to the original "text" for ornamentation. His recordings and live performances of Verdi (*Nabucco,* for example), Puccini *(Tosca),* and other composers have at times employed a heavy-handed approach in order to achieve the most authentic rendition of the composer's original work, leaving the vocalists little latitude to interpret. In contrast to Muti, Chailly is known as a committed modernist who has boldly interpreted twentieth-century compositions. Named assistant conductor at La Scala at age 19, Chailly then traveled widely and debuted as conductor at La Scala at age 25. He then launched a recording career and won appointments as conductor of the London, Berlin, and Vienna philharmonic orchestras.

As important a place as Italian composers and conductors have established, it would be unwise to ignore the great postwar performers of classical music and opera. Among the most acclaimed opera singers of the postwar era are sopranos Mirella Freni, Renata Scotto, Renata Tebaldi, Katia Ricciarelli, and Anna Antonacci; mezzo-soprano Cecilia Bartoli; tenors Giuseppe Di Stefano, Franco Corelli, Carlo Bergonzi, and Luciano Pavarotti; and baritones Piero Cappuccilli, Tito Gobbi, and Renato Bruson. Freni first achieved distinction with her 1963 performance of Mimi in *La Bohème* staged at La Scala by Franco Zeffirelli. Freni has been a regular at La Scala and at the Metropolitan Opera. Scotto won fame at age 23 when she replaced Maria Callas as Amina in La Scala's 1957 Edinburgh performance of Bellini's *La Sonnambula.* In her long career, Scotto is best known for her performances as Mimi, Violetta in *La Traviata,* Cio-Cio-San in *Madama Butterfly,* Lucia in *Lucia di Lammermoor,* and Lady Macbeth in *Macbeth.* Renata Tebaldi debuted for Toscanini at La Scala in 1946 and at the Met in 1955. A rival of Callas, Tebaldi is best remembered for her performances as Mimi, Violetta, Tosca in *Tosca,* and Minnie in *La Fanciulla del West.* Ricciarelli established herself and her supple voice in the 1970s by performing the *bel canto* repertoire of Verdi, Puccini, and Rossini, most notably at La Scala and the Met (while recording for CBS and RCA). Antonacci's impassioned acting and a commanding voice made her a unique presence in Italian opera. She is known particularly for her renditions of eighteenth- and early nineteenth-century works, especially Rossini, and her revival of lesser-known operas. Bartoli began as a child performer and established herself both through Decca recordings in the early 1990s and by performing around the world where she became best known for her renditions of Rossini and Mozart.

Of the postwar tenors, Di Stefano was the first to achieve fame, debuting in 1947 at La Scala in *Manon Lescaut* and in 1948 at the Met in *Rigoletto.* His most notable performances came as Faust, Rodolfo in *La Bohème,* Des Grieux in *Manon,* and the Duke of Mantua in *Rigoletto.* Corelli achieved notoriety with his 1951 performances at Spoleto and the *Maggio Musicale* in Florence. Shortly thereafter, Corelli debuted in Rome and at La Scala, singing opposite Maria Callas in Spontini's *La vestale,* then expanded his career throughout Italy and across Europe. Often compared to the legendary Enrico Caruso, Corelli performed at the Met every season from 1961 through 1976.

Carlo Bergonzi is celebrated as an interpreter of Verdi's operas, having recorded all the composer's tenor arias. He has performed numerous other roles as well, especially Puccini, exhibiting remarkable versatility in a career that spanned more than 40 years. Pavarotti won worldwide acclaim in the 1960s for his energetic attack on several roles, including Edgardo in Donizetti's *Lucia di Lammermoor* and Arturo in Bellini's *I puritani.* Pavarotti's fame soared when he participated in Italy's World Cup festivities in 1990, and his showmanship and penchant for publicity assure that he remains a major figure in the opera world, even if his voice may have diminished. Pavarotti announced his intention to retire on his seventieth birthday in 2005.[5]

Baritones Piero Cappuccilli, Tito Gobbi, and Renato Bruson have excelled for more than three decades. Like Bergonzi, Cappuccilli specialized in Verdi, performing Verdi's *I vespri siciliani* in Palermo in 1958, then debuting at La Scala in 1964 *(Lucia di Lammermoor)* and Covent Garden in 1967 (Verdi's *La traviata*). Gobbi is known also for interpreting Verdi, and developed a wide-ranging repertory that includes Puccini and celebrated roles in *Barber of Seville* and *Don Giovanni.* Bruson debuted at Spoleto in 1961 at age 25; at the Met in 1969 in *Lucia di Lammermoor;* at La Scala in 1972 in *Linda di Chamounix;* and at Covent Garden in *Un ballo in maschera* in 1976.

In addition to vocalists, a number of Italian classical instrumentalists have distinguished themselves in the postwar period. Notable are pianists Arturo Benedetti Michelangeli and Maurizio Pollini, violinist Uto Ughi, and flutist Severino Gazzelloni. Michelangeli is considered one of the century's greatest and most eccentric pianists. A child prodigy from Brescia, Michelangeli studied medicine, then enlisted in the Italian Air Force, and ultimately was held prisoner by the Germans. After the war, he taught piano and won a reputation for his skillful transcriptions, arrangements, and piano renditions of Brahms, Bach, Beethoven, Chopin, and Debussy. After studying at the Milan Conservatory and winning the Warsaw Chopin competition, Pollini studied with Michelangeli. Pollini has performed worldwide and is known especially for his interpretations of contemporary compositions including Boulez. Ughi was another child prodigy, debuting in a recital at the Teatro Lirico in Milan at age seven. Ughi studied with George Enescu (who had previously taught Yehudi Manuhin), then toured Europe, Australia, and the United States, playing antique violins—a 1744 Guarneri del Ges and a 1701 Stradivarius—while performing the classics at music festivals and concerts with the world's most renowned orchestras.

Like many great Italian musical figures, Gazzelloni studied and taught at the Accademia di Santa Cecilia in Rome. He debuted on flute in 1945 in Rome, where he held the chair of first flutist in the RAI orchestra for three decades. Gazzelloni performed a vast repertoire ranging from baroque to the most innovative, avant-garde music in many venues worldwide, while establishing a reputation as one of Italy's great instrumental soloists.

FOLK AND POPULAR MUSIC

There are clear connections between the somewhat artificially defined categories of Italian serious and popular music. Italian popular music can be said to consist of the *canzonetta* ("little" or light songs), *canzone d'autore* (songs

Stradivari viola maker, Cremona. Courtesy of the author.

composed by identifiable songwriters), folk music, political songs, blues, various types of jazz and rock, and newer forms known as *posse* and rap. The recent popular forms have often led to fusion, as is the case with reggae and hip hop. Traditionally, music critics have been dismissive of *canzonette* as escapist songs with little artistic merit geared toward a lowest-common-denominator commercial audience. Sociologists and historians have looked more objectively at the function of *canzonette* as providing real insight into culture. In fact, in the turbulent 1960s and 1970s, protest songs that borrowed from the past achieved great popularity. The Christian Democratic Party adapted the hit song "Volare" to their 1958 campaign, altering the chorus to *"Votare DC"* ("vote DC"), while young communists could be heard singing the popular Resistance song "Bella Ciao," derived from several old ballads.[6]

Just as critics and scholars have often ignored *canzonette,* they have similarly tended to treat folk songs with disdain. It was not until after World War II that an archive of field recordings of Italian folk music was assembled. On the other hand, Neapolitan popular songs have earned special consideration and fame, particularly "Santa Lucia," "Funiculì funiculà," and "O Sole mio" ("My Sun"), all before the twentieth century. Many of the best known have classical roots, traced to such composers as Donizetti and Bellini.[7]

Just as origins of popular songs can be discovered in tradition, so popular traditions have cross-fertilized with classical forms. Andrea Bocelli, blind since age 12, worked as a lounge singer, then, after completing his law degree,

Youth *banda musicale* performing in Arezzo. Courtesy of the author.

began vocal studies with Franco Corelli. Bocelli first made a reputation by touring in 1993 with blues singer Zucchero and his band, then four years later released the wildly successful *Romanza* album. Although his operatic technique has been questioned by critics, Bocelli has achieved undisputed success in bringing opera to a new audience by "crossing over" with his 1998 album *Aria*.[8] The acclaimed flutist Severino Gazzelloni also experimented with contemporary music, especially in electronic renditions. And several Italian festivals, most notably the Spoleto Festival, have incorporated contemporary forms of music and dance alongside the classical. Other festivals are dedicated specifically to nonclassical music, such as the jazz festivals in Umbria (Perugia), Siena, Bessano, and Coridonia; blues festivals in Pistoia and Salerno; rock festivals in Arezzo, Cremona, and Umbria; Rome's world music festival; and the famous San Remo festival. Every year since 1951, reporters and fans have gathered at this town on the coast of Liguria to attend performances of Italian popular music. Although inconsistent in quality, the music serves to reinforce the tradition of Italian popular song.

Another performer who bridges the musical genres is Gianna Nannini. Best known as one of Italy's leading popular musicians who has recorded more than 20 albums, Nannini further solidified her reputation with performances at Italy's 1990 World Cup. After studying piano at Lucca and composition and philosophy at the University of Milan, she composed a score for a cinematic version of *A Midsummer Night's Dream* (in which she also acted) and two short operas, *Eberhard Schöner* and *Palazzo dell'Amore (Palace of Love)*. In 1994, Nannini earned her doctorate from the University of Siena with a thesis on traditional Tuscan music.

Jazz migrated to Italy from the United States as part of its general introduction to Europe in the 1920s and 1930s. However, as part of Fascist cultural policy that emphasized autarchy (national self-sufficiency) and, after 1938, Fascist racial policy, the Italian government attempted to stop the influx of this "alien" art form and to Italianize those existing influences: thus the African-American Louis Armstrong became Luigi Braccioforte and the Jewish-American Benny Goodman, Beniamino Buonuomo. An Armstrong recording of "St. Louis Blues" reputedly was slipped past censors when the name was given a religious connotation in translation: "Le tristezze di San Luigi" ("The Sadness of Saint Louis"). In spite the censors and partly via the Voice of America radio broadcasts, jazz won popularity among university students and even within the inner circles of Fascism, including the Duce's son, Romano, who became a jazz pianist after the war. During the Allied invasion of the peninsula in 1943, American troops brought along the music of the big bands, introducing "swing" to Italians. Early Italian jazz artists include Cinico Angelini and Pippo Barzizza (known for conducting their famous radio orchestra), Natalino Otto (who produced many hit vocals, including "Il ritmo d'amore," "The Rhythm of Love"), and Gorni Kramer, who continued to write and vocalize swing.[9]

At the same time that the be-bop of Charlie Parker and Dizzy Gillespie stormed the jazz scene in the United States, the Roman pianist-vibraphonist Sergio Battistelli, the pianist-drummer Miro Graziani, trombonist Riccardo Laudenzi, tenor saxophonist Aldo Masciolini, drummer Luciano Schiccheri, and bassist Ennio Carretta were among those Italian jazz musicians who introduced a number of the new forms of jazz to Italy.

American influences in jazz and popular music combined with the advent of television fueled the careers of a number of Italian performers in the 1950s, including Renato Carosone, Fred Buscaglione, Domenico Modugno, and a number of female vocalists. Carosone employed the swing style in several 1950s hits, including the sarcastic "Tu vuo'fa l'americano" ("So You Want to be an American"). Buscaglione began as a jazz violinist, incorporating bebop, Afro-Cuban, and Brazilian elements before becoming a popular singer, utilizing urban working-class themes to provide an alternative to the light *canzonette* that were favored and rewarded by the famous San Remo festival. Modugno broke through at San Remo in 1958 with "*Volare,*" which developed into a hit that sold in excess of 22 million copies. Cinema also contributed to the popularity of jazz in Italy as such film directors as Francesco Rosi and Ettore Scola introduced jazz-based scores in their movies, utilizing the compositions of Piero Piccioni, Armando Trovajoli, and others.

Among the female vocalists who crossed over from jazz to pop, Mina (Mina Anna Mazzini) utilized her agile soprano voice to achieve great success, particularly in television variety shows. Other popular women artists were Ornella Vanoni, Milva (Maria Ilva Biolcati), Rita Pavone, who reached a wide audience on the Ed Sullivan show in 1965, Caterina Caselli, who launched her career at San Remo in that same year, and the glamorous Patty Pravo (Nicoletta Strambelli), whose "La Bambola" sold 9 million copies in the mid-1960s.

By the 1960s, Italian pop music diversified. Some artists found a more rebellious, alienated, youth-oriented edge, exemplified by Adriano Celentino (who was compared to Jerry Lee Lewis) and the heartthrob Gianni Morandi. At the same time, with emerging social discontent in Italy's cities, a new genre of *cantacronache* ("news singers") emerged, first in Turin, to address contemporary issues, usually from a left-wing political posture that spawned a counter-culture of urban folk ballads. Best known of these folk artists were Giovanna Daffini, who appeared regularly at folk festivals and revived many traditional songs, and Giovanna Marini, whose haunting "Lamento per la morte di Pasolini" ("Lament for the Death of Pasolini") provided a memorable tribute to the murdered poet. At the same time, a new genre of Italian cabaret music developed, particularly with the songs of actor-dramatist Dario Fo and surgeon-turned pianist Enzo Jannacci who, in 1991, won a prize at San Remo for his performance of "La fotografia" ("The Photograph") and more recently has turned to jazz. And finally, a new breed of singer-songwriters emerged from Genoa, including Luigi Tenco, Piero Ciampi, Gino Paoli, and Fabrizio De Andrè, all producing nonconformist music in rejection of the materialism of the Economic Miracle. Of the group, De Andrè, who provided a memorable collection of acoustic songs in Genoese dialect, was by far the most gifted.

Just as might be expected, Italian popular music of the 1970s reflected many of the musical influences of the era, including blues, progressive rock, and fusion. Of the Italian artists of that decade, Lucio Battisti stands out. His collaborations with lyricist Mogol (Giulio Rapetti) reached a devoted audience, particularly with their appeals to the sexual frustrations of young males. Also enormously successful was Zucchero (Adelmo Fornaciari, nicknamed "Sugar") who won notoriety at several music festivals and released his debut album, "Un po' di Zucchero" ("A Little Sugar") in 1983. Success enabled Zucchero to attract experienced players from around the world, including former Bruce Springsteen keyboardist David Sancious. Zucchero's breakthrough album, "Blue's," sold over 1.3 million copies. Touring to support the album, Zucchero sang duets with Joe Cocker, to whom he has been compared, and performed with Miles Davis, Eric Clapton, and B. B. King.

The 1980s brought rock musicians to the forefront. Among them were the crooner Luciano Ligabue and the Florentine group Litfiba, featuring vocalist Piero Pelù, that has been compared to Pearl Jam. At the same time a new generation of vocalists emerged, including Nada (Nada Malanima); Fiorella Mannoia, who won the 1987 San Remo prize with her rendition of "Quello che le donne non dicono" ("What Women Don't Say"); Ann Oxa, another San Remo winner whose soft pop style has accounted for numerous gold and platinum albums; and Nino D'Angelo, whose melodic renditions in the traditional style of the Neapolitan love ballad continue to attract great attention in Italy.

More recently, Italian rap, hip-hop, acid jazz, and reggae have created enthusiastic audiences and have combined to create a new genre of Italian popular music. The biggest name in Italian hip-hop is Jovanotti (Lorenzo Cherubini), whose early rapping in English was panned as derivative and poorly executed, but whose recent work is more original. *Rap italiano* developed in the late 1980s in the *centri sociali* (social centers) that left-wing youth occupied as part of a nationwide movement, proclaiming *"Il potere è come lo spazio; si prende non si chiede"* ("Power is like space; you don't ask for it, you take it.") A number of rap groups became associated with specific *centri sociali*, including Lionhorse Posse from Milan, the Isola All Stars from Bologna, Rome's *Onda*

Rossa Posse, and Messina's *Nuovi Briganti* (New Brigands). By the mid-1990s, Italian artists were rapping in their own language and dialect and fusing rap, reggae, and world music elements with traditional Italian music in the context of socially and politically relevant lyrics. At the same time, Jovanotti found a much more successful direction, as his career matured. His 1992 release *Lorenzo* that included the hit "Radio Rap" took the popular music scene by storm. Success led to Jovanotti's commitment to social and international causes, teaming with Pavarotti and U2's Bono to raise money for charity, which in turn led to approval of his music by the Vatican.[10]

In its various forms, jazz continues to sustain audiences, as confirmed by the continuing international popularity of the Umbria Jazz festival, founded in 1973 in Perugia. Among Italian jazz artists enjoying current success are saxophonist Rosario Giuliani ("Connotazione Blue"), saxophonist-composer Pietro Tonolo ("Portrait of Duke"), bassist Giovanni Tommaso ("Secondo Tempo"), vocalist Roberta Gambarini, and trumpeter Enrico Rava ("Shades Of Chet"). In the 1960s, Tommaso left his native Lucca for New York where he played with Sonny Rollins, Max Roach, Kenny Clarke, Chet Baker, and others. A Torinese, Gambarini studied at the New England Conservatory and won the Thelonious Monk vocal competition, before moving to New York recently. She has collaborated with such luminaries as Herbie Hancock, Hank Jones, the Heath Brothers, and James Moody. Rava toured with Americans Mal Waldron and Steve Lacy before moving to New York in 1967. Rava now performs widely and records with his own band.[11]

Jazz band performance, Perugia. Courtesy of the author.

CONTEMPORARY THEATER AND DANCE

Theater and dance did not keep pace with literature and music in the first half of twentieth-century Italy. There are several explanations. Two decades of Fascist censorship took a significant toll on theater, which at the same time had been regarded in Italy more as entertainment than art. As a result, theater had seldom addressed serious social issues and had perpetuated a traditional emphasis on literary language delivered by principal actors. Thus Italian theater had produced only one playwright with an international reputation, Luigi Pirandello, and had never developed a mass audience. The same can be said for Italian dance, which similarly remained mired in a tradition that reproduced classical ballets but little notable modern dance. At a time when French, British, German, and American writers, directors, and choreographers created powerful modern works, Italian theater and dance appeared stagnant.

Soon after the fall of Fascism and the liberation of the peninsula, however, a burst of new energy animated both theater and dance. One of the first indications that theater had begun to regenerate was the advent of Vito Pandolfi's "people's theater." Inspired by a similar French concept, Pandolfi envisioned a new nationwide campaign that would place government-subsidized companies in every town with a population of 100,000 or more. The "people's theater" would draw mass audiences, encourage experimentation, and thus stimulate a renaissance in drama.

The first manifestation of Pandolfi's vision was the now famous *Piccolo Teatro* (Little Theater) in Milan, founded by Giorgio Strehler and Paolo Grassi in 1947, with the commitment to provide drama that would appeal to all social classes while addressing serious issues.[12] The *Piccolo Teatro* of Milan succeeded remarkably, establishing a superb reputation for creativity while staging performances of works by some of the era's renowned playwrights such as Eugene Ionesco, Samuel Beckett, and Bertolt Brecht. Other little theaters, known generally as *stabili,* spread around the country, and new authors and directors emerged, including Diego Fabbri; Luigi Squarzina *(Il seduttore, The Seducer);* Vitaliano Brancati, whose *La governante (The Governess)* was censored for addressing issues of homosexuality; and, most notably, Eduardo De Filippo. De Filippo, affectionately known simply as Eduardo, brought his long experience with Neapolitan theater and *commedia dell'arte* to bear on pertinent postwar issues, writing, staging, and acting in his original works such as *Napoli milionaria! (Millionaire from Naples), Le voci di dentro (The Inner Voices),* and *Il sindaco del Rione Sanità (The Local Authority).* De Filippo's best works were widely recognized for their sensitive portrayal of the despair of the human condition.[13]

Another bright spot in postwar Italian theater was the founding of Vittorio Gassman's theater school in Florence. Gassman had studied at the National Academy of Dramatic Arts in Rome and won a brilliant reputation for his interpretation of classical texts—he was known as Italy's Sir Laurence Olivier—as well as of the experimental works of writers such as Pasolini. Gassman made the transition to the big screen, breaking through in *Riso Amaro* (*Bitter Rice,* 1948) and appearing in more than 100 films, none of which displayed his comedic skills more convincingly than *I soliti ignoti* (*Big Deal on Madonna Street,* 1958).[14]

However, with the exception of De Filippo and Gassman, and in spite of the efforts of the other notable postwar dramatists, Italian theater did not win wide acclaim. Except for the *stabili* in Genoa and Milan, few of the others achieved distinction, particularly because the public funding usually was awarded on the basis of political favor rather than artistic merit. Conservative influence and even censorship by postwar Christian Democratic governments doomed the *stabili,* which ultimately failed to achieve Pandolfi's concept of mass-based, socially relevant theater.

The decade of the 1960s saw the convergence of a number of forces that transformed Italian theater rather dramatically. Even if the *stabili* ultimately failed, their experimentation breathed life into what had been a moribund institution. The infusion of foreign plays and the emergence of De Filippo and the other promising authors and directors made the repertoire of the Italian stage more fresh, creative, and socially relevant, while the "boom" of the 1950s provided needed resources. Then came the jolt of the 1967 protests, which engendered a prolonged era of social radicalism and political violence that thrust the theater, like much of Italian society and culture, into crisis. One product was the drama of the absurd, which in turn brought the theater great criticism; another was the re-emergence of dialect plays, largely because the language was more accessible to ordinary Italians, many of whom had been introduced to "standard" Italian by television only in the mid-1950s. Another result of the insurgency was the emergence of avant-garde theater.

Mounting criticism of Italian theater in various journals and within the community of actors, authors, and directors led to the founding of a number of experimental groups called *colletivi* (collectives), committed to dramatizing political and social issues. The *colletivi* rejected the "star" system in favor of an ensemble approach, repudiated overly formal language in favor of dialect and vernacular, and encouraged both innovation and spontaneity. And while the quality of these new productions varied widely, the new air of experimentation opened the door to remarkably original talents such as Luca Ronconi, Carmelo Bene, and the husband-and-wife partners Dario Fo and Franca Rame.[15]

The director Luca Ronconi won acclaim for his 1963 production of the Renaissance epic poem *Orlando Furioso.* Most innovative in Ronconi's productions was his use of unconventional spaces such as *piazze* (public squares) where members of the audience were encouraged to share space with the actors, who, in turn, performed in several different spaces simultaneously. Ronconi continued his experimentation at his Prato Theater Laboratory outside Florence and in numerous opera productions.

Among the avant-garde, Carmelo Bene has proven the most flamboyant of an audacious assortment of Italian dramatic artists. Called the *enfant terrible* of Italian theater and routinely criticized both for his plays and his behavior, Bene has undoubtedly exercised a significant impact on contemporary drama. Bene first won notoriety as an actor in the 1950s, developing a maniacal style by which he confronted his audiences in a series of explosive spectacles, including his adaptation of *Dr. Jekyll and Mr. Hyde,* an erotic version of *Pinocchio,* and his *Cristo '63 (Christ '63),* which was immediately censored. In each case, Bene deconstructed the original text in producing a daring interpretation, often bordering on madness, that utilized a wide range of voice, from shouts to screams and whimpers. In spite of—or more likely because of—his reputation for brilliance and audacity, Bene was named theatrical director of the Venice Biennale, the frequently controversial international arts festival.[16]

More gifted and influential than Bene—and no less adventurous—is Dario Fo. Long involved in theater as an actor, Fo began writing plays in the 1960s, then turned away from entertainment during the turbulent final years of the decade in favor of a politicized, radical theater. With his wife and fellow actor Franca Rame, Fo founded several alternative theatrical troupes that performed for workers in the face of threats by political opponents, adapting to contemporary political theater such medieval traditions as storytelling and mime. In this period, Fo's *Morte accidentale di un anarchico (Accidental Death of an Anarchist)* and his *Mistero buffo (Funny Mystery)* monologues played to the delight of large, left-wing crowds while provoking censorship from the government for their irreverent political messages. Eventually, Fo was allowed to return to television, and his work won acclaim outside Italy. In 1997, Fo was awarded the Nobel Prize for literature.[17]

The contributions of Fo, Ronconi, Bene, and the other avant-garde dramatists established Italian alternative theater as an accepted form, bringing new audiences into what had been a staid tradition. By 1980, feminist theater had also begun to make its mark, especially with the works of Dacia Maraini (see also Chapter 6), Franca Rame, and Natalia Ginzburg (see also Chapter 6). Maraini founded several women's theatrical groups, including *La compagnia blu* (The Blue Company), later known as *Teatroggi,* and the *Teatro della Mad-*

dalena. Rame's feminist monologues included *Parti Femminili (Female Parts)* and *una donna sola (A Woman Alone).*

Dance

Like Italian theater, postwar Italian dance operated within the classical tradition and largely in the shadows of the more celebrated artists of the nineteenth century, such as Carlotta Brianza, Carlo Blasis, Fanny Cerrito, Carlotta Grisi, and Enrico Cecchetti. Although such innovative companies as Diaghilev's Ballets Russes, Isadora Duncan, and Mary Wigman performed, they failed to exercise the modernizing influence in Italy that they had spread elsewhere, and Italian dance remained largely static. Modernist cultural currents within the Futurist and Fascist movements influenced dance, but not altogether beneficially. Typical of their assault on convention, Futurists lambasted classical ballet in their 1917 *Manifesto della Danza Futurista (Manifesto of Futurist Dance).* The Fascist regime's record is mixed; while it founded two ballet institutions, the Opera Ballet School and the Royal School of Dance, Fascist censorship and repression drove into exile a number of supporters of ballet. Italy has never boasted a national ballet company, and most companies existed for the convenience of opera houses such as La Scala and the Rome Opera.[18]

Of the contemporary performers of classical ballet, no Italian has shone more brightly than Carla Fracci. Fracci studied at the ballet school of the Teatro alla Scala, where she created the roles of Juliet in Cranko's *Romeo and Juliet* and Elvira in Massine's *Don Giovanni.* She soloed with the London Festival Ballet, the Royal Ballet, the Stuttgart Ballet, and the Royal Swedish Ballet and, beginning in 1967, danced as principal guest artist of the American Ballet Theatre. Celebrated for her interpretation of the classic romantic roles in such standards as *Les Sylphides* and *L'Après Midi d'un Faune,* Fracci partnered with Rudolf Nureyev, Mikhail Baryshnikov, and Erik Bruhn. Fracci's interpretation of *Giselle* became legendary, drawing adoring audiences who treated her as an Italian national treasure. Fracci served as director of ballet in Naples and Verona before accepting a similar position with the Balletto dell'-Opera di Roma.

Recently, several small, independent ballet companies have enjoyed success. Among them are Aterballetto of Reggio Emilia, directed successively by Vittorio Biagi, Amedeo Amodio, and Mauro Bigonzetti. Aterballetto built its reputation on experimental choreography introduced by such notable artists as Glen Tetley and Alvin Ailey. Like Aterballetto, the *Collettivo di Danza Contemporanea* of Florence utilized experimentation and guest choreographers such as the Russian Evgheny Polyakov and the Belgian Micha Van Hoecke to develop a reputation

Carla Fracci performing "Giselle," "*Maggio Musicale Fiorentino.*" Courtesy of the author.

and, in 1985, to create the *Balletto di Toscana* (Ballet of Tuscany). Alternatives to ballet called *danza nuova* ("New dance") and *danza libera* (free dance) in Italy developed as far back as the 1920s when art patron Riccardo Gualino imported such foreign artists as Wigman, Bella Hutter, and Jia Ruskaya. After World War II, Ruskaya was named director of the *Accademia Nazionale di Danza* (National Academy of Dance) in Rome. One important successor to the *danza libera* movement was the *Teatrodanza Contemporanea di Roma* (Contemporary Dance Theater of Rome) founded in 1972 by Elsa Piperno and Joseph Fontano, who introduced Martha Graham technique to Italy.

In spite of Italy's rather sparse international reputation for modern dance, Italian companies and choreographers have distinguished themselves at least regionally. The influence of American contemporary dance in the 1970s touched off a "dance boom" that produced a number of new groups and a new mix of choreographic styles. Sosta Palmizi is a Turin-based company that has been at the forefront of experimental choreography in Italy for a number of years. The company originated in 1984 as a result of the work of the American expatriate Carolyn Carlson, a student of Alwin Nikolais and a devotee of Wigman's German expressionist school. In the absence of a strong Italian audience for modern dance, Sosta Palmizi has traveled widely, and in 2004 the company relocated to Cortona in Tuscany. Raffaella Giordano and Giorgio Rossi, both charter members, have provided most of the choreography for the company. Carlson's influence extends also to the Aldes company of Lucca whose founder and director, Roberto Castello, was both an original member of Sosta Palmizi and a student of Carlson. In 1984, Virgilio Sieni and Fabrizio Monteverde debuted their choreography and, in doing so, began to fashion what has been recognized as an Italian style.[19]

Company Excursus was founded by choreographer Ricky Bonavita and dancer Theodor Rawyler in 1988 with headquarters in Rome and Biel-Bienne, Switzerland. Excursus has performed Bonavita's choreography—surrealistic images derived from ordinary gestures—in Paris as well as in Italy and Switzerland. A number of other Italian modern dance companies have gained international recognition. Among them are the Egribiancodanza Company of Rome, Insania Dance Company of Ancona, and the Keos Dance Company of Viareggio. In addition, two festivals have regularly brought international acclaim since the 1950s. The Festival of the Two Worlds in Spoleto has showcased international contemporary dance, while the Nervi Dance Festival has regularly presented ballet companies from around the world. Each summer, dance festivals are to be found throughout the peninsula along with the television dance program *"Maratona d'estate"* (Summer Marathon), promising to continue the popularity generated by the "dance boom" initiated in the 1970s.

NOTES

1. Richard Andrews, "Theatre," in *The Cambridge History of Italian Literature,* ed. Peter Brand and Lino Pertile (Cambridge: Cambridge University Press, 1999), 284–86; Albert N. Mancini, "Narrative Prose and Theatre," in *The Cambridge History of Italian Literature,* ed. Peter Brand and Lino Pertile (Cambridge: Cambridge University Press, 1999), 327–29.

2. Andrews, "Theatre," 288–92.

3. David Kimball, "Opera since 1800," in *The Cambridge History of Italian Literature,* ed. Peter Brand and Lino Pertile (Cambridge: Cambridge University Press, 1999), 450.

4. Hindley, Geoffrey, ed., *The Larousse Encyclopedia of Music* (New York: Excalibur Books, 1981), 418–20.

5. Jay Nordlinger, "Farewell, Fat Man," *National Review,* April 5, 2004, 58–59.

6. Marcella Filippa, "Popular Song and Musical Cultures," in *Italian Cultural Studies,* ed. David Forgacs and Robert Lumley (New York: Oxford University Press, 1996), 327–43.

7. Alessandro Carrera, "Folk music and popular song from the nineteenth century to the 1990s," in *The Cambridge Companion to Modern Italian Culture,* ed. Zygmunt Barański and Rebecca J. West (Cambridge: Cambridge University Press, 2001), 326.

8. John Kersey, "Bocelli," in *Encyclopedia of Contemporary Italian Culture,* ed. Gino Moliterno (London: Routledge, 2000), 69–70.

9. Marcello Sorce Keller, "Popular Music in the Early Twentieth Century," in *The Garland Encyclopedia of Music,* ed. Timothy Rice, James Porter, and Chris Goertzen, vol. 8, *Europe* (New York: Garland Publishing, 2000), 618–19.

10. Joseph Sciorra, "Hip Hop from Italy and the Diaspora: A Report from the 41st Parallel," *Altreitalie* 24 (January–June, 2002): 86–104; Saskia Reilly, "Rap, Funk and Politics Italian-Style," *Europe* (June 2000): 34.

11. Javier Antonio Quiñones Ortiz, "Giovanni Tommaso," All About Jazz, http://www.allaboutjazz.com/iviews/gtommaso.htm; "Roy Hargrove Quintet + The Roberta Gambarini Quartet Town Hall," All About Jazz, http://www.allaboutjazz.com/php/news.php?id=3315; Andrey Henken, "Trumpeter Enrico Rava," http://www.allaboutjazz.com/php/article.php?id=1003.

12. "Paolo Grassi," *The New York Times,* March 15, 1981.

13. Roberto Tessari, "Actor Training in Italy," *New Theatre Quarterly* 4, no. 14 (1988): 184–85.

14. "Vittorio Gassman," *The New York Times,* June 30, 2000; William Van Watson, "Gassman," in *Encyclopedia of Contemporary Italian Culture,* ed. Gino Moliterno (London: Routledge, 2000), 251; Tessari, "Actor Training in Italy," 188–90.

15. Federica Sturani, "Theatre," in *Encyclopedia of Contemporary Italian Culture,* ed. Gino Moliterno (London: Routledge, 2000), 581–85; Mario Prosperi, "Contemporary Italian Theatre," *The Drama Review* 22, no. 1 (1978): 17–26.

16. Prosperi, "Contemporary Italian Theatre," 22; Bernadette Luciano, "Bene," in *Encyclopedia of Contemporary Italian Culture,* ed. Gino Moliterno (London: Routledge, 2000), 55–56.

17. William Weaver, "Italian Theatre's Gifted Rebels With a Cause," *The Financial Times* (London), January 11, 1990.

18. Giannandrea Poesio, "The Cinderella of the Arts," in *Europe Dancing,* ed. Andrée Grau and Stephanie Jordan (London: Routledge, 2000), 100–104.

19. "Italians Embrace Modern Dance," *Toronto Star,* December 17, 1990; "A Quiet Entrance by Italian Companies," *The New York Times,* October 15, 2003; Poesio, "The Cinderella of the Arts," 108–9.

8

Art, Architecture, and Design

IF IT CAN BE SAID that postwar Italian achievement in some areas of cultural production—music and painting, for example—have proven disappointing in comparison to its glorious past, that cannot be said for design, a field in which Italians have asserted themselves as clear leaders. In fact, successes in the furniture and fashion industries are major reasons for Italy's prosperity.[1] In part that record of excellence is a product of the long and distinguished history of art, architecture, and design in Italy and particularly its rich traditions of craftsmanship and small-scale production of textiles such as silk. It was in fact this strong artistic tradition that contributed most notably to the virtuosity of modern Italian design.

Italian design developed late and without a great deal of philosophical debate until after World War II. One early twentieth-century exception might be the Futurists, but their manifestos and projects were more often defiant political and social assertions than aesthetic theories. Because they failed markedly to influence industrial production, Futurist designs remain relegated to museums and art history texts. The *Novecento* (1900s) movement might have proved a second example of theoretical foundation, but their link to the Latin past proved too great a burden and their influence remained limited. Rationalism was an important movement in Europe, advocating simple, functional forms, free of ornamentation and national identity. And while it produced its Italian architects, rationalism's influence on Italian design proved minimal.[2]

During the two decades of Fascist rule, a debate over architectural styles persisted, providing ample evidence that the regime fell short of full cultural

orthodoxy. Modernists viewed themselves as the force that would drive not
only a new style, but a new society, while architects and designers of the *Novecento* movement linked severe contemporary lines with the classical past. The
Milan Triennale, held in a building designed in the *Novecento* style by Giovanni Muzio, provided a showcase for *Novecento* designs every three years
beginning in 1933. American influences also contributed to Italian style during the interwar years, but while American design was primarily commercial
in application, the Italian context more directly merged political and social
influences with industrial.[3]

One characteristic of postwar Italian painting, architecture, and design was
to be its diversity. These forms of modern artistic expression most often represented self-conscious statements of reform and a general rejection of the
political and social status quo, and thus tended to be somewhat polemical in
direction and jealously defiant of any single Italian "school," as artists constantly reinvented themselves. Furthermore, the defeat of the Italian left by
the Christian Democratic Party in the elections of 1948 created a sense of
alienation among many of the artists, architects, and designers who, like
other intellectuals, were committed to a leftist political agenda. Shut out of
power, they resorted to their crafts as a means to reform society. Although
they never forged a consensus of style, they did agree on the uses of their art
as a mechanism to reject the Fascist past, extend the heroic tradition of the
Resistance, and forge a new culture and society. And if in other forms of artistic expression change was the only constant, in the world of fashion design
this axiom was all the more obvious. The concept of fashion, a special case of
design, cannot exist without an awareness of change.[4]

ITALIAN PAINTING IN THE POSTWAR ERA

As was generally the case across Italian culture, artists were intent on making an emphatic break with the era of Fascism and war. As a result, accom-
panying the explosion of artistic creativity were intense debates over
aesthetics, the role of artists in society, and the responsibility of artists to
engage the era's political and social questions in their work. This debate produced a number of artistic manifestos and endless polemics in the burgeoning journals of the day and in the popular press. Behind all the debates
was the ideological polarization produced by the emerging Cold War, illustrated in Italian politics by the ongoing political and cultural battle between
Catholics and communists. And although Catholics prevailed at the polls
through the victories of the Christian Democratic Party, communists succeeded in establishing supremacy in intellectual circles and "high" or formal
culture. Marxists and many other left-wing intellectuals demanded that

artists commit themselves to socially pertinent works parallel to the neorealism of writers and filmmakers. Neorealists condemned "escapist" art in all its forms, favoring social realism. However, as might be expected, there was no conformity among artists, and ideological disagreements persisted along with a variety of styles. One obvious split opened between figurative art, often favored by neorealists for its ability to convey a clear political message, and nonfigurative or abstract art, more attuned to the European and American avant-garde. Just after the war, a diverse group of Italian artists, who agreed primarily in their opposition to Fascism, organized in Rome, Milan, and Venice the *Fronte nuovo delle arti* (New Front of the Arts).

The Sicilian Renato Guttuso was a member of the *Fronte nuovo,* a resolute communist, and Italy's outstanding figurative painter of the postwar era. He had painted since adolescence in the mid-1920s and had emerged as a force because of his persistent call for artists to engage history. While on military duty in Milan, Guttuso befriended a number of intellectuals, including Elio Vittorini and Salvatore Quasimodo, the beginning of an enduring series of relationships with leading Italian artists, including the writer Alberto Moravia. Guttuso's prolific output of large-scale works, landscapes, nudes, and still-life compositions contributed to his growing reputation and an array of prizes. In the 1930s he completed two famous works, *Fucilazione in campagna* (Execution by Firing Squad in the Countryside), dedicated to the murdered Spanish poet Federico Garcìa Lorca, and *Fuga dall'Etna* (Flight from Etna), which won the prestigious Bergamo prize in 1938. Guttuso's best-known painting, *Crocifissione* (Crucifixion), condemned by the Vatican, is recognized as a modern masterpiece. Guttuso, who completed the work in 1941, explained that he wished to show "the torment of Christ" at a moment of wartime suffering, reinforcing his commitment to engage his art in political struggles.

The tension between Italian realistic and abstract art continued through the 1940s, manifested in both words and paintings. That tension intensified toward the end of the decade, eventually leading to an open breach. In 1947, three Marxist artists, Carla Accardi, Piero Dorazio, and Giulio Turcato, established in Rome the *Forma* (Form) group that was committed to abstract art, in opposition to realists such as Guttuso and to the official social realism of the Communist Party. The next year proved decisive.

In 1948, the *Alleanza della Cultura* (Alliance of Culture) organized in Bologna an exhibition of postwar art. The show featured the works of Guttuso and such other prominent artists as Renato Birolli and Antonio Corpora in an effort to explore the various styles and to encourage the development of a contemporary visual language. Although this was the first national exhibition of the postwar era, it also marked one of the final occasions when abstract and realistic art coexisted in the same prominent exhibition.

It was also in 1948, at the Venice Biennale, that the definitive breach opened, as abstract artists and groups expanded their presence, leaving figurative artists isolated from the "cutting edge" of art-making. Illustrative of the new prominence of nonfigurative art, the artist Lucio Fontana founded in Milan the movement of spatialism with the publication of his *Primo Manifesto di spazialismo* (First Manifesto of Spatialism), one of several such proclamations. In his writing and painting Fontana emphasized space, movement, and time, especially the spatial context of art. Other indications of the triumph of abstraction included the founding in Rome of the journal *Arti Visive* (Visual Arts), committed to abstract art, and two groups of nonfigurative artists, *Gruppo Origine* and the abstract gallery known as *Fondazione Origine*. Among the leaders of these movements were Ettore Colla, Alberto Burri, and Giuseppe Capogrossi. Colla was a sculptor who made the transition from figurative to abstract works, using found materials to rediscover their basic geometrical identity apart from their function. His *Genesi* featured sharp surfaces that gave the impression of a terrifying machine.[5] Burri began making art while a prisoner of war in Texas during World War II. In his work he made use of a variety of media, combining such materials as burnt wood and plastic. After winning the Bergamo prize with a figurative work, Capogrossi moved decisively toward abstraction with his neocubist *Le due chitarre* (Two Guitars) at the Venice Biennale of 1948.

Figurative artists did not disappear. Guttuso continued to produce and exhibit widely. Marino Marini sculpted bronze, terracotta, and stone images—dancers, female nudes, portrait busts, and, most notably, the horse and rider. Marini managed to address contemporary themes, especially the prospect of nuclear holocaust, while maintaining contact with the Greek and Etruscan sculptural heritage. Nonetheless, experimentation dominated the Italian art of the 1950s and 1960s as artists repudiated tradition in favor of new forms and international influences. At the same time, the Economic Miracle created enough new wealth that galleries and museums multiplied and demand grew for artistic works, particularly those that reflected new and international styles. Although they had moved away from realism, Italian artists and critics continued to engage in ideological polemics, debate the role of art in renewing culture, and challenge the status quo by their innovative works.

The decade of the 1960s saw a move away from ideologically driven art toward an even greater emphasis on experimentation. Interest in exhibits increased and patrons focused on novel and imaginative painting, sculpture, and multimedia compositions. At the same time, Italians turned outward for inspiration, particularly to the pop-art of artists such as Andy Warhol who featured the icons of consumer capitalism. As evidenced by the Venice Biennale of 1964, Marxist ideology had largely been displaced by a general criticism of the crassness of the new mass-consumer-driven materialism that had accompanied the booming prosperity, burgeoning popularity of television, and proliferation of American-style situation comedies, commercials, and game shows.

The Venice Biennale of 1968, which coincided with a global surge in radicalism, featured the works of a number of young Italian artists who portrayed overt political statements in sympathy with the Italian students' movement. An example is Enrico Baj's 1972 *Funerali dell' anarchico Pinelli* (Funeral of the Anarchist Pinelli) in tribute to a young man who had died in police custody after having been wrongly accused of a notorious 1969 bank bombing in Milan. Baj attained notable success by constructing figurative satires of Italian society and politics. The protests of 1967–68 led to an extended period of violence, which, in turn, moved many Italian artists away from explicit political themes to experimentation with form.

Among the more notable and audacious of the new experimental artists was Pietro Manzoni. Originally a figurative artist like many experimentalists, he was influenced by the spatialism of Fontana. Manzoni engaged in conceptual art, often jolting conventional sensitivities with such works as inflated balloons that he called *Fiato d'artista* (Artist's Breath) and almost-naked bodies that he signed as *Living Sculptures.*

Manzoni is regarded as a precursor to the *arte povera* (poor art) movement that began in 1967 with an exhibition in Genoa. Curated by Germano Celant, the show displayed the works of a number of artists including Alighiero Boetti, Luciano Fabro, and Giulio Paolini. Boetti's work showed influences of pop art as well as *arte povera* and reflected a unique application of ordinary objects, such as he displayed in his *Arazzo* (Tapestry), a world map on which the nation states are identified by the colors and designs of their flags. Fabro is known for employing figurative elements in highly imaginative designs, most notably in his series called *Italia,* each part of which features an inverted Italian peninsula rendered in unconventional materials such as iron, leather, and glass. Paolini moved from *arte povera* toward conceptual art, focusing on the relationship between artist and observer. In his *Giovane che guarda Lorenzo Lotto* (Young Man Looking at Lorenzo Lotto), Paolini photographed the portrait, reversing the roles of artist and viewer.

The term "poor art" evoked a number of connotations. The works consistently drew upon subjective expressions, often incorporated ordinary and found objects, and were often—although not always—crudely executed rather than elaborately developed. In addition, Celant and the artists generally shared a disdain for the art of highly-valued masterpieces that were purchased by a wealthy elite; thus, this seditious art—or "guerrilla art," as Celant termed it—was created for a mass audience. On the other hand, the *arte povera* movement never did clearly articulate an agenda and exercised little recognizable influence on Italian politics. By the 1980s, the movement had become passé and was overcome—as was much of Italian abstract art—by a revival of figurative art.

The move toward a new figurative art emerged most dramatically at the 1980 Venice Biennale, setting the tone for the 1980s and subsequent decades. A group of artists whose work was celebrated at that show, including Francesco Clemente, Mimmo Paladino, Emilio Cucchi, and Sandro Chia, were labeled the *Transavanguardia* (transavantgarde) by critic Bonito Oliva. Oliva meant to distinguish this new movement from previous avant-gardes, implying that this group transcended, or surpassed, other modernists. Clemente is a self-trained Neapolitan who, like others in the *Transavanguardia,* combined figurative and abstract elements as a means of personal expression in his paintings, often using icons from classical and Renaissance traditions. Like Clemente, Paladino incorporates ancient elements in his work, which now includes sculpture, prints, and mixed-media as well as painting. Paladino's work often invokes mystery, as in the fanciful human and animal forms of *Sull'orlo della sera* (On the Edge of Evening). Cucchi moved from conceptual art to a more figurative, expressionist approach in the 1980s, then expanded into marble reliefs, frescoes, mosaics, and small drawings. He is known especially for imaginative installations of his work in galleries. Like other artists of the *Transavanguardia,* Sandro Chia incorporates images from other schools of art in his work, primarily in the bold, sharp lines and vivid colors that he calls "graffiti." The *Transavanguardia* movement is considered by many art historians to be the most important in Italy since the Futurist movement of the early twentieth century.[6]

Art in Italy, as in the rest of Europe and the United States, was fragmented in the final decades of the twentieth century to the point that it defies generalization about styles and trends. An influential exhibition in Genoa in 1982, *Una generazione postmoderna,* announced the arrival of the "Post-modern Generation" in Italian art. It was an eclectic show, typifying a certain lack of direction and lack of historical context, rejecting both ideology and history in favor of personal, introspective themes.

However, the realignment and rapid integration of Europe resulting from the collapse of the Soviet Union and the end of the Cold War in the early 1990s created a renewed awareness of the relationship between art and history. A number of exhibitions demonstrated a new inquiry into issues of totalitarianism, war, and inhumanity and a new curiosity about the contemporary world. In one such 1995 exhibition, Genoa featured *Art of Freedoms, of Antifascism, of War and Liberation in Europe,* signifying a new awareness of historical context and a new social consciousness among Italian artists.

CONTEMPORARY ITALIAN ARCHITECTURE

Italian architects, like painters, sculptors, photographers, filmmakers, and other creative artists, found themselves very much engaged in the events of the Resistance to Fascism and Nazism, the liberation of the peninsula, and the hopes and fears that absorbed Italians in the immediate postwar era. In fact architects were directly engrossed in the period because of the stark reality of physical destruction and the pressing need to provide new buildings. It has been reported that only 10 percent of Italian dwellings had bathrooms by 1950.[7] As the renowned architect Ernesto Nathan Rogers declared, he and his colleagues had to rebuild "the house of man," especially in light of the large number rendered homeless by the war.[8] Although they were alike in believing that their profession could provide the vision and the physical framework for constructing a new democratic society and a new moral order, Italian architects disagreed along conceptual lines. Hence a debate raged that was both an extension of a past dialectic and a precursor of a looming one: what should be the connection between the new buildings and their historical context? One contingent argued for exact reconstruction; the other advocated a new urban design for the destroyed areas, using the slogan *"Indietro non si torna"* (You can't turn back).[9]

An example is the rebuilding of the Ponte Santa Trinità in Florence. As they retreated from Florence in August 1944, German troops destroyed five of the six bridges crossing the Arno, including the Ponte Santa Trinità, a Renaissance masterpiece, as well as the buildings that lined the streets approaching the bridges. When the return of order to the city led to discussions about renovation, compromise prevailed, resulting in the painstakingly accurate reconstruction of the Ponte Santa Trinità and the use of historical references in materials and designs in the rebuilding of the *centro storico* (the historical center). Similar deliberations occurred in Milan and other cities. Some progressive architects objected to the rebuilding of Florence in conformity to its historic style, arguing that, in doing so, the city had missed the opportunity to reconfigure itself in accord with their modernist vision.

Another example of the demands on postwar architects was the need to construct memorials to victims of war and Nazi and Fascist atrocities. In Milan, the renowned modernist firm of BBPR (Ludovico Barbiano di Belgioioso, Enrico Peressutti, and Ernesto Nathan Rogers—Giuliano Banfi had died in a concentration camp in 1944) constructed a transparent, metal, cubic monument that contained ashes from various concentration camps, a strong abstract statement in favor of rationalist architecture.

In contrast to the austere abstraction of the BBPR memorial in Milan, a Roman architectural team led by Mario Fiorentino and Giuseppe Perugini designed and executed a powerfully moving memorial to the 385 Roman prisoners who were executed at the Ardeatine caves by German troops in March 1944. The memorial to the Ardeatine massacre leads the visitor through the caves into the shrine on a journey that represents the tragedy in more literal terms, evoking a strong, visceral response. In a sense, these two contrasting solutions to similar challenges are indicative of the coexistence of diverging, and sometimes conflicting, schools of thought in postwar Italian architecture.

The trauma of World War II influenced Italian architecture in other ways as well. Three distinct theories or "schools" of architecture can be identified in the immediate postwar era: neorealism, organic architecture, and rationalism. Neorealist architecture was a part of the broader neorealist movement that was especially prevalent in cinema and literature at the time, and an extension of the left-wing influence on Italian culture in the wake of the liberation of the peninsula. Neorealist architects rejected the classical tradition as both elitist and tainted by the Fascist preference for classical themes; they favored the simpler styles of traditional, rural building, which they invested with a certain moral character and democratic political value.

The organic architecture movement in Italy predates World War II. It shared with the neorealists a commitment to democratizing Italy and was most ably and energetically represented by Bruno Zevi, a protege of the American architect Frank Lloyd Wright. Zevi founded the Association for Organic Architecture (APAO) in 1945 in Rome. Applying Wright's organic concepts to the demands of postwar construction proved both difficult and controversial. One example is found in the Tiburtino, a working-class district in the sprawling suburbs of Rome, where a firm headed by Ludovico Quaroni and Mario Ridolfi built a housing complex. Rejecting the rigid, rectilinear design favored by the rationalist school, the Quaroni-Ridolfi firm varied the angles of windows and balconies and the orientation of the buildings. Influenced by Zevi, Ridolfi's postwar work symbolized his shift from rationalism to organic architecture. Quaroni was acknowledged as one of the driving forces behind postwar modernism and realism, of which his *Nuova Stazione di Roma Termini* (New Rome Railroad Station) is considered an exemplary work.[10]

The rationalist school was a revival of prewar modernism, whose inspiration came from Central Europe, particularly Walter Gropius and the Bauhaus tradition, and whose advocates had vied with the classical architects within the Fascist regime. The rationalists rejected neorealist design as parochial and oblivious to advanced international influences. They proposed a modern style of simple, functional forms based on new materials, including concrete and steel. Italy's leading rationalist architect of the era was Giulio Carlo Argan, who argued that Italy should reject its regressive past in favor of integration into the broader European community. In opposition to Zevi's Rome-based, organic APAO, the rationalist school made its greatest impact in Milan where two groups led the way. The Movement of Architectural Studies (MSA) engaged in continuing analysis of Italy's architectural challenges. An excellent example of Milanese rationalist architecture is found along the Via Dessié, where the housing developments of Luigi Figini and Gino Pollini are angular cubes, with exposed frames and flat roofs, representative of the rationalist approach. Figini and Pollini developed a reputation as leaders of the rationalist school in their use of strong and complex geometric shapes and textured surfaces. Particularly notable was their apartment-office building on the Via Broletto and the church of the Madonna of the Poor in Milan and their collaboration with Adriano Olivetti in the design of the Olivetti factory at Ivrea. The other important Milanese rationalist group was Architetti Riuniti (AR), which produced a comprehensive regional plan in July 1945, designed to control suburban sprawl and real estate speculation.

The 1948 national elections, the first under the new republican constitution, provided a rude awakening for the architectural community that was intent on building the new Italy. With the hardening Cold War engulfing Italian politics, the DC, with strong support from the United States, won control of power and launched its own housing construction program (through the INA-Casa agency) that shared little with any of the dominant architectural schools. One problem with the party-driven approach was that it was designed to be labor intensive, employing as many Italians as possible. Consequently, most of the designs advocated by groups such as MSA and AR were not feasible, because they required the most advanced methods and materials, which exceeded the training of most of the workers hired by INA-Casa. Consequently, such groups as MSA and AR eventually withered away in the face of mass production methods.

A housing boom in the 1950s, when the number of rooms roughly quadrupled, placed an urgent demand on the community of Italian architects. With the late-1950s surge in growth known as the Economic Miracle, the demand for architectural designs—often spurred by commissions from Italian firms—continued, stimulating debates over land use and urban planning. At the same time, Italian architecture attracted worldwide attention both for originality and variety of design as well as for the sheer volume of new construction. One critic referred to Italian postwar design as "pure poetry."[11] Some notable accomplishments exemplify the best of the era. Pier Luigi Nervi's design for the *Palazetto dello Sport* (sports complex), built for the 1960 Rome Olympic games, won admiration both for his aesthetic statement and his bold use of reinforced concrete. Just off the Autostrada del Sole outside Florence stands Giovanni Michelucci's renowned church of San Giovanni Battista (sometimes known as "St. John of the Autostrada"), with its bold, sweeping, contemporary lines and organic interior spaces that invoke impressions of caves and groves of trees as spaces for traditional worship. As the result of a brilliant career in building, urban planning, teaching, and editing, Michelucci is often considered the finest Tuscan architect of the twentieth century.[12]

The very individuality that made Italian architectural design of the 1950s and 1960s exceptional also makes easy generalization difficult. In spite of the wide variety of designs, several common features are evident. One characteristic of Italian architecture of the period is what has been referred to as its "mural" character, in other words the Italians' use of opaque walls as a significant design element—in contrast to the transparent, glass walls favored in Europe and the United States at the time, and often considered a defining characteristic of modern architecture. Architect Ernesto Nathan Rogers, editor of the journal *Casabella,* persuasively defended Italian architects for their intent to design within physical, social, and historical context and their preference for "continuity" between past and present. Rather than rejecting modern architectural traditions of Gropius and the Bauhaus, Rogers argued, the Italians were simply expanding and adapting modern norms. The light and transparent aesthetic of modern architecture, Rogers noted, was incapable of sustaining the weight of Italian history, which was an essential component of any modern Italian design. Rogers and his colleagues at BBPR introduced their concepts of modern architecture to the conservative Politecnico of Milan.

Also important in extending and critiquing modernism was the Istituto Universitario di Architettura di Venezia (IUAV, University of Venice Institute of Architecture), directed by the notable educator and architect Giuseppe Samonà and by one of the great architects of the century, Carlo Scarpa. Samonà's commitment to urban planning is evident in his structures including the Bank of Italy in Padua. Scarpa converted historic buildings to museums and designed a number of exhibitions, including many of the Venice Biennale. Inspired in part by Frank Lloyd Wright and in part by the Venetian tradition of craftsmanship, Scarpa moved away from modernism to complex, highly expressive designs. Among other important examples of his work are the Banca Popolare of Verona and the Olivetti showroom in Venice. One of the more successful IUAV students was Gino Valle, who returned from his studies at Harvard University to found the Studio Architetti Valle and to design structures in and around Udine. In his more recent work, Valle has stressed both color and the importance of designing for humans, even in the most grandiose structures.

The renowned Milanese architect Gio Ponti demonstrated his embrace of divergent trends in two notable structures. Engineered by Nervi and Arturo Danusso, Ponti's stunning Pirelli tower vaulted skyward, a dramatic prism in the "light" style of the glass tower favored by the European modernists. In contrast, BBPR's Torre Velasca provided a contemporary interpretation of the historic fortress, suggesting embattlements and grounded in much heavier, imposing fashion. Over his long career, Ponti proved himself the consummate artist-as-architect, integrating architecture, industry, and culture. While organizing the Milan Triennale exhibits Ponti founded and edited the influential journal *Domus*.

By 1970 much of the postwar enthusiasm in the artistic community had given way to disillusionment. Italian architects had often been forced to compromise their idealistic visions in the face of pragmatic demands, often the result of commissions that expected firms to provide comfort and convenience with little, if any concern for greater social questions. Too often the stark lines of modernism had lent themselves to cheap imitation and the use of inferior materials with the result that many tired of the drabness and lack of embellishment in the steel-and-concrete rectangles that had become too often the lowest-common denominator in the application of Bauhaus principles to Italian buildings. Within the community of Italian architects, the escalating violence and terrorism of the 1970s fractured the myth that modernism was contributing to ever-evolving progress. At the same time, a new generation of Italian architects emerged, partly as a product of the student protests. This new breed offered the megastructure, a comprehensive, integrated design that incorporated living pods into a massive complex, and often integrated new-left social theory into their designs.

Among the firms that offered this radical new vision were Group 9999 and two Florentine studios, Superstudio and Archizoom. The theoretician for Superstudio was Adolfo Natalini who stressed the dialectical relationship between buildings and their contexts, while the guiding genius at Archizoom was Andrea Branzi, who repudiated the popular trend toward functional architecture in favor of a new aesthetic derived from symbolism and allegory and executed with natural materials. In 1983 Branzi founded the acclaimed Domus Academy in Milan; three years later he affiliated with the European Union effort to promote design in Europe. Branzi's work set the tone for the movement known as post-functional design that would become an important force in Italy.

Natalini, Branzi, and many other architects working in the last decades of the century can be considered part of the postmodern movement. Postmodernist architecture, like postmodernism in general, defies definition. Instead of agreeing on an orthodoxy, postmodern architects resolve to reject what went before, particularly rationalism and the uncompromising modernism represented by Walter Gropius's Italian disciples who adhered to the maxim that "form follows function." A part of that rejection was an admission of failure. In particular, it had become readily apparent that although the great rationalist and modernist firms had produced living quarters for millions of people and, at best, had won international acclaim for their "poetic" designs, the buildings themselves all too often had become social failures. Social critics argued that the redundancy of design and the arid aesthetic had deprived occupants of a sense of individuality and solace. That criticism led to a growing sense among Italian architects that they had too often turned their backs to the nation's heritage in pursuit of iconoclastic design. Thus one element in postmodern architecture is to borrow from the past, incorporating elements from more than one era, reintroducing complexity and wit into design. The result was not a style, but a myriad of original styles, often eclectic and labeled "postmodern."

A number of Italian architects have excelled in the postmodern era, striking out in various directions. Gaetana Aulenti earned international notoriety with her conversion of a Parisian railway station into an art museum, the Musée d'Orsay, and has continued to focus on art museum design and restorations, including Michelucci's Santa Maria Novella train station in Florence. Mario Bellini moved into architecture and urban planning from design, where he had served as chief industrial designer for Olivetti. In the 1980s, while serving as editor of *Domus,* Bellini designed buildings in Italy, the Middle East, and Japan for which he was recognized for his poetic and innovative structures. Two professors of architecture from Turin, Roberto Gabetti and Aimaro Oreglia d'Isola, had established reputations for their designs of the Turin Stock Exchange and other residential and public buildings in the Piedmont region before demonstrating their concept of total design of both the building and its furniture at the LIS bookstore. Ignazio Gardella, whose earlier rationalist works won acclaim, began to move away from the orthodoxy of modern design with his house on the Zattere promenade in Venice and his reconstruction of the Carlo Felice theater in Genoa. Francesco Venezia incorporates unique organic influences into his postmodern work, particularly natural materials, including geological strata, from the area around Naples and Sicily. An example is his Museum in Gibellina Nuova where he thoughtfully incorporated remnants of an earthquake-devastated house into the courtyard wall of the museum.

In addition to their work, several Italian architects of the postmodern era have been especially important in theoretical design and intellectual discourse. Franco Purini of the Faculty of Architecture at the University of Rome has accomplished highly imaginative designs while executing a number of them, including an apartment house in Naples-Marianella. An important journal is Guido Canella's *Architettura e città (Architecture and the City)*. In the contemporary era, Italian urban planners, architects, and designers have often worked collectively, approaching tasks from the same basic assumptions. Often working in the same firm, they reduced a project to its simplest form. At best, according to a leading designer and critic, each conceptualized their approach as part of an integrated whole, wherein the building design fit inside the urban plan and, in turn, the furniture design conformed to the same concept, using similar materials and reflecting the general purpose. Lines of distinction between architects and designers are thus blurred, and while their loftiest goals of reforming society and culture surely failed, they did manage to create a distinct approach or "stylistic code" that was quickly translated by thousands of craftsmen into popular household objects, including vinyl chairs and slender chrome table legs, that helped to define "modern Italy."[13]

ITALIAN DESIGN IN THE CONTEMPORARY WORLD

The emergence of Italian design as a standard in the late twentieth-century world can be traced to dual origins. It is rooted in long-established Renaissance traditions of art and craftsmanship, but it is also the immediate product of the emergence of a robust material culture in the decades following World War II, which wed the artistic tradition to Italy's expanding industrial base. The concept of design as a separate process from execution also is a product of the modern era, when specialization enabled greater efficiency in the mass production of goods. Mass production was driven by mass consumption, which in turn was stimulated by the appeal of elegant designs and the advertising of well-designed products in the mass media.

The shape of Italian design was likewise the product of several influences. Modernist styles of architecture, painting, and sculpture had won favor during the early decades of the century and had been embraced to some extent by the Janus-faced aesthetic of the Fascist regime, simultaneously looking to the past for classical styling and to the future for innovation. With the ignominious fall of Mussolini and Fascism and its defeat by the heroic forces of the Italian Resistance, Italian designers advocated an aesthetic that embraced anti-Fascist ideology while consciously rejecting all physical symbols of the disgraced regime.

Although architects took the lead in postwar design—building apartments to house the homeless—designers of consumer appliances, household furnishings, and vehicles followed suit, especially as Marshall Plan aid flowed into the country and the economy began to recover. Politically powerless, designers forged a working relationship with industry that provided them the means to accomplish cultural reform. Much of Italian industry was small in size, innovative, and agile, and thus it easily adapted to experimental designs. B&B Italia, Cassina, and Zanotta are examples of small companies that adapted to changing postwar conditions.

Another important key was the availability of a nucleus of master designers experienced in a rationalist aesthetic that lent itself to the demands of the period. The favored designs of the 1950s were simple, usually adaptable to mass production, and frequently executed in plastic, chrome, and ceramics. Enough of these designs were so original in concept and stunning in shape as to win immediate attention as the "Italian line," creating a powerful image both to Italian consumers and to the outside world, and thereby enabling Italian manufacturers to distinguish themselves from their competitors. Among the designs that won wide acclaim were Pininfarina's Alfa Romeo coupé 1900, the Piaggio 1947 Vespa motor scooter, Gio Ponti's Pavoni *espresso* machine, and Marcello Nizzoli's "Lexicon 80" Olivetti typewriter. At the same time, Italy's first major assembly line at the Fiat factory began to produce the small, affordable *Cinquecento* (500) and *Seicento* (600) models, so that by the mid-1960s, Italians owned more than 5 million cars, while industrial production more than doubled between 1958 and 1963. These remarkable gains in production, accompanied by growing demands for Italian exports, provided an unprecedented outlet for Italian designers.[14]

Like other aspects of Italian life, design evolved as both a mobilizing force behind the development of the general culture and a reflection of change. Consequently, as American support elevated the fortunes of the Christian Democratic Party and billions of dollars in Marshall aid stimulated economic development, the American "Fordist" model of large-scale, assembly-line production was encouraged by the U.S. government, which also summoned Italians to embrace the modern American political model of democracy built on a shared consumer prosperity. These American capitalistic values of material comfort and conspicuous consumption began to manifest themselves in Italian design, as evidenced by the statement by the famous architect Gio Ponti: "Our ideal of the 'good life' and the level of taste and thought expressed by our homes and manner of living are all part of the same thing."[15]

This materialistic ethic was most strikingly illustrated in designs for the home, especially in furniture and lighting. Emblematic of the period were the wood and glass furniture of Carlo Mollino, chairs designed by Marco Zanuso, Vico Magistretti, Joe Colombo, and Osvaldo Borsani—often featuring leather and chrome or brightly colored, molded plastic—and the sculptured lamps of Achille and Pier Giacomo Castiglioni and Gino Sarfatti, the latter influenced by the mobiles of Alexander Calder. Italian designers were

BBPR's Torre Velasca in Milan. ©Enzo & Paolo Ragazzini/CORBIS.

celebrated, creating a demand for products bearing their names, not only to satisfy household needs, but to stand as art objects. Full-colored illustrations in such Italian magazines as *Domus, Abitare,* and *Stile Industria* and in the international design press distributed the images widely, contributing to burgeoning demand in Italy and around the Western world where prosperity fueled more extravagant household purchases.

Together these Italian designs represented a bold commitment to modernism that consciously rejected the traditional shapes found in Italian homes in the past, and firmly established the image and reputation of Italian design. At the same time, Italian designers largely avoided the "Fordist" model of mass production in favor of an Italian niche market more in alignment with Italian traditions. Most were architects working individually or in small units, largely dissociated with large industry. The result was that through the mid-1960s, the Italian design movement proved a major strength of the Italian economy and an important source in shaping a postwar Italian culture.

As the progress of the Economic Miracle began to show signs of faltering in the face of spreading strikes and student protests of the late 1960s, Italian designers rejected much of the postwar tradition. At the same time, they reflected a loss of direction and confidence as the movement split in disparate directions. Many Italian designers abandoned the elitist approach of rejecting consumer culture, instead accepting the reality of its presence and the need to work within it, producing consumer commodities while maintaining a critical perspective.[16] At the same time, a movement emerged that was to be known as antidesign, rejecting the American model in which designers simply supported the process of production. Spurred by new architectural and design firms such as Archizoom and Superstudio, this movement rejected the individual designer-driven traditions of the postwar period and touched off a flurry of innovation.

The most influential pacesetter of the antidesign movement was Austrian native Ettore Sottsass. Sottsass developed experimental designs in furniture and worked as a consultant for Olivetti where he designed typewriters and an early-generation computer. Sottsass believed that design ought to establish its own force and cultural identity separate from industry. Sottsass and the antidesign studios succeeded in dramatically influencing Italian design, particularly by inserting humor and by challenging existing concepts. An example is the sack *(Sacco)* chair marketed by the Zanotta company in 1969. Filled with polyurethane particles and known widely in the United States as the "bean bag chair," the *Sacco* was intended explicitly to ignore the luxury market in furniture and defied the assumption that design required permanent shape. As provocative as the antidesign movement proved to be, however, it found most of its objects relegated to art galleries rather than furniture stores.

The 1980s saw the re-emergence of Sottsass as the innovator driving the new Memphis group, which burst on the scene in Milan in 1981. Sottsass, Michele de Lucchi, and others succeeded in reestablishing Italy at the forefront of innovative and provocative design and attracted many non-Italian designers to Milan, reinforcing Italy's presence in the design world. Italian influence was further amplified by the proximity of factories that proved readily able to transform design into product.

But by the final decade of the century, Italian designers found themselves facing stiff challenges from Europe and Asia at the same time that the world of design was becoming so internationalized as to threaten the status that the great Italian designers of the 1950s and 1960s had established. In a sense, their work has been so influential and widely imitated that it lost some of its unique identity.[17] At the same time, as Italian post-industrial capitalism faces the crisis of unregulated growth and urban sprawl, Italian designers and architects once again are challenged, much as they were in 1945, not only to reform design, but to alter the environment in which they work.

POSTWAR ITALIAN FASHION DESIGN

Clothing styles have long been regarded as reflections of commerce and symbols of society, particularly as they have identified class and gender. Since the Renaissance, Italians in particular have "dressed for success," so that social historians have refused to dismiss fashion as superficial; instead they have weighed the psychological implications of the search for beauty along with the social, economic, and political implications of style. Thus fashion design may be viewed, like architecture and painting, as a reflection of social and political change, and the successes and failures of the fashion industry, important as it has become, as a benchmark of economic well-being.[18]

Within the tradition of design, the powerful presence of Italian fashion merits special consideration. As well-known as are the designers of Italian automobiles and household furnishings, they have not surpassed such designers of clothing and accessories as Gucci, Fendi, Krizia, Ferragamo, Pucci, Valentino, Prada, Armani, Versace, Ferrè, and Dolce and Gabbana. Much of their success came in the last decades of the twentieth century, as the demand grew for ready-to-wear designer labels. Traditionally, Italy had remained in the shadow of Paris, which had dominated fashion since the sixteenth century. In fact, Parisian designers had regularly used Italian craft houses to sew garments, and in turn, some Italian designers had moved their operations to Paris, as Elsa Schiaparelli did in the 1930s. However, throughout the twentieth century, Italians had produced prized accessories, dating from the purses of Guccio Gucci (1906) and the shoes of Salvatore Ferragamo (1927).[19]

More than 20 years of Fascism and war left the Italian fashion industry in a shambles, as Fascist policies of autarchy, League of Nations sanctions, the decline of world trade, and the demands of war more or less shut it down. The regime was committed to creating a standard Fascist image that included the somewhat incongruous ideal of a woman both athletic and domestic. To support that image, the regime created the Ente Nazionale della Moda (National Fashion Board) in Turin in 1932 for the purpose of creating an "Italian fashion." However, the regime found itself constantly on guard against the subversive influences of both French and American styles, the latter imported via Hollywood movies.

As was the case with architecture and design in general, the fashion industry blossomed after the war in response to American capital and the emergence of an integrated international fashion network and, as a result, Italian fashion and the "Italian look" gained worldwide recognition. The symbols of Italy's breakthrough into the upper tier of world fashion were its first world-class runway shows, held in Florence in 1950–52 as a result of the efforts of the Florentine aristocrat and businessman Giovanni Battista Giorgini. As a result of the publicity generated by the press and the response of fashion store buyers from around the world, Italian clothing sold in large volume and clothing manufacturers enthusiastically purchased the rights to Italian designs. Italian clothing became known for the quality of its fabrics and craftsmanship and for the innovative styles of its evening wear. The "Italian look" established itself; no longer could Paris claim the almost exclusive right to be known as the world fashion capital.

Concurrent with Giorgini's shows at historical sites such as the Pitti Palace were a number of movies shot in Rome that featured such stars as Ava Gardner, Sophia Loren, and Gina Lollobrigida wearing Italian fashions on the big screen. One feature that distinguished the "Italian look" was its brilliant selection of fabrics—evident in the designs of Emilio Pucci—often created by skilled artists using labor-intensive, highly colorful, hand-executed designs. Also emblematic of the "Italian look" was the preeminence of casual wear, which provided a popular alternative to the sometimes pretentious look of Parisian high fashion. Italian clothing established a reputation as carefree, sophisticated, comfortable, and flattering.

Among the pioneers of postwar Italian design were Pucci, the Sorelle Fontana (Fontana Sisters: Giovanna, Micol, and Zoe), and Simonetta Visconti. Pucci's use of stretch fabrics provided a memorable line of casual wear for the home. The Sorelle Fontana were especially known for their wedding dresses, evening gowns, and film costumes, as evidenced in the wardrobe of Ava Gardner in Joseph Mankiewicz's *The Barefoot Contessa* (1954). The alluring Simonetta enjoyed notable success in designing cocktail dresses, which she promoted, especially in the United States, with great aplomb. The most original designer of this era, however, was the Roman Roberto Capucci, whose silk evening gowns demonstrated dramatic lines that made his work easily distinguishable.

The exit to Paris of Simonetta and Capucci created opportunities for a new generation of Italian designers, including Valentino (Valentino Garavani), Irene Galatzine, Federico Forquet, and Patrick de Barentzen, whose success was bolstered not only by Italy's Economic Miracle, but by expanding global prosperity in the late 1950s. In Italy, the importance of presenting an elegant image *(bella figura)* became widely accepted. At the same time, Valentino's designs, particularly his pants-suits and short dresses, were much in demand outside Italy, especially in New York. Galatzine, known especially for socializing with First Lady Jacqueline Kennedy, became famous for her "palazzo pajamas," which became emblematic of the luxurious and glamorous casual styles of Italian fashion of the 1960s. Forquet and Barentzen burned brightly for a few years on the strength of spectacular designs, but then faded. Forquet was known for his bold fabrics and evening outfits, including jumpsuits. Before the end of the 1960s, both Barentzen and Galatzine went bankrupt. Over that decade, Rome challenged Florence as Italy's fashion headquarters, international competition peaked, and the trend toward ready-to-wear clothing forced the decade's acclaimed designers to make major adjustments.

Among the designers who successfully made the transition to the ready-to-wear era was Elio Fiorucci, whose stores appealed to the growing demand from young shoppers. By the end of the 1970s, Italian design had begun to specialize in luxury sportswear, an important niche in the changing clothing market. Max-Mara was an early example of what was to become a growing northern presence in the Italian fashion industry. Under the Max-Mara label, the Maramotti family of Reggio Emilia had been producing high-quality, ready-to-wear coats and suits since 1951 and became known for its "total look" marketed to urbane, professional women. Gianfranco Ferrè, born near Milan, brought his experience in architecture and furniture design to the world of ready-to-wear fashion in 1978, establishing a reputation for elegant executive attire. During the 1970s transition to ready-to-wear, Milan displaced Florence and Rome as the design capital of Italy, if not of the world. The first to move to Milan were Missoni and Krizia, both of whom opened boutiques and contributed to Milan's reputation as an international fashion center. Ottavio and Rosita Missoni won fame for their colorful knits and imaginative, practical designs. Krizia (Mariuccia Mandelli) focused on smart, practical clothing for women before developing a clothing empire. As part of the process by which the Italian fashion industry survived its crisis of the early 1970s, individual designers abandoned production and began to team with clothing factories, both under their names and anonymously. Armani bought SIMINT, for example, and Ferré combined with Marzotto. By the end of the decade, Italian design houses, led by Benetton, began to excel in global marketing. Luciana and Giuliana Benetton, with brothers Gilberto and Carlo, expanded their virgin wool knitwear business to Paris in 1970 as a first step toward an emerging global empire.

By 1980, the prevailing stars in the Italian design world were Giorgio Armani and Gianni Versace, and with them came a renewed emphasis on men's fashion. Armani had worked for Cerruti in the 1960s before launching his own menswear line in 1974 and opening Emporio Armani and Armani Jeans in 1984. He became known both for the androgynous "power" clothing for women and for the unstructured look of the 1980s, which he crafted of soft, elegant fabrics. Armani has exercised a major influence on international design over the past decades. Versace moved to Milan in 1978 where his sister and brother joined him in his design business. Fascinated by the American market, Versace broke in emphatically with miniskirted suits, broad-shouldered jackets, and the sensual style that became his trademark. Versace's violent death in 1997 left the design house under the capable artistic direction of his sister Donatella.

At the end of the twentieth century, the Italian fashion industry retained its reputation for innovative, elegant, and comfortable designs and high-quality production, driven largely by a traditionally strong textile industry. Gucci and Prada survived a period of consolidation to retain a strong presence at the end of the century. Under the highly visible inverted "G" logo, the Gucci group overcame familial discord, personal tragedy, and hostile takeover attempts under the leadership of CEO Domenico de Sole and artistic director Tom Ford. The recent departure of both leaves Gucci in a state of uncertainty. At

Prada, Miuccia Prada and Patrizio Bertelli have expanded the familial enterprise from leather accessories to mass-marketed, ready-to-wear clothing,
including their Miu-Miu and Prada Sport lines, and into the highly visible
America's Cup of international yacht racing.

Among the more recent houses to win attention are Gigli, Moschino, and
Dolce and Gabbana. Romeo Gigli set himself apart as a "minimalist" in fashion design, providing soft and supple clothing in rich colors of linen, wool,
cashmere, and silk. Gianfranco Moschino left Versace in 1983 to launch a
line of casual wear that employed bold designs and challenged many conventions of style by combining disparate elements in the same outfits. Before his
death in 1994, Moschino became known for his commitment to social
causes. The Sicilian Domenico Dolce and the Milanese Stefano Gabbana
opened a design studio in 1982. They claimed to produce clothing for "real"
women—as opposed to supermodels—and began to market widely in the Far

Women's fashions, Lucca. Courtesy of the author.

East. By 1990, Dolce and Gabbana had become identified with a new generation of Italian design.

The history of Italian design in the post-World War II era suggests that although Italians will be challenged by the forces of globalization, their tradition of craftsmanship and small-scale textile industries will carry them well. Furthermore, as the driving force of design is change, Italian textiles will both be influenced by the dynamics of the next decades—ever-growing European integration, for example—and will produce a colorful and imaginative reflection of those changes.

NOTES

1. Rinaldo Gianola, "Design and Fashion: Driving Forces of Italy," in Luigi Settembrini, *1951–2001: Made in Italy?* (Milan: Skira International Corporation, 2001), 101.

2. Andrea Branzi, "Italian Design and the Complexity of Modernity," in *The Italian Metamorphosis, 1943–1968,* ed. Germano Celant (New York: Guggenheim Museum Publications, 1994), 598–99.

3. Penny Sparke, "Design in Italy since 1866," in *The Cambridge Companion to Modern Italian Culture,* ed. Zygmunt Barański and Rebecca J. West (Cambridge: Cambridge University Press, 2001), 272.

4. Eugenia Paulicelli, "Fashion: Narration and Nation," in *The Cambridge Companion to Modern Italian Culture,* ed. Zygmunt Barański and Rebecca J. West (Cambridge: Cambridge University Press, 2001), 284.

5. Max Staples, "Colla," in *Encyclopedia of Contemporary Italian Culture,* ed. Gino Moliterno (London: Routledge, 2000), 119.

6. Max Staples, "Clemente," "Cucchi," "Chia," "Paladino," "Transavantgarde," in *Encyclopedia of Contemporary Italian Culture,* ed. Gino Moliterno (London: Routledge, 2000), 115–16, 145, 107, 415, 599–600.

7. Gianola, "Design and Fashion," 102.

8. Dennis Dourdan, "Rebuilding the House of Man," in *The Italian Metamorphosis, 1943–1968* ed. Germano Celant (New York: Solomon R. Guggenheim Museum, 1994), 586; Penny Sparke, "Design in Italy," 273.

9. Dourdan, "Rebuilding the House of Man," 586–87.

10. Fassil Zewdou, "Ridolfi," in *Encyclopedia of Contemporary Italian Culture,* ed. Gino Moliterno (London: Routledge, 2000), 510–11; Gordana Kostich, "Quaroni," in *Encyclopedia of Contemporary Italian Culture,* ed. Gino Moliterno (London: Routledge, 2000), 485–86.

11. Dourdan, "Rebuilding the House of Man," 591.

12. Gordana Kostich, "Michelucci," in *Encyclopedia of Contemporary Italian Culture,* ed. Gino Moliterno (London: Routledge, 2000), 365–66.

13. Branzi, "Italian Design," 602–3.

14. Sparke, "Design in Italy," 273; Branzi, "Italian Design," 603; Gianola, "Design and Fashion," 102.

15. Gio Ponti, "Italy's Bid on the World Market," *Interiors,* February 1953, 79.

16. Branzi, "Italian Design," 605–6.

17. Sparke, "Design in Italy," 280–81.

18. Paulicelli, "Fashion," 284–85; Nicola White, *Reconstructing Italian Fashion* (Oxford: Berg Publishers, 2000), 1–7.

19. Valerie Steele, "Italian Fashion and America," in *The Italian Metamorphosis, 1943–1968* ed. Germano Celant (New York: Solomon R. Guggenheim Museum, 1994), 496; Steele, *Fifty Years of Fashion* (New Haven, Conn.: Yale University Press, 1997).

9

Cinema and Mass Media

IN THE MORE THAN 60 YEARS since the end of World War II, Italian mass communications has both shaped and been molded by the dramatic modernization of Italy. First Italian movies portrayed postwar devastation and poverty. Then movies and television presented images of the new prosperity that spread in the Economic Miracle of the 1950s. The images propelled consumer demand; in turn, consumption patterns influenced the media, particularly as Italians forsook movie houses in favor of their newly acquired television sets. This dynamic interaction of a changing population and a rapidly expanding media has played a significant role in the development of the post-Fascist state and what has been called the "Second Republic" that began to emerge after the *Tangentopoli* ("kickback city" or "bribesville") scandals of the early 1990s. The scandals rocked the political system when news spread that hundreds of party leaders and businessmen had been arrested on charges of bribery. In the aftermath of *Tangentopoli*, calls for fundamental change created the opportunity for the rise to power of media mogul Silvio Berlusconi, who used his ownership of advertising, television, and print media to win Italy's highest political office twice. Berlusconi's rise symbolized the merging of media and politics at a level never before known in Italy and alarmed many critics who viewed this combination as a threat to democratic institutions.

EARLY ITALIAN FILM

Film has played an important role in Italian culture and, likewise, Italian filmmakers have contributed significantly, if unevenly, to the history of cinema. It has been proposed that the study of film, as well as other mass media, requires consideration of technological and artistic changes in production and distribution as well as consumption patterns of audiences. In the earliest days of Italian cinema, filmmakers built their own equipment and showed their films wherever they could. However, as the novelty of seeing images wore off, cinematographers began to hire professional actors and to develop more complete plots to retain the interest of viewers.[1]

In the infancy of silent movies, before Hollywood emerged after World War I to dominate the industry, Italian productions made an indelible mark. Filoteo Albertini patented the Albertini Kinetograph in 1895 and produced what has been considered "the first feature film with a complex plot," *La Presa di Roma* ("The Taking of Rome," 1905). The founding of Italy's first major production company, CINES, in 1906 enabled worldwide distribution of Italian movies, most notably Giovanni Pastrone's *Cabiria* (1914), which won wide acclaim for its artistic merit and established Pastrone as Italy's first great director. Among his innovations, Pastrone introduced the "tracking shot" by moving the camera along a trolley. Although the first Italian directors indulged in a variety of formats including comedy and adventure, *Cabiria* typified their melodramatic renditions of themes from classical history, a popular genre in early Italian film. The speed of production was striking; Italian filmmakers made more than 550 films in 1915 to lead the world in cinematic exports.[2]

The parallel post-World War I emergence of Hollywood and Benito Mussolini would be intrinsically linked and would influence Italian filmmaking for two decades. Competition from imported films, primarily from the United States, plunged Italian production to a mere dozen films in 1930 from the hundreds produced in the early years of the decade, leading to the collapse of the industry. Aware of the importance of film, Mussolini began to reorganize the industry, block Hollywood imports, limit the number of days when imports could be shown, and demand that imports be dubbed into Italian. In turn, Hollywood suspended operations in Italy, giving Italian movie makers a captive market. The response was abundant. Italians produced more than 700 films during the two decades of Fascism, most designed either as documentary or entertainment rather than propaganda. However, the Fascist regime subsidized films approved by script-readers who insisted that Italy be portrayed favorably.

In a number of ways, the Fascist era proved greatly significant in developing Italian film. The regime built a first-rate studio complex, Cinecittà (Cinema City), and a film school, Centro Sperimentale di Cinematografia (Experimental Center of Cinematography), both of which make important contributions to the Italian film industry even today. At the same time, several journals, one edited by Mussolini's son Vittorio, provided criticism, while the government launched the Venice film festival to spotlight Italian cinema. Most of the films produced in the Fascist era, although not overtly propagandistic—with the exception of a few like Alessandro Blasetti's *Vecchia Guardia* ("Old Guard") that celebrated the Fascist March on Rome—were either patriotic or comic. An example of indirect propaganda was Carmine Gallone's *Scipione l'Africana*, an epic celebration of the Roman incursion into North Africa to win the Punic Wars that transparently celebrated the 1935 Fascist invasion of Ethiopia and the declaration of the Italian Empire. In addition to Blasetti, the other best-known director of the Fascist era was Mario Camerini who specialized in sophisticated comedies such as *Darò un milione (I'll Give a Million)* and *Signor Max (Mister Max)*, both featuring Vittorio De Sica. In addition to De Sica, two other comedic actors excelled. Erminio Macario and Totò (Antonio De Curtis) won nationwide popularity, the former as everyman befuddled by the complexities of life; the latter, the Neapolitan clown whose mime and improvised tongue-twisters made this Chaplin-like character the most revered comic actor in Italian history. Although frequently dismissed by historians as escape from the problems of the Fascist era, the comedies of the 1930s fit into a long comedic tradition in Italian film that began before World War I and traced its origins to the *commedia dell'arte* of the early modern era. Comedic films were a part of a resurgence of Italian cinema that accounted for 100 productions per year by 1942, aided by the regime's monopoly of distribution that forced Hollywood, once again, to withdraw from the Italian market.

Equally important was the experience gained by those who would emerge as the most famous directors of the celebrated neorealist films of the era following the fall of Fascism. For example, the young Roberto Rossellini, destined for fame as a neorealist *auteur*, filmed a series of documentaries for the Italian military. In pseudo-documentaries such as *La nave bianca (The White Ship)*, Rossellini developed techniques that he and other neorealists later made famous: placing nonprofessional actors in a context of historical fiction, and using black-and-white images filmed on location.

Moreover, the place of cinema in Italian culture remained fixed, integrated into the theater stage and the music hall, as actors and singers regularly gave live performances as a prelude to the featured film. In that same era, cinema was largely confined to the cities. The culture of cinema would abruptly change in the first years after the war.

ITALIAN CINEMA SINCE WORLD WAR II

When the Allies invaded in 1943, they moved directly to reintroduce American movies. After converting Cinecittà to a refugee facility, the Allied government ended restrictions against imported films and "dumped" more than 2,000 Hollywood films at prices well below market value. At the same time, Hollywood companies discovered that they could take advantage of the lower costs of filming in Italy.

In the immediate aftermath of Fascism and World War II, Italian cinema made a remarkable recovery. First came the Italian production of inexpensive films made under duress, which began to win international acclaim for their social realism and their artistic merit. This phenomenon, known as Italian neorealist cinema, featured works of innovative brilliance by Rossellini, De Sica, Luchino Visconti, and others whose masterpieces changed the course of film history. Critics and historians debate the extent to which Italian neorealists shared artistic and philosophical tenets; however, although they issued no manifesto or canon of cinematic neorealism, their work does exhibit common characteristics, some ideologically driven, others simply imposed by the difficult conditions under which they worked.[3]

Most neorealist directors, whether members of the Italian Communist Party or not, shared the left-wing philosophy of much of the Italian Resistance movement. Thus they were committed to political engagement, and they most frequently portrayed the struggles of poor Italians trying to survive against powerful forces: wartime devastation, Fascism, Nazism, and the re-emerging and oppressive bourgeoisie. Stylistically, these directors rejected the elaborate productions and escapism that dominated much of Hollywood filmmaking in favor of simple, direct assaults on such pressing social issues as the wartime devastation and poverty that pervaded the peninsula. They generally employed the documentary style in which they had been trained during the Fascist era and made frequent use of nonprofessional actors filmed on location, often using primitive equipment without benefit of much editing. The result, when overlaid on compelling plots that emphasized the heroism of ordinary Italians, was sometimes brilliant.

Among the finest of the many neorealist films are Rossellini's *Roma città aperta (Open City)* and *Paisà (Paisan)*, De Sica's *Ladri di biciclette (The Bicycle Thief)*, and Visconti's *La terra trema* ("The Earth Trembles"). In *Roma città aperta,* Rossellini documents both the despair and elation shared by Romans as partisans conspire in clandestine efforts to liberate the city from Nazi occupiers. With the assistance of scripts by a youthful Federico Fellini, a cast of nonactors, and memorable performances by Anna Magnani and Aldo Fabrizi, Rossellini shot the film in the streets of Rome immediately after the Allies liberated the city. The film earned worldwide acclaim, won the best picture award at the 1946 Cannes Film Festival, and, in contrast to most other neorealist films, became a commercial success.

Although similar in many respects—most notably the immediacy of the documentary technique and the use of nonprofessional actors—Rossellini's *Paisà* differs in structure from *Roma, città aperta.* A montage of six episodes—

one of which brings together an African American soldier and a Neapolitan street urchin—*Paisà* portrays the clash and ultimate accommodation of American and Italian cultures during the Allied invasion of the peninsula. Just as important, at a time when Italians were struggling to rediscover their national identity in the wake of more than two decades of Fascism and war, Rossellini provided a series of representations of authentic Italian culture, a contribution that has been called a "civic function" of cinema.[4]

Vittorio De Sica's *Ladri di Biciclette* employs standard neorealist techniques of documentary style and nonprofessional actors in a heartrending story of an unemployed father who has found a delivery job, only to lose it when his bicycle is stolen. The movie serves both as an exposé of the terrible conditions of the postwar era and an implicit call for profound social and political change that will provide the means for this good but despairing father to support his family. The young amateur Enzo Staiola provides a memorable performance as the son who assists his father in the desperate search.

Luchino Visconti, one of the more ideologically driven of the neorealist directors, made a masterpiece of a Giovanni Verga novel *(I Malavoglia)* in *La terra trema.* In addition to the standard neorealist techniques (he cast fishermen from the Sicilian village of Aci Trezza), Visconti insisted on using the Sicilian dialect and a slow pace with a stationary camera to fix and ennoble the simple peasant culture.

As critically acclaimed as the greatest of the neorealist films were, most failed at the box office in Italy, suggesting that ordinary Italians were much more interested in the glamour and escapism provided by Hollywood than in the realistic portrayal of their own lives. However, as the new Italian government reintroduced protectionist laws, Italian production began to recover. At the same time, a number of directors tired of employing the same techniques and hard-driving social and political ideology that appealed to an intellectual elite and left-wing critics but few others. As a result, by the mid-1950s, Italian cinema underwent a transition from the stark social commentary of neorealism to the more introspective, psychological works of the former neorealists Rossellini *(Viaggio in Italia, Journey to Italy)* and Michelangelo Antonioni *(Cronaca di un amore, Story of a Love Affair)* and the first movies of Fellini *(I vitelloni, The Young and the Passionate)*. All explored private dimensions of the inner self, particularly the themes of alienation and sexual fantasy, that reflected dominant themes of contemporary European philosophy. Fellini, in particular, drew upon themes of mythology and spirituality in two Oscar-winning films, *La Strada* (*The Road,* 1954) and *Le notte di Cabiria* (*The Nights of Cabiria,* 1956).

As a result of these and other changes, Italian cinema reached new heights of artistic and commercial success by 1960, spreading to the rural South and provincial towns, often taking center stage in the cultural life of Italy. While the veterans Rossellini, Visconti, Antonioni, and Fellini continued to excel, they were joined by a brilliant new breed headed by the visionaries Pier Paolo Pasolini and Bernardo Bertolucci and including Marco Bellocchio, Gillo Pontecorvo, Ermanno Olmi, Francesco Rosi, Elio Petri, and the Taviani brothers, Paolo and Vittorio. Many of their works were provided the prestigious label "art films" and regularly awarded prizes at the world's best-known festivals, while they themselves were toasted as great *auteurs*. At the same time, the industry turned substantial profits, selling 700 million tickets per year and attracting American capital investment. Particularly profitable were the lucrative export markets, and by 1970, Italy was producing more films annually than the United States.

An important portion of those revenues in the decade of the 1960s was generated by the successes of three additional genres—never mistaken for "art films"—traditionally popular comedies, the new "spaghetti westerns" made famous by Sergio Leone, and the toga *(peplum)* films that recalled Italy's success with classical themes in the silent era. Comedies, called *commedia all'italiana,* although often unfairly dismissed by critics and intellectuals of the left, provided a significant commentary on Italian mores and social conventions, particularly in their satirical treatment of Italian stereotypes such as the "Latin lover" and the coddling mother. Perhaps the best example is Pietro Germi's *Divorzo all'italiano (Divorce Italian Style)* which satirized both Sicilian customs and the pressures that resulted from the absence of legal divorce in Italy. In the film, a Sicilian nobleman (Marcello Mastroianni) must trick his wife (Daniela Rocca) into adultery so that he can murder her—a crime of honor for which he will be given a light sentence in the Sicilian tradition— and marry his mistress. In addition to Germi, a number of directors of *commedia all'italiana* enjoyed success in the sixties. Among them were Mario Monicelli, Luigi Comencini, and Dino Risi. Each could choose from an abundant stable of talented comedic actors. Mastroianni, Rocca, Vittorio Gassman, Alberto Sordi, Nino Manfredi, Monica Vitti, Claudia Cardinale, Sophia Loren, and others constituted a brilliant resource whose combined skills could not be matched outside Hollywood.

The "spaghetti western" is a different case altogether. Underappreciated and critically panned in its day, this genre has been reassessed in the light of its considerable success. In this case, one director, Sergio Leone, was almost exclusively responsible for the success of the genre. Leone's first film, *Un pugno di dollari (A Fistful of Dollars),* was the most successful of more than 400 westerns produced in Italy in the late sixties and early seventies and almost single-handedly catapulted to fame the young Clint Eastwood. Leone's success can be explained by his reinvention of the western, whose popularity had waned in Hollywood, by twisting the characterization so that the traditional white-hatted "good guy" is proven equally greedy and violence-prone as the classic villain. Filled with pointless violence and patronizing sight gags, the spaghetti westerns were accompanied by Ennio Morricone's distinctive sound tracks that featured original combinations of gunfire and other sound effects combined with Sicilian folk instruments. *A Fistful of Dollars* netted more than 15 times its production costs, and although it may have been the most successful, the 450 Italian westerns produced enormous profits and are given credit for reviving the western from obscurity.[5]

Peplum films shared a number of characteristics with spaghetti westerns. They offered gratuitous violence, appealed largely to male audiences, imported American actors such as muscleman Steve Reeves—and brought in substantial profits at the box office. Instead of the American west, *peplum* films were set in some unidentified "classical" era with mythical heroes and voluptuous heroines who prevailed against overwhelming odds. Examples are Blasetti's *Ulisse (Ulysses),* starring Kirk Douglas and Anthony Quinn, and Pietro Francisci's *Le fatiche di Ercole (Hercules),* featuring Reeves. American companies bought the distribution rights to many *peplum* films, promoted them, and then sold the television rights. Italian companies made more than 300 of these films from the late 1950s through the 1960s, bringing substantial financial benefit to the film industry.[6]

Also in the 1960s, the Italian genre of "art film" maintained its critical reputation while continuing its popularity with audiences around the world. In some respects, directors such as Fellini and Antonioni exceeded the success of the neorealists, while some of the leading neorealists made the transition to other methods. One example is Visconti's *Il gattopardo (The Leopard),* in which the director transformed a novel set in nineteenth-century Sicily into a slowly developing, richly-layered, and subtle masterpiece—very unlike his neorealist works and very successful. Maintaining his commitment to link his films to history and present an ideological statement, Visconti emerged from neorealism to make his most important films: *Rocco e i suoi fratelli (Rocco and His Brothers), La caduta degli dei (The Fall of the Gods),* and *Morte a Venezia (Death in Venice).* In the same decade, Antonioni featured brilliantly innovative black-and-white photography in *L'avventura (The Adventure), La Notte* (The Night), and *L'eclisse (Eclipse),* then experimented with surrealistic color in *Il deserto rosso (The Red Desert),* and in 1966 made *Blowup (Blow-Up).* Fellini's *La dolce vita (The sweet life)* brilliantly satirized the newly prosperous urban middle class of the Economic Miracle and signaled his examination of the theme of human decadence.

In fact, none of the post-neorealists matched Federico Fellini, whose movies from this era combined various elements with highly original results. Exploring the depths of fantasy, sexuality, and introspection, Fellini made

Otto e mezzo (8 1/2), Giulietta degli spiriti (Juliet of the Spirits) and *Satyricon (Fellini Satyricon)* between 1960 and 1971. In many of his works, Fellini relied heavily on influences from European literature and opera, linking film to the more traditional media. He has been said to have represented "unfettered creativity"[7] and "'authorship'at its purest."[8]

While Visconti, Antonioni, and Fellini were dominating Italian cinema in the 1960s, a number of gifted young directors appeared who were variously linked to neorealism through technique and ideology, but who were also prepared to establish highly original contributions. Together they produced a body of memorable movies, including Pasolini's *Il vangelo secondo Matteo (The Gospel According to Matthew)*, Pontecorvo's *La battaglia di Algeri (The Battle of Algiers)*, Bertolucci's *Prima della rivoluzione (Before the Revolution)*, and Rosi's *Salvatore Giuliano* and *Tre fratelli (Three Brothers)*. Pasolini's *Il vangelo* shows that while he embraced parts of the neorealist approach, he redefined realism in terms that included dreams and fantasy and combined them in highly original, nonlinear sequences, as might be expected in a Marxist rendition of a biblical story. Pontecorvo applied some of the neorealist quasi-documentary techniques to a portrayal of the anticolonial revolution in Algeria, making regular use of flashbacks and handheld camera shots. In Bertolucci's *Prima della rivoluzione,* he adapts Stendahl's novel *The Charterhouse of Parma* to a more contemporary encounter of a young, middle-class

Director Frederico Fellini on set of *Fellini's Cassanova.* Courtesy of Photofest.

intellectual with the theories of Karl Marx. Rosi's *Giuliano* is a boldly political, quasi-documentary treatment of the infamous Sicilian outlaw, and a cinematic venture into the political connections between the Sicilian *mafia* and the Christian Democratic Party, which were later reaffirmed by a series of scandals and subsequent judicial inquiries. The director's *Three Brothers* is an allegory that treats with affection the social conventions of Italy's rural past.

As was true with most aspects of Italian culture, the insurrectionist turmoil of 1968 influenced film for more than a decade. As a result, many directors who had moved away from politically charged movies (or, like Fellini, had never been so inclined), now focused on political themes that carried ideological messages. Among them were Fellini, Pasolini, Bertolucci, and the Taviani brothers. Fellini's *Amarcord,* although not as ideologically driven as some, recorded a scathing condemnation of Fascist conformity in a provincial town, satirizing sexual immaturity in particular. In his adaptations to the screen of literary masterpieces, Pasolini's *Medea* and *Il Decamerone (The Decameron)* carry heavy political criticisms of modern industrial culture. In the former, the director utilizes Euripides' classical tragedy as a mechanism to investigate the interplay between industrialized and preindustrial cultures; in transforming Boccaccio's classic from its original setting in Florentine bourgeois society to the contemporary Neapolitan underclass, Pasolini explores sexual themes and in the process levels criticism at the repressed sexuality of the middle class. In *Il conformista,* Bertolucci employs all his directorial skills to interpret Moravia's novel of the shaping of the assassin of well-known anti-Fascists Carlo and Nello Rosselli. In *Padre Padrone,* the Taviani brothers provide an autobiographical interpretation of a Sardinian shepherd's ambition to pursue a career in linguistics.

During the polarized decade initiated by the tumult of 1968, many Italian directors made traditional comedies, though often layering them with social satire and a sardonic twist. Most prominent among the directors of this genre of dark, biting comedy is Ettore Scola who made a series of exceptional films. Among them were *C'eravamo tanto amati (We All Loved Each Other Very Much),* *Una giornata particolare (A Special Day),* and *La terrazza (The Terrace).* The most ambitious by far was *C'eravamo tanto amati* in which Scola addressed not only postwar social and political change but the parallel evolution of Italian cinema. Another remarkable example of the bittersweet comedy of the 1970s was Franco Brusati's *Pane e cioccolata (Bread and Chocolate),* a scathing indictment of the conditions under which migrants worked and lived in Switzerland.

Notable also in the 1970s were the audacious, irreverent works of Lina Wertmüller, most notably *Film d'amore e d'anarchia (Love and Anarchy),* *Travolti da un insolito destino nell'azzurro mare d'agosto (Swept Away),* and her controversial masterpiece, *Pasqualino Settebellezze (Seven Beauties).* Wertmüller managed to draw upon familiar techniques and images from the Italian comedic tradition (coarse humor delivered by stock characters, for example) while employing bold imagery and biting satire. There is no better example of this than her *Pasqualino Settebellezze,* which treated comedically a story set in a concentration camp. Needless to say, while she and the film received critical accolades for daring, they were nearly overwhelmed by criticism for insensitivity and exploitation. One film of the era that won widespread acclaim for its sensitive treatment of Jewish families in a northern Italian city in the face of the evolution of anti-Semitic policies was Vittorio De Sica's *Il giardino dei Finzi-Contini (The Garden of the Finzi-Continis),* the Oscar winner for Best Foreign Film of 1972.

When Bernardo Bertolucci made *1900* in 1977, he perhaps signaled an impending departure from the dark comedies of Scola and Brusati and the startling imagery of Fellini and Wertmüller to a period when Italian directors would make epic dramas more consistent with Hollywood style. Although an ambitious attempt to encompass a century of Italian social history, *1900* carries a strong social-political message that has been aptly described as "a Marxist *Gone With the Wind.*"[9] A more warmly accepted Bertolucci epic was *L'ultimo imperatore (The Last Emperor),* winner of nine Oscars, including Best Picture and Direction. Another Italian epic was Sergio Leone's final film, *C'era una volta in America (Once Upon a Time in America),* in which Leone attempted to transform the Hollywood gangster film, as he had transformed the western, by focusing on the Jewish mob instead of the Italian *mafia.*

In spite of these successes, the decade of the 1970s was not kind to the Italian movie industry. When Hollywood reorganized its production and distribution systems, American movies began to recapture the Italian market, reinforcing the tradition of Italian consumption of American popular culture. At about the same time, Italy's deregulation of its television industry produced profound results. Television offerings expanded, as the many new stations scrambled to import American movies, situation comedies, soap operas, and game shows. Attendance at movie theaters dropped off, capital resources dried up for the production of the kind of films that had brought fame to the Italian movie business, and the Italian public refocused on the "world in the box." Between 1975 and 1996, ticket sales dropped 94 percent. Cinema no longer monopolized the imagination of the Italian public and lost its primacy in influencing mass culture; it was now replaced by what has been termed *videocrazia* (videocracy), directly attuned to the powerful pull of the (often imported) images of conspicuous consumption in the eyes of a newly prosperous public. The Italian movie industry, in a desperate effort to compete, often imitated the formulas of the emerging video culture.[10]

The death of Federico Fellini in 1993 marked the passing of an era in Italian film. Witnessing Fellini's coffin lying in state, a celebrated journalist wrote: "people were really mourning the virtual death of Italian cinema."[11] The immediate postwar years had featured the stark brilliance and powerful humanistic and political message of neorealism; the following era had highlighted the sheer genius of Fellini, Pasolini, and Bertolucci. Italian film had generated an irrefutable reputation for excellence in acting and in all aspects of direction and production. By the time of Fellini's death, Italian companies were producing about 100 films annually, one-third of the peak production levels of the 1960s; ticket sales dropped over the same period to one-seventh of their mid-1960s sales, with 80 percent of ticket revenues going to Hollywood. Movie houses and distribution of films in Italy now were controlled by a few cartels, including the Cecchi Gori group and the media conglomerate of future prime minister Berlusconi. Consequently, the artistic films for which Italian directors became famous are now few in number and confined largely to small-scale, low-budget, "minimalist" cinema—referred to by one observer as "unexportable and often invisible little films, cute films, and trash"—leaving the future of a once-proud industry in doubt.[12]

What was widely viewed as the marginalization of Italian cinema was at least partially resolved by the emergence in the 1990s of yet another generation of Italian directors, referred to as a "new wave" of *auteurs.* The best among them are Giuseppe Tornatore, Gabriele Salvatores, Gianni Amelio, Nanni Moretti, and Roberto Benigni; with them lies the hope that the powerful legacy will not be lost. Tornatore made the immensely successful *Nuovo cinema Paradiso (Paradise Cinema),* a brilliant treatment of Italian history through its history of cinema (Jury Prize at Cannes; Best Foreign Film at the Oscars). In recapturing the allure of the movies to a child in provincial Sicily, Tornatore made a triumphant return to authentic, indigenous Italian cinema. Salvatores won the Oscar for Best Foreign Film in 1991 with *Mediterraneo,* a story of Italian soldiers stranded on a Greek island during World War II that happily invokes the tradition of *commedia all'Italiana.* Amelio won a Grand Jury prize at Cannes with *Porte aperte (Open Doors),* an adaptation of a Sciascia novel about Fascist injustices. This recent revival of Italian film includes notable 2004 works by two venerable producers: Luciano Emmer's *Una lunga, lunga, lunga notte d'amore (A Long, Long, Long Night of Love)* and Ermanno Olmi's *Il mestiere della armi (The Possession of Arms).*What this new generation of post-Fellini Italian *auteurs* is said to share is a creative impulse that rejects the Hollywood method as the universal formula for success.[13]

What distinguishes Moretti and Benigni from the rest of the new breed of directors is their experience as actors, which has served them well as they have expanded their careers. Moretti has been called "the Italian Woody Allen" for the offbeat wit he displayed in his autobiographical *Caro Diario (Dear Diary)*, 1994 Grand Prize winner at Cannes. Moretti won the Grand Prize again in 2001 with *La stanza del figlio (The Son's Room)*. Benigni initially won recognition for succeeding the late Peter Sellers as Inspector Clouseau in the Pink Panther role, then broke through spectacularly as a director with *Johnny Stacchino*, a farcical satire of the mobster film that broke all Italian box office records. Benigni's greatest achievement to date is *La vita é bella (Life is Beautiful)*, a dramatic comedy about the Holocaust that scored at Cannes and won three Oscars. Benigni is given credit for creating a new, hybrid genre by integrating elements of the *commedia all'italiana* with historical memory of enormous tragedy, and thus constructing "a powerful, destabilizing mixture of laughter and tears."[14]

THE TRADITION OF ITALIAN NEWSPAPERS

Italian newspapers have evolved from the era of the *Risorgimento* when they exhibited certain characteristics that have proven durable, especially what critics have called their provincialism and elitism. At the time of unification, no national press emerged; instead, most newspapers were regional in scope, financed by regional interests or particular political factions for whom they spoke, as was the case with *La Nazione* of Florence, champion of Baron Bettino Ricasoli and the Tuscan *Risorgimento*. Moreover, Italian papers exhibited little interest in providing news coverage or in expanding circulation. Instead, they appealed to Italy's relatively small middle class of educated readers by continuing the earlier tradition of literary prose that tended to be extravagant in style and moralizing in tone. Readership was and remains modest in comparison to other industrialized countries, with only the region of Lombardy comparing favorably to the European norm. As the expansion of literacy provided new opportunities for the development of a popular press, none developed, with the exception of several minor and largely unsuccessful papers. It is said that the number of readers has remained constant at about 5 million since 1915.[15]

The Fascist dictatorship's press laws reduced newspapers to subservience, and the number of papers fell from 120 to 70 during the decade of the 1930s. The end of Fascism and Allied military occupation created a burst of interest in information and a resurgence in daily publishing, so that there were 136 newspapers by 1946. However, this surge in activity still did not create a popular, mass press; instead, *Il Giornale* of Rome introduced the *terza pagina* (third page), which examined cultural issues and was emulated by other papers such as *Il Corriere della Sera* (Milan) and *La Stampa* (Turin). Although most remained regional, the latter two, along with *La Repubblica* (Rome), developed enough of a broad-based readership to qualify as national newspapers. Nevertheless, even they maintained a local and regional focus.

Thus Italian newspapers remain largely elitist in their style and readership, a tradition that largely endures in the twenty-first century. Italy defines journalism as a profession legally equivalent to law and medicine and is the only state in the European Union that requires its journalists to pass an examination and join a regulatory body *(Ordine dei Giornalisti)* before practicing. "Il bello scrivere" (beautiful writing) remains the standard, even if it produces long sentences and sometimes extravagant prose, and Italian journalists are respected and well rewarded according to a national union contract. Instead of a mass daily press, what emerged after liberation were three daily sports papers—*Il Corriere dello Sport, La Gazzetta dello Sport,* and *Tuttosport*—and a series of illustrated weekly magazines, featuring photographs and simplified language, that developed broad appeal. The most prominent of this "glossy" press are *L'Espresso, Panorama, Il Mondo,* and *Europea* (sometimes described as "highbrow") and the so-called "family weeklies," *Oggi, Gente,* and *Domenica del Corriere.*

THE EMERGENCE OF ITALIAN RADIO AND TELEVISION IN THE ERA OF RAI MONOPOLY

From the start, Italian radio enjoyed monopoly status and was funded by a combination of license fees and advertising revenue. The Fascist government had in 1924 granted a monopoly for radio broadcasting to the URI (*Unione Radiofonica Italiana,* Italian Radio Union) and three years later to the EIAR (*Ente Italiano per le Audizioni Radiofoniche,* Italian Corporation for Radio Reception). The URI broadcasts featured music, drama, news, and talk, but the expense of owning a radio receiver slowed the spread of Italian radio, which lagged behind the rest of Western Europe. Mussolini proclaimed that he "wanted a radio in every village." By the mid-1930s, radio had become more popular; the regime trumpeted its conquest of an Ethiopian empire on the radio, and broadcasts of sporting events began shortly thereafter. By 1937 an inexpensive receiver, the *Radioballila,* was marketed, rendering the medium readily available in homes. During World War II, EIAR broadcast unrealistically rosy accounts of the success of Italian armed forces, which Italians discovered to be unreliable by listening to broadcasts from London and Moscow. Immediately after the war, radio served as the first mass medium for Italians, playing a positive role in reorganizing the national culture after 20 years of Fascism and the physical suffering and malaise brought on by invasion and defeat. Gathering in bars and factories, Italians developed some common understanding of both the suffering endured throughout the country and the first hopeful signs of recovery. It has also been noted that radio broadcasts contributed to the standardization of the Italian language, particularly in the South.[16]

The first experimental Italian television transmissions were broadcast in 1953; the next year, the first national television network, the state-owned and operated RAI (originally known as *Radio Audizioni Italia,* later as *Radiotelevisione Italiana*) began broadcasting. For the first 20 years, Italian television remained a government monopoly, maintaining the status granted to URI and EIAR. During the two decades of RAI's monopoly, the dominant Christian Democratic Party controlled RAI and used it to influence public opinion and maintain power. The rules by which RAI was granted a monopoly required it to inform, entertain, and educate.[17]

By the late 1950s, television, known as *il cinema dei poveri* (the cinema of the poor), challenged movies for an audience, as Italians gathered around small screens in neighborhood bars all over the peninsula to watch a steady diet of game shows and dubbed American movies. Ironically, at the very time Italian moviemakers had begun to reach a mass audience, television largely displaced cinema, forcing the closing of movie houses. Eventually, the film industry would recover, partly by utilizing the assets of television. In the 1970s, RAI began producing films, and by the 1990s Italian television companies were investing in film production. Television also provided a major outlet for cinema, broadcasting between 5,000 and 10,000 films annually by the mid-1990s.

Critics argued that the proliferation of television stations led to a debasing of popular culture and often looked scornfully on much of popular television programming. Among the most popular early formats were the quiz show, the talk show, and the *telenovela* (soap opera). The immense popularity of the quiz show "Lascia or raddoppia?" (Double or Nothing) made it a phenomenon of national culture and a subject of detailed coverage in the national press. Talk shows flourished beginning in 1976 with Maurizio Costanzo's *Bontà loro* (With Their Kind Permission) which brought together celebrities and ordinary folk in wide-ranging, late-night discussions. Costanzo continued with several other talk shows culminating in 1982 in the innovative *Maurizio Costanzo Show.* The popularity of the format brought a number of new shows, including Raffaella Carrà's *Pronto Raffaella* (Hello, Raffaella) that used the telephone call-in approach; *L'amore è una cosa meravigliosa* (Love Is a Many Splendored Thing), *Stranamore* (Strangelove), *Amici* (Friends), and numerous others, including two soccer talk shows, *Il processo del lunedì* (Monday's Tribunal) and *Galagoal.* The melodramatic *telenovelas,* produced inexpensively in South and Central America, began to win audiences in the 1980s. Among the most popular was *Anche i ricchi piangono* (Rich People also Cry), which built a large daytime audience on Rete A.

Whether it degraded culture or not, the new television broadcast market clearly changed the cultural role of Italian movies. Italian cinema largely abandoned its civic function—contributing to the understanding of what it meant to be Italian—in response to the sudden demand for movies as "filler" to occupy the countless hours of broadcast time. It was highly unlikely, for example, that the new video culture would produce another movie such as Rossellini's *Paisà*.

Although some critics who panned early television clearly did so from the standpoint of cultural elitism—and thus were out of touch with the tastes of the public—the case for the impact of televison on Italian culture is especially convincing in one sense. An original, authentic Italian cultural product—the cinema of the quarter-century following World War II—was largely replaced by imported movies and "a constant diet of [televised episodes of] *Happy Days, Dallas,* and *Bay Watch* [sic.]," that had nothing to do with indigenous Italian culture.[18] Additionally, critics have noted that the concept of cinema as public spectacle was lost once movies were broadcast into homes and made available for rental as videos.

Radio underwent a transition in the 1950s as well. There were three stations, all public: *Programma Nazionale* (National Program), *Secondo Programma,* and *Terzo Programma,* a cultural offering. The proliferation of transistor radios (which became status symbols) allowed various family members to select individual programming and to move away from the large, family-centered console. By 1955, nearly 20 million Italians listened to radio for an average of four hours per day, with listenership heaviest in the North.[19]

During the Cold War, the DC governments controlled all political programming on Italian radio, so that the opposition PCI was forced to broadcast *Oggi in Italia* (Today in Italy) from Prague. At the same time, the emergence of television brought ominous prospects. Although RAI radio featured new dramatic and musical offerings as well as live news broadcasts and phone-in shows (such as *Chiamate Roma 3131,* Call Rome 3131), television's popularity largely relegated the radio to a second-class status of providing background sound.

In November 1961, the Italian government launched RAI 2. RAI director and former Christian Democrat newspaper editor Ettore Barnabei led RAI 2 toward informational and educational programming. The next year, a dramatic incident on live television touched off a nationwide debate on censorship of the medium. During the airing of the popular Saturday night program *Canzonissima,* the playwright-actor Dario Fo and his wife Franca Rame, who were hosting their seventh episode of the predominantly musical show, walked out during the live broadcast to protest the censorship of one of their satirical political sketches. The Fo-Rama incident emphasized the fact that RAI was heavily censored from within, and actually led to more prere-cording of programs for the purpose of censoring them.

As a news source, Italian television in the 1950s and 1960s proved inade-quate, so that many Italians continued to rely upon newspapers. RAI broad-casts regularly reported the Christian Democratic government's activities without analysis or alternative points of view.

ITALIAN MEDIA IN TRANSITION

A series of laws and court decisions in the early 1970s, beginning with the expiration of RAI's monopoly in 1972, signaled changes in the traditional landscape of Italian radio, television, and newspapers. Consolidation of the newspaper business had begun as early as the 1950s, when the Confindustria (the industrial employers' alliance) began acquiring financial papers; contin-ued in the 1960s as several prominent families (the chemical industry's Nino Rovelli and oilman Attilio Monti) purchased dailies; and persisted in the 1970s when the chemical giant Montedison and the publisher Rizzoli obtained theirs. Fears spread that the replacement of independent, profes-sional newspaper publishers by conglomerates might subject the press to cor-porate manipulation and threaten journalistic quality and independence. In fact, although there is little evidence of overt interference, several well-known editors have been forced out.[20]

In 1974 the Constitutional Court ruled in support of more pluralistic media, thus favoring private local radio and television broadcasting and open-ing the door to entrepreneurial efforts to begin commercial broadcasting based on advertising revenues, altering the fundamental environment in which media operated. As a result, the airwaves were opened. In radio, where the costs were relatively modest, programming proliferated, leaving RAI's control only a memory. At first there was *radio pirate* (pirate radio) and *radio libere* (free radio), including Radio Libera in Florence and Radio Canale 96 in Milan. Within 3 years there were more than 1,500 radio stations and within 20 years there were more than 4,000 broadcasting, at the national, regional, and local levels. Among the new stations were "democratic" stations such as Radio Alice (Bologna) and Radio Radicale (Rome) with politically radical messages—including Marxism and advocacy of drug use—which frequently brought them into conflict with police.

Televison progressed more gradually, as deregulation opened broadcasting, not yet to market forces, but to political competition. While a number of businessmen launched networks of local stations, Silvio Berlusconi succeeded dramatically. Through his Canale Cinque (Channel 5), Berlusconi cleverly had identical videotapes delivered to all his local stations so that, by broadcasting them simultaneously, they were effectively a national network. He also imported a massive volume of American recorded programming, most notably "Dallas," which he bundled with advertising through Publitalia, his advertising company. And he raided RAI to recruit several of its most popular personalities. As a result of efforts by Berlusconi and others, RAI was forced to compete with the new unregulated commercial channels for advertising revenue while maintaining its privileged status.

After extensive negotiations among the leading political parties, Law 103 of April 1975, while maintaining RAI's monopoly as a "public service" broadcaster, transferred its control from the prime ministers (and thus from DC governments) to the Parliament. In the Parliament, the leading parties apportioned power among themselves, a system known as *lottizzazione* ("parceling out") that passed for the pluralism that the court had ordered. As a result, a patronage system developed. The DC kept control of RAI 1, the Socialist Party took RAI 2, and, when it was created in 1979, RAI 3 (except for local news programming) was awarded to the PCI. The respective television news arms (TG1, TG2, and TG3) were awarded similarly to the three parties. A 1991 study published in the popular journal *Panorama* confirmed that this partisan affiliation lasted at least a decade.[21]

In the mid-1980s existing networks won the ability to broadcast nationwide, opening a new era in Italian electronic media. Again, Berlusconi both facilitated and took great advantage of the changing conditions. His Fininvest company bought two stations, Italian Uno and Rete Quattro. When prosecutors challenged Berlusconi's emerging media empire, the PSI developed a scheme to protect his interests. The so-called "Berlusconi Decree" was implemented by Socialist Prime Minister and Berlusconi ally Bettino Craxi in a decree of December 1984. The decree was confirmed by a law of February 1985 that extended legal standing to both local and national private television stations and by the Broadcasting Act (Mammi law) of 1990 that placed limits on media ownership.

By 1990, corporate holding companies were moving to consolidate media properties, including Berlusconi's move to add newspapers and magazines to his television assets. Thus seven corporate groups had emerged by the early 1990s to dominate media ownership in Italy. A group headed by the Agnelli family's Fiat corporation included the Rizzoli publishing house, the television station Telemontecarlo, a number of newspapers (including *Il Corriere della Sera* and *La Gazzetta dello Sport,* both of Milan, and *La Stampa* of Turin) and magazines, giving them about 20 percent of the markets for both daily and weekly press. The Mondadori group, controlled by Carlo De Benedetti of

Olivetti, owned *La Repubblica* and a number of other dailies, giving them about 14 percent of the newspaper market, and enough weeklies (including *L'Espresso* and *Panorama*) to account for about 18 percent of that market. A third holding company, the Rusconi group, owned about 13 percent of the market in weekly publications, while a fourth, the Poligrafici group, owned *Il Resto del Carlino* (Bologna), *La Nazione* (Florence), *Il Tempo* (Rome), and enough other newspapers to account for about nine percent of the daily market. The Ferruzzi group, headed by Raul Gardini, published *Italia Oggi* and *Il Messaggero* (Rome), giving them about six percent of the market. In the South, the Banco di Napoli group dominated. And, finally, Berlusconi's Fininvest group took over most of Mondadori (*La Repubblica* and *L'Espresso* were separated by a 1991 court decision), about 16 percent of the market in weekly publications, and four national television networks (Canale 5, Italia Uno, Rete Quattro, and Rete Italia).

Corporate consolidation was so concentrated by 1990 that it has been observed that "four men could determine what information Italians were privy to"—Agnelli, De Benedetti, Gardini, and Berlusconi.[22] Through his advertising company, Publitalia, and the ownership and control of Italian media assets through Fininvest, Berlusconi had positioned himself as a major force in Italian public life. In response to consolidation, both Parliament and the courts moved to place restrictions of cross-media ownership.

Italian Mass Media in the Berlusconi Era

In 1992, Parliament passed legislation granting national broadcast rights to the three RAI channels, Berlusconi's three Fininvest channels, and three additional channels, Telemontecarlo, Videomusic, and Rete A, providing formal confirmation to the newly emerging mixed public-private system. This system was called duopoly, because the state controlled RAI while Berlusconi controlled private broadcasting. Meanwhile, as RAI adjusted to compete with the entertainment and commercial sponsorship of the Fininvest channels, it lost its uniqueness and its dominance of news broadcasting. By 1993, RAI held 48 percent of the "prime time" audience, while Berlusconi's channels drew 44 percent.[23]

With the breakdown of the old party system in the early 1990s, the PCI's successor, the PDS (*Partito Democratico della Sinistra,* or Democratic Party of the Left), threatened new regulation of media ownership. Determined to protect his own interests and sensing a political opening, Berlusconi created a new political organization, *Forza Italia,* and mobilized his extensive advertising and communication empire in a campaign for prime minister. Once elected, Berlusconi could control RAI, giving him almost total command of

Italian television (Telemontecarlo remained independent) and televison advertising, significant control over the weekly magazine industry, and part ownership of one of the two major daily newspapers. In spite of avowing to divest himself of his media holdings and sell them to Australian media tycoon Rupert Murdoch, Berlusconi has not done so and, in fact, has used them repeatedly to his political advantage.[24]

Beyond the realm of Berlusconi's media empire, although there are no cable channels, several pay-per-view channels (Tele+1 and Tele+2) are available from Mediaset. Political parties continue to publish newspapers that shape members' opinions, most prominently the DC's *Il Popolo,* the PSI's *Avanti!,* the PCI's *L'Unità* (which at the height of the Cold War counted a circulation of 500,000). The Vatican publishes its *L'Osservatore Romano.* Other "fringe" publications existed, particularly on the left, including *Lotta continua,* which attempted to reach those alienated from the mainstream press. Radio stations, which originally responded to television by providing alternative programming, eventually settled into a pattern of providing news, talk, and music targeted at a youthful audience. Local commercial stations abound, while RAI maintains five national stations: Radiouno, Radiodue, Radiotre, Stereo RAI, and Radio Verde RAI. This formula provided radio a space in the rapidly developing world of media, but one in which its advertising revenues—along with those of the newspapers—diminished sharply in a culture whose people watch more hours of television programming than any other in Europe. Television has now established itself as the primary news source, while the print media struggle to compete, having allowed television to set their agenda. On the other hand, by the mid-1990s, Italian radio enjoyed a resurgence, adding about 1 million new listeners per year. One survey showed that each day 35 million Italians listened to radio.[25]

Criticism of the state of Italian television mounted with the Tangentopoli scandals and the subsequent collapse of the political parties in the early 1990s. Fairness in the reporting and analysis of public affairs (known as *par condicio*) remains a topic of continuing debate between the two prevailing political groups, and criticism of Berlusconi's pervasive control of media resources remains an issue, fueled by repeated conflict-of-interest charges and Berlusconi's own condemnation of his critics and his apparently imperious treatment of his own employees. Numerous proposals for antitrust legislation and attempts to impose some norms to assure fair coverage of politics have failed. Given the importance of the electronic media in the political arena, a vague tradition of regulation, and Berlusconi's dominance of both the television industry and the political system, structural changes do not appear imminent. However, Berlusconi's hold on power is tenuous. His support for the U.S. war in Iraq has proven unpopular and he has not been able to deliver on his promised economic reforms. An ongoing dispute between his two principal coalition partners, the *Alleanza Nazionale* and the Lega Nord, threaten to bring down his government. If the center-left opposition can organize effectively—apparently behind European Union president and former prime minister Romano Prodi—it may not only return to power but may also develop the impetus to restructure Italian media in a more rational way. At the same time, it may be more realistic to understand the changes that have accompanied the mounting corporate influence in the Italian media as merely symptomatic of global trends toward consolidation and the subjection of media to market forces.[26]

NOTES

1. Christopher Wagstaff, "Cinema," in *Italian Cultural Studies,* ed. David Forgacs and Robert Lumley (New York: Oxford University Press, 1996), 216.

2. Peter Bondanella, "Italian Cinema," in *The Cambridge Companion to Modern Italian Culture,* ed. Zygmunt Barański and Rebecca J. West (Cambridge: Cambridge University Press, 2001), 215; Wagstaff, "Cinema," 219–23.

3. Wagstaff, "Cinema," 220.

4. Millicent Marcus, *After Fellini* (Baltimore, Md.: Johns Hopkins University Press, 2002), 10.

5. Bondanella, "Italian Cinema," 228–29; Wagstaff, "Cinema," 224.

6. Wagstaff, "Cinema," 224.

7. Marcus, *After Fellini,* 3.

8. Massimo Riva, "Old Masters, New Trends: Contemporary Italian Cinema in the Light of Neo-Realism," in *Journal of Modern Italian Studies* 8, no. 2 (Summer 2003): 285.

9. Bondanella, "Italian Cinema," 239.

10. Riva, "Old Masters, New Trends," 291–92, citing Pierre Sorlin, *Italian National Cinema, 1896–1996* (London: Routledge, 1996).

11. Marcus, *After Fellini,* 3 (quoting Daniel Singer).

12. Marcus, *After Fellini,* 7 (quoting Lino Miccichè); Wagstaff, "Cinema," 228; Riva, "Old Masters, New Trends," 294.

13. Riva, "Old Masters, New Trends," 285, 292; Marcus, *After Fellini,* 11, 199–213.

14. Marcus, *After Fellini,* 284.

15. Robert Lumley, "Peculiarities of the Italian Newspaper," in *Italian Cultural Studies,* ed. David Forgacs and Robert Lumley (New York: Oxford University Press, 1996), 199–207; Lumley, "Newspapers," in *Encyclopedia of Contemporary Italian Culture,* ed. Gino Moliterno (London: Routledge, 2000), 402; Audrey Parnell, "The Press in Postwar Italy," in *European Insights: Postwar Politics, Society, and Culture* (Amsterdam: North-Holland, 1991), 200–201.

16. Jan Kurz and Gino Moliterno, "Radio," in *Encyclopedia of Contemporary Italian Culture,* ed. Gino Moliterno (London: Routledge, 2000), 489–90; Christopher Wagstaff, "The Media" in *The Cambridge Companion to Modern Italian Culture,* ed. Zygmunt Barański and Rebecca J. West (Cambridge: Cambridge University Press, 2001), 305.

17. Elena Dagrada, "Television and its Critics: A Parallel History," in *Italian Cultural Studies,* ed. David Forgacs and Robert Lumley (New York: Oxford University Press, 1996), 234; Wagstaff, "The Media," 293–94.

18. Marcus, *After Fellini,* 4–9.

19. Kurz and Moliterno, "Radio," 490.

20. Parnell, "The Press in Postwar Italy," 206–10; Lumley, "Peculiarities of the Italian Newspaper," 210.

21. "RAI Lottizzazione: Giornalisti," *Panorama,* September 15, 1991, 52; Wagstaff, "The Media," 299–300; Paul Statham, "Broadcasting," in *Encyclopedia of Contemporary Italian Culture,* ed. Gino Moliterno (London: Routledge, 2000), 76.

22. Wagstaff, "The Media," 305.

23. Statham, "Broadcasting" and "RAI," in *Encyclopedia of Contemporary Italian Culture,* ed. Gino Moliterno (London: Routledge, 2000), 76–77, 494; Dagrada, "Television and its Critics," 243–46; Parnell, "The Press in Postwar Italy," 207–8.

24. Statham, "RAI," 494.

25. Lumley, "Peculiarities of the Italian Newspaper," 199–211; Statham, "Broadcasting," 76; Wagstaff, "The Media," 294, 303–9; "Radio" in *Encyclopedia of Contemporary Italian Culture,* ed. Gino Moliterno (London: Routledge, 2000), 492.

26. Lumley, "Peculiarities of the Italian Newspaper," 211; "Berlusconi Burlesque," *The Economist,* October 11, 2003; "The Opposition Finds Its Man," *The Economist,* November 15, 2003; "Former Fascists Seek Respectability," *The Economist,* December 6, 2003; "Berlusconi Rebuffed," *The Economist,* January 17, 2004; "It's a Riot," "The Re-Entry Man," "Berlusconi's Desperate Gamble," *The Economist,* April 3, 2004; "Prodi's Problem," *The Economist,* June 19, 2004; "Berlusconi Risks His Bacon," *The Economist,* July 10, 2004.

Glossary

AC Milan   One of Italy's most successful soccer teams, purchased by media mogul Silvio Berlusconi in 1986.

Alleanza Nazionale   Heir to the neo-fascist MSI, a political party that has achieved influence under the leadership of vice-prime minister Gianfranco Fini.

"Anni di piombo" (Years of Lead)   Extended wave of violence carried out by both left- and right-wing extremist factions during the 1970s.

Anniversario della liberazione   June 2, the day Italians celebrate the founding of the Republic in 1946.

APAO (Association for Organic Architecture)   Roman firm founded in 1945 by Bruno Zevi, a protégé of the American architect Frank Lloyd Wright, that applied Wright's organic concepts to the demands of postwar construction.

Archizoom   Florentine design studio, led by Andrea Branzi, who repudiated the popular trend toward functional architecture in favor of a new aesthetic derived from symbolism and allegory and executed with natural materials.

Arcigay   Dominant Italian gay liberation and advocacy organization.

Arte povera (poor art)   Movement that began with a 1967 exhibition curated by Germano Celant in Genoa, characterized by subjective expressions, often incorporating ordinary and found objects, often crudely executed.

Avant garde movement   The movement among writers, visual artists, and filmmakers of the late 1950s and 1960s that boldly manipulated language, time, and space. Prominent were Umberto Eco, Pier Paolo Pasolini, Elio Vittorini, and Michelangelo Antonioni.

The "Azzurri"   The Italian national soccer team, so named because of their blue uniforms.

BBPR   Renowned Milanese architectural firm of Ludovico Barbiano di Belgioioso, Enrico Peressutti, Ernesto Nathan Rogers, and Giuliano Banfi that created some of the most notable postwar structures in Italy.

"Il bello scrivere" (beautiful writing)   Standard in Italian newspaper writing, sometimes blamed for long sentences and extravagant prose.

Calcio   Soccer, Italy's favorite sport.

Calcio Storico Fiorentino   Annual historical Florentine football match, which resembles rugby more than soccer, and features teams from four quarters of the city.

Campanilismo   Intense pride in the bell tower, or *campanile,* of one's town.

Carabinieri   National police force.

Carnevale   Annual festival preceding the Lenten season that features costumes, masked balls, parades, and feasts, most notably in Venice.

Centro Culturale Virginia Woolf   An important feminist cultural center located in Rome.

Cinecittà (Cinema City)   Film studio complex built by the Fascist regime, an important training ground for Italians who directed films in the postwar era.

Cinquecento ("Topolino")   Small Fiat 500 automobile that became enormously popular in the postwar era.

Clientelism   System of client-patron relationships that has traditionally influenced Italian politics.

Colletivi (collectives)   Experimental theater groups founded in the 1960s that were committed to dramatizing political and social issues, known for an ensemble approach, dialect and vernacular language, innovation, and spontaneity.

Commedia dell'Arte   Popular Italian theater of the sixteenth and early seventeenth centuries that featured stock characters such as *I dottori* (the doctors), *Il notaio* (the notary public), and *Pulcinella* (the "Punch" character of the "Punch and Judy" puppet show).

La cucina di casa (la cucina casalinga)   Home cooking.

Danza libera (free dance)   Like "New dance," a modern alternative to ballet that began in the 1920s and continued with such groups as the *Teatrodanza Contemporanea di Roma* (Contemporary Dance Theater of Rome).

DC (Christian Democratic Party)   Roman Catholic political party that dominated Italian political power through various arrangements for a half century after the creation of the Republic.

Ferragosto   Most important Italian summer holiday, celebrated in mid-August, a time when Italians flee en masse from the cities to the shores and the mountains.

Festa di San Giuseppe (St. Joseph's Festival)   Traditional festival that provides an interlude in the Lenten season of fasting.

Feste   Festivals of various types, including saints' days, celebrations of the harvest, and civic feasts.

Fiat   The largest private company in Italy, this automotive conglomerate has been in business for more than one hundred years and is owned by the Agnelli family of Turin and now controlled by Ferrari's Luca Cordero di Montezemolo.

Forza Italia!   Political movement founded by Silvio Berlusconi (and a standard cheer, "Go Italy!" for the national football team).

Fronte nuovo delle arti (New Front of the Arts)   Group organized after World War II by Italian artists, featuring Renato Guttuso, who had opposed Fascism.

Fuori (Fronte Unitario Omosessuale Rivoluzionario Italiano)   Italy's first gay liberation movement.

Futurists   Group of early twentieth-century Italian writers, artists, and intellectuals who forcefully rejected tradition, especially humanist values, while exalting the aesthetic of the machine and glorifying conflict and combat.

Giro d'Italia   Italy's major bicycle race, second in importance only to the *Tour de France.*

Gondolieri   Gondola captains, regularly visible in Venice and most notable in the fall festival known as *La Regata Storica* (the historical boat race).

Gruppo 63   Movement of experimental writers (including Umberto Eco), musicians, and painters committed to a radical critique of society and experimentation with language and structure.

Lega Nord (Northern League)   Political organization led by Umberto Bossi that has built a strong political base by campaigning against the South as a region characterized by political corruption and criminal activity.

Lyric opera   The grand, romantic style of opera popularized in Italy in the mid and late-19th century, most successfully in the compositions of Giovanni Verdi.

Mafia   Criminal organizations that, along with the *camorra* and *'ndrangheta,* developed from a rural movement opposed to landlords, then shifted its operations to urban and suburban development by controlling labor and construction contracts, and finally expanded into a wide range of international crime, including narcotics, arms trafficking, money laundering, and finance.

Maggio Musicale   Florentine music festival, one of the most important in Italy.

Malocchio   Evil eye. Superstitious belief that some persons cast a curse by looking at a victim.

"*Mammismo*"   Excessive reliance on mothers' protection of adult males based on the reluctance of adult males to leave the nurturing environment of the matriarchal home.

Memphis group   Milanese design firm featuring Ettore Sottsass and Michele de Lucchi that re-established Milan and Italy at the forefront of innovative design in the 1980s.

Natale   Christmas.

Neorealismo (neorealism)   Movement in Italian arts—especially literature and cinema—that returned to realism for inspiration, focusing on the lives of ordinary people to portray the heroic struggles of Italians against the brutality of Fascism and war.

Opera buffa (comic opera)   Light, humorous form of opera, popular in the eighteenth century, in which the spoken word was interspersed with song.

Osso bucco   Veal shin bone with the marrow inside, cooked slowly in wine, stock, onions, and tomatoes and served on rice; a favorite Milanese dish.

Palio delle Contrade   One of Italy's most renowned and picturesque festivals, a horse race dating from the thirteenth century, celebrated twice annually in the Piazza del Campo in Siena.

Parmigiano Reggiano   Italy's most renowned cheese, a buttery, granular, aged variety that is produced in the provinces of Parma, Reggio Emilia, Modena, Bologna, and Mantova.

Pasqua   Easter Sunday.

PCI (Italian Communist Party)   Party of European communism (Eurocommunism) that provided the main opposition to the DC in the half century after the creation of the Republic.

***Peplum* films**   Set in some unidentified "classical" era with mythical heroes and voluptuous heroines who prevailed against overwhelming odds, these films offered gratuitous violence, appealed largely to male audiences, imported American actors such as muscleman Steve Reeves, and brought in substantial profits at the box office.

Piccolo Teatro   Famous "Little Theater" founded in Milan by Giorgio Strehler and Paolo Grassi in 1947 with the commitment to provide drama that would appeal to all social classes while addressing serious issues.

Il Politecnico   Created in 1945 by Elio Vittorini, *Il Politecnico* was the most influential Marxist review of the era, ranging widely from literature and art to politics and sociology.

Primo Maggio   May Day, a traditional Italian holiday.

Prosciutto di Parma   Most famous Italian cured ham.

PSI (Italian Socialist Party)   Partner in many Christian Democratic (DC) governments during the years of DC dominance, the PSI was discredited in the Tangentopoli scandals and lost its political influence as a result.

RAI (Radiotelevisione Italiana)   Originally known as *Radio Audizioni Italia,* the state-owned and operated media company was originally granted a monopoly (expired in 1972) but now must compete with commercial stations; it now consists of three television and four radio stations.

La Resistenza (the Resistance Movement)   Successful Italian resistance (1943–45) to German occupation by Italian partisans who overthrew the remnants of the Fascist state and gained important cultural and political influence in the aftermath of World War II.

Risorgimento ("resurgence" or "rebirth")   Nineteenth-century movement for Italian unification that culminated in the acquisition of Rome in 1870. Italy unified through military and diplomatic means primarily at the expense of Austria, the Neapolitan Bourbons, and the papacy.

Risotto alla milanese   Rice with saffron slowly simmered with butter, onions, wine, and stock, a favorite dish in Lombardia.

Sagre   Festivals that originated as ancient pagan rituals and continue to be celebrated with spring and summer harvests.

Scuderia Ferrari (team Ferrari)   Italy's Formula One racing enterprise, founded by the legendary Enzo Ferrari and most recently led to a series of constructor's championships by German-born driver Michael Schumacher.

"Spaghetti westerns"   Genre of Italian film made famous by Sergio Leone—*Un pugno di dollari (A Fistful of Dollars)* was the most successful of more than 400—launching the film career of the young Clint Eastwood and reinventing the struggling Hollywood western.

Spoleto Festival dei Due Mondi (Spoleto Festival of Two Worlds) Founded by Giancarlo Menotti in 1958, the festival has developed a reputation for featuring artists from around the world who have incorporated contemporary forms of music and dance alongside the classical.

Stabili Experimental, publicly-funded little theaters that emerged in the period after World War II, especially notable in Genoa and Milan.

Tangentopoli ("kickback city" or "bribesville") Scandals of the early 1990s that rocked the political system when news spread that hundreds of party leaders and businessmen had been arrested on charges of bribery.

Tifosi Italy's "feverish" fans, known especially for their enthusiasm at Formula One auto races.

Transavanguardia (transavantgarde) Movement to resurrect figurative art that emerged at the 1980 Venice Biennale and set the tone for the '80s, including artists Francesco Clemente, Mimmo Paladino, Emilio Cucchi, and Sandro Chia.

ultràs Fanatical soccer fans.

Unione Donne Italiane (Italian Women's Union or UDI) A group, dominated by communist women, that acted as the precursor of the Italian feminist movement.

Bibliography

Allum, Percy. "Catholicism." In *The Cambridge Companion to Modern Italian Culture,* ed. Zygmunt Barański and Rebecca J. West. Cambridge: Cambridge University Press, 2001.

Allum, Percy. "Italian Society Transformed." In *Italy Since 1945,* ed. Patrick McCarthy. New York: Oxford University Press, 2000.

Andrews, Richard. "Theatre." In *The Cambridge History of Italian Literature,* ed. Peter Brand and Lino Pertile. Cambridge: Cambridge University Press, 1999.

Aust, Derek, with Mike Zollo. *Italian Language, Life and Culture.* London: Hodder and Stoughton, 2000.

Barański, Zygmunt, and Rebecca J. West, eds. *The Cambridge Companion to Modern Italian Culture.* Cambridge: Cambridge University Press, 2001.

Barolini, Helen. *Festa.* New York: Harcourt Brace Jovanovich, 1988.

"Berlusconi Burlesque." *The Economist,* October 11, 2003.

"Berlusconi Rebuffed." *The Economist,* January 17, 2004.

"Berlusconi Risks His Bacon." *The Economist,* July 10, 2004.

"Berlusconi's Desperate Gamble." *The Economist,* April 3, 2004.

Birnbaum, Lucia Chiavola. *Liberazione della donna, Feminism in Italy.* Middletown, Conn.: Wesleyan University Press, 1986.

Bobbio, Norberto. *Ideological Profile of Twentieth-Century Italy.* Princeton, N.J.: Princeton University Press, 1995.

Bondanella, Peter. "Italian Cinema." In *The Cambridge Companion to Modern Italian Culture,* ed. Zygmunt Barański and Rebecca J. West. Cambridge: Cambridge University Press, 2001.

———. *Umberto Eco and the Open Text.* Cambridge: Cambridge University Press, 1997.

Borradori, Giovanna, ed. "Introduction." In *Recoding Metaphysics: The New Italian Philosophy.* Evanston, Ill.: Northwestern University Press, 1988.

Brand, Peter, and Lino Pertile, eds. *The Cambridge History of Italian Literature.* Cambridge: Cambridge University Press, 1999.

Branzi, Andrea. "Italian Design and the Complexity of Modernity." In *The Italian Metamorphosis, 1943–1968,* ed. Germano Celant New York: Guggenheim Museum Publications, 1994.

Brown, Adam, and Andy Walsh. "Football Supporters' Relations with Their Clubs: A European Perspective." *Soccer & Society* 1, no. 3 (Autumn 2000): 88–94.

Caesar, Michael. "Contemporary Italy (since 1956)." In *The Cambridge History of Italian Literature,* ed. Peter Brand and Lino Pertile. Cambridge: Cambridge University Press, 1999.

Capatti, Alberto, and Massimo Montanari. *Italian Cuisine: A Cultural History.* Trans. Aine O'Healy. New York: Columbia University Press, 1999.

Carrera, Alessandro. "Folk music and popular song from the nineteenth century to the 1990s." In *The Cambridge Companion to Modern Italian Culture,* ed. Zygmunt Barański and Rebecca J. West. Cambridge: Cambridge University Press, 2001.

Celant, Germano, ed. *The Italian Metamorphosis, 1943–1968.* New York: Solomon R. Guggenheim Museum, 1994.

Clark, Martin. *Modern Italy, 1871–1982.* London: Longman Group, Ltd., 1984.

Croce, Benedetto. *Estetica come scienza dell'espressione e linguistica generale: Teoria e storia.* Milan: Sandron, 1902.

———. *Materialismo storico ed economia marxistica.* Milan: Sandron, 1900.

———. *Saggio sullo Hegel seguito da altri scritti di storia della filosofia.* Bari: Laterza, 1906.

———. *Storia della storiografia italiana nel secolo decimonono.* Bari: Laterza, 1921.

———. *Storia d'Europa nel secolo decimonono.* Bari: Laterza, 1932.

———. *Storia d'Italia dal 1871 al 1915.* Bari: Laterza, 1928.

———. *Teoria e storia della storiografia.* Bari: Laterza, 1917.

———. *That Which Is Living and That Which Is Dead in the Philosophy of Hegel* (1907). Trans. Douglas Ainslie. London: Macmillan, 1915.

———. *The Philosophy of Giambattista Vico.* Trans. R. G. Collingwood. London: Howard Latimar, Limited, 1913.

Dagrada, Elena. "Television and its Critics: A Parallel History." In *Italian Cultural Studies,* ed. David Forgacs and Robert Lumley. New York: Oxford University Press, 1996.

de Biasi, Rocco. Review of *La partita di calcio,* by Christian Bromberger. *Journal of Modern Italian Studies* 5, no. 3 (Fall 2000): 415–17.

De Felice, Renzo. *Mussolini.* 8 vols. Turin; Einaudi, 1965–98.

De Grazia, Victoria. *How Fascism Ruled Women: Italy, 1922–1945.* Berkeley: University of California Press, 1992.

De Mauro, Tullio. "Linguistic Variety and Linguistic Minorities." In *Italian Cultural Studies,* ed. David Forgacs and Robert Lumley. New York: Oxford University Press, 1996.

D'Epiro, Peter, and Mary Desmond Pinkowish. *Sprezzatura*. New York: Random House, Inc., 2001.

Di Scala, Spencer. *Italy From Revolution to Republic*. 3rd ed. Boulder, Colo.: Westview Press, 2004.

Dogliani, Patrizia. "Sport and Fascism." *Journal of Modern Italian Studies* 5, no. 3 (Fall 2000): 327–43.

Dombroski, Robert. "The Rise and Fall of Fascism (1910–45)." In *The Cambridge History of Italian Literature*. Ed. Peter Brand and Lino Pertile. Cambridge: Cambridge University Press, 1999.

Domenico, Roy. *The Regions of Italy*. Westport, Conn.: Greenwood Press, 2002.

Dourdan, Dennis. "Rebuilding the House of Man." In *The Italian Metamorphosis, 1943–1968,* ed. Germano Celant. New York: Solomon R. Guggenheim Museum, 1994.

Eco, Umberto. "*Intentio Lectoris:* The State of the Art." In *Recoding Metaphysics: The New Italian Philosophy,* ed. Giovanna Borradori. Evanston, Ill.: Northwestern University Press, 1988.

———. *The Role of the Reader: Explorations in the Semiotics of Texts (Advances in Semiotics)*. Bloomington: Indiana University Press, 1979.

Farrell, Joseph. *Leonardo Sciascia*. Edinburgh: Edinburgh University Press, 1995.

Field, Carol. *Celebrating Italy*. New York: HarperCollins Publishers, 1997.

Filippa, Marcella. "Popular Song and Musical Cultures." In *Italian Cultural Studies,* ed. David Forgacs and Robert Lumley. New York: Oxford University Press, 1996.

Finn, Gerry P. T., and Richard Giulianotti. *Football Culture*. London: Frank Cass, 2000.

Fleishman, Jeffrey. "Italians Fight U.S. Use of Death Penalty." *Philadelphia Inquirer,* August 20, 2000.

Forgacs, David, and Robert Lumley, eds. *Italian Cultural Studies*. New York: Oxford University Press, 1996.

"Former Fascists Seek Respectability." *The Economist,* December 6, 2003.

Fremantle, Ann. *The Papal Encyclicals in Their Historical Context*. New York: Mentor Books, 1956.

Garelli, Franco. "Destra cattolica or cattolici di destra?" *Il Mulino* 44, no. 358 (March–April 1995): 252–65.

Gatt-Rutter, John. "The Aftermath of the Second World War (1945–56)." In *The Cambridge History of Italian Literature,* ed. Peter Brand and Lino Pertile. Cambridge: Cambridge University Press, 1999.

Gianola, Rinaldo. "Design and Fashion: Driving Forces of Italy." In *1951–2001: Made in Italy?* by Luigi Settembrini. Milan: Skira International Corporation, 2001.

Gibson, Mary. "New Perspectives on Italian Women's History." *Journal of Women's History* 8, no. 2 (summer 1994): 169–80.

———. *A History of Contemporary Italy: Society and Politics, 1943–1988*. London: Penguin Books, 1990.

Ginsborg, Paul. *Italy and Its Discontents*. New York: Palgrave Macmillan, 2003.

Giusti, Eugenio. "Gay Movement." In *Encyclopedia of Contemporary Italian Culture,* ed. Gino Moliterno. London: Routledge, 2000.

"Gli stranieri regolarmente presenti in Italia." http://www.istat.it.

Gordon, Robert S. C. "*Impegno* and Modernity: 'High' Culture." In *Italy Since 1945,* ed. Patrick McCarthy. New York: Oxford University Press, 2000.

Gramsci, Antonio. *Quaderni del carcere.* Turin: Einaudi, 1948–51.

Hazan, Marcella. *The Classic Italian Cookbook.* New York: Alfred A. Knopf, 1993.

Heller, Richard. "Big Kick." *Forbes,* July 8, 2002.

Henken, Andrey. "Trumpeter Enrico Rava." http://www.allaboutjazz.com/php/article.php?id=1003.

Hindley, Geoffrey, ed. *The Larousse Encyclopedia of Music.* New York: Excalibur Books, 1981.

Howard, Judith Jeffrey. "The Civil Code of 1865 and the Origins of the Feminist Movement in Italy. In *The Italian Immigrant Woman in North America,* ed. Betty Boyd Caroli, Robert F. Harney, and Lydio F. Tomasi. Toronto: The Multicultural History Society of Ontario, 1977.

Hughes, H. Stuart. *Consciousness and Society.* New York: Alfred A. Knopf, 1958.

"Italians Embrace Modern Dance." *Toronto Star,* December 17, 1990.

"It's a Riot." *The Economist,* April 3, 2004.

"John Paul Makes First Papal Address to Italy's Parliament." *The New York Times,* November 15, 2002.

Keller, Marcello Sorce. "Popular Music in the Early Twentieth Century." In *The Garland Encyclopedia of Music,* Vol. 8, *Europe,* ed. Timothy Rice, James Porter, and Chris Goertzen. New York: Garland Publishing, 2000.

Kersey, John. "Bocelli." In *Encyclopedia of Contemporary Italian Culture,* ed. Gino Moliterno. London: Routledge, 2000.

Kimball, David. "Opera since 1800." In *The Cambridge History of Italian Literature,* ed. Peter Brand and Lino Pertile. Cambridge: Cambridge University Press, 1999.

Kostich, Gordana. "Michelucci." In *Encyclopedia of Contemporary Italian Culture,* ed. Gino Moliterno. London: Routledge, 2000.

———. "Quaroni." In *Encyclopedia of Contemporary Italian Culture,* ed. Gino Moliterno. London: Routledge, 2000.

Kurz, Jan, and Gino Moliterno. "Radio." In *Encyclopedia of Contemporary Italian Culture,* ed. Gino Moliterno. London: Routledge, 2000.

Lepschy, Anna Laura. *The Italian Language Today.* 2nd ed. London: Routledge, 1992.

Livorni, Ernesto. "Montale." In *Encyclopedia of Contemporary Italian Culture,* ed. Gino Moliterno. London: Routledge, 2000.

Luciano, Bernadette. "Bene." In *Encyclopedia of Contemporary Italian Culture,* ed. Gino Moliterno. London: Routledge, 2000.

Lumley, Robert. "Newspapers." In *Encyclopedia of Contemporary Italian Culture,* ed. Gino Moliterno. London: Routledge, 2000.

———. "Peculiarities of the Italian Newspaper." In *Italian Cultural Studies,* ed. David Forgacs and Robert Lumley. New York: Oxford University Press, 1996.

Mancini, Albert N. "Narrative Prose and Theatre." In *The Cambridge History of Italian Literature,* ed. Peter Brand and Lino Pertile. Cambridge: Cambridge University Press, 1999.

"Marco Pantani." *The Economist,* February 28, 2004.

Marcus, Millicent. *After Fellini.* Baltimore, Md.: Johns Hopkins University Press, 2002.

Margry, Peter Jan. "Merchandising and Sanctity: The Invasive Cult of Padre Pio," *Journal of Modern Italian Studies* 7, no. 1 (Spring 2002): 88–115.

McCarthy, Patrick, ed. "The Church in Post-war Italy." In *Italy Since 1945.* New York: Oxford University Press, 2000.

———. "*Forza Italia:* Old Problems Linger On." In *Italian Politics,* ed. Roberto D'Alimonte and David Nelkan. Boulder, Colo.: Westview Press, 1997.

———. *Italy Since 1945.* New York: Oxford University Press, 2000.

———. "Sport and Society in Italy Today." *Journal of Modern Italian Studies* 5, no. 3 (Fall 2000): 322–411.

Mieli, Mario. *Homosexuality and Liberation: Elements of a Gay Critique.* Trans. David Fernbach. London: Gay Men's Press, 1980.

Mudge, Lewis S. "*Veritatis Splendor* and Today's Ecumenical Conversation." *The Ecumenical Review* 48, no. 2 (April 1996): 158–62.

Noble, Kate. "No Money, No Kickoff." *Time* (Europe), September 2, 2002, p. 104.

Nordlinger, Jay. "Farewell, Fat Man." *National Review,* April 5, 2004.

"The Opposition Finds Its Man." *The Economist,* November 15, 2003.

Ortiz, Javier Antonio Quiñones. "Giovanni Tommaso," *All About Jazz.* http://www.allaboutjazz.com/iviews/gtommaso.htm.

Pace, Enzo. *L'unita dei cattolici in Italia.* Milan: Editore Guerini Associati, 1995.

"Paolo Grassi." *The New York Times,* March 15, 1981.

Parmeggianni, Francesca. "Gadda." In *Encyclopedia of Contemporary Italian Culture,* ed. Gino Moliterno. London: Routledge, 2000.

Parnell, Audrey. "The Press in Postwar Italy." In *European Insights: Postwar Politics, Society, and Culture.* Amsterdam: North-Holland, 1991.

Passerini, Luisa. "Gender Relations." In *Italian Cultural Studies,* ed. David Forgacs and Robert Lumley. New York: Oxford University Press, 1996.

Patriarca, Silvana. "Gender Trouble: Women and the Making of Italy's 'Active Population,' 1861–1936." *Journal of Modern Italian Studies* 3, no. 2 (Summer 1998): 144–63.

Paulicelli, Eugenia. "Fashion: Narration and Nation." In *The Cambridge Companion to Modern Italian Culture,* ed. Zygmunt Barański and Rebecca J. West. Cambridge: Cambridge University Press, 2001.

Pintor, Giame. "L'Ultima lettera" (November 28, 1943). Quoted in *Ideological Profile of Twentieth-Century Italy,* by Norberto Bobbio. Princeton, N.J.: Princeton University Press, 1995.

Pitkin, Donald. *The House That Giacomo Built.* Cambridge: Cambridge University Press, 1985.

Podiliri, C., and C. Balestri. "The *Ultras,* Racism and Football Culture in Italy." In *Fanatics!,* ed. Adam Brown. London: Routledge, 1998.

Poesio, Giannandrea. "The Cinderella of the Arts." In *Europe Dancing,* ed. Andrée Grau and Stephanie Jordan. London: Routledge, 2000.

Poli, Emanuela. "Italian Media and Telecommunications Authority." *Journal of Modern Italian Studies* 5, no. 3 (Fall 2000): 371–93.

Ponti, Gio. "Italy's Bid on the World Market." *Interiors,* February, 1953.

"Pope Asks Jews for Forgiveness at Wailing Wall." *The Independent* (London), March 27, 2000.

"Pope Beatifies Monk Persecuted by Church." *The Independent* (London), May 3, 1999.

"Pope Brings Anti-Mafia Message to Sicily." *Chicago Sun-Times,* November 23, 1995.

Porro, Nicola. "Italian Sports: Between Government and Society." In *National Sports Policies,* ed. Laurence Chalip, Arthur Johnson, and Lisa Stachura. Westport, Conn.: Greenwood Press, 1996.

Porro, Nicola, and Pippo Russo. "Berlusconi and Other Matters: The Era of Football-Politics." *Journal of Modern Italian Studies* 5, no. 3 (Fall 2000): 348–71.

"Prodi's Problem." *The Economist,* June 19, 2004.

Prosperi, Mario. "Contemporary Italian Theatre." *The Drama Review* 22, no. 1 (1978): 17–26.

"A Quiet Entrance by Italian Companies." *The New York Times,* October 15, 2003.

"The Re-Entry Man." *The Economist,* April 3, 2004.

Reilly, Saskia. "Rap, Funk and Politics Italian-Style." *Europe* (June 2000): 34.

Rendell, Matt. "The Long, Lonely Road to Oblivion." *The Observer,* March 7, 2004.

Richards, Charles. *The New Italians.* London: Penguin Books, 1995.

Richardson, Brian. "Questions of Language." In *The Cambridge Companion to Modern Italian Culture,* ed. Zygmunt Barański and Rebecca J. West. Cambridge: Cambridge University Press, 2001.

Riedel, Stephen. "Gay Writing." In *Encyclopedia of Contemporary Italian Culture,* ed. Gino Moliterno. London: Routledge, 2000.

Riva, Massimo. "Old Masters, New Trends: Contemporary Italian Cinema in the Light of Neo-Realism." *Journal of Modern Italian Studies* 8, no. 2 (Summer 2003): 284–98.

Roberts, David D. *Benedetto Croce and the Uses of Historicism.* Berkeley: University of California Press, 1987.

―――. "Maggi's Croce, Sasso's Gentile and the riddles of twentieth-century intellectual history." *Journal of Modern Italian Studies* 7, no. 1 (Spring 2002): 116–44.

Root, Waverley. *The Food of Italy.* New York: Vintage Books, 1992.

"Roy Hargrove Quintet + The Roberta Gambarini Quartet Town Hall." All About Jazz. http://www.allaboutjazz.com/php/news.php?id=3315.

"Saints before soaps on Italian TV." http://news.bbc.co.uk/1/hi/world/europe/2814287.stm.

Salvadori, Massimo L. "Foreword." In *Ideological Profile of Twentieth-Century Italy,* by Norberto Bobbio. Princeton, N.J.: Princeton University Press, 1995.

Sassatelli, Roberta. "The Commercialization of Discipline: Keep-Fit Culture and its Values." *Journal of Modern Italian Studies* 5, no. 3 (Fall 2000): 396–411.

Sassoon, Donald. *Contemporary Italy.* 2nd ed. New York: Addison Wesley Longman, 1997.

Scabini, Eugenia, and Vittorio Cigoli. "Young Adult Families." *Journal of Family Issues* 18, no. 6 (November 1997): 608–26.

Sciorra, Joseph. "Hip Hop from Italy and the Diaspora: A Report from the 41st Parallel." *Altreitalie* 24 (January–June 2002): 86–104.

Severino, Emanuele. "The Earth and the Essence of Man." In *Recoding Metaphysics: The New Italian Philosophy,* ed. Giovanna Borradori. Evanston, Ill.: Northwestern University Press, 1988.

Sgritta, Giovanni B. "The Italian Family: Tradition and Change." *Journal of Family Issues* 9, no. 3 (September 1988): 372–96.

Slaughter, Jane. *Women and the Italian Resistance, 1943–1945.* Denver, Colo.: Arden Press, 1997.

Sorlin, Pierre. *Italian National Cinema, 1896–1996.* London: Routledge, 1996.

Sparke, Penny. "Design in Italy since 1866." In *The Cambridge Companion to Modern Italian Culture,* ed. Zygmunt Barański and Rebecca J. West. Cambridge: Cambridge University Press, 2001.

Staples, Max. "Chia." In *Encyclopedia of Contemporary Italian Culture,* ed. Gino Moliterno. London: Routledge, 2000.

———. "Clemente." In *Encyclopedia of Contemporary Italian Culture,* ed. Gino Moliterno. London: Routledge, 2000.

———. "Colla." In *Encyclopedia of Contemporary Italian Culture,* ed. Gino Moliterno. London: Routledge, 2000.

———. "Cucchi." In *Encyclopedia of Contemporary Italian Culture,* ed. Gino Moliterno. London: Routledge, 2000.

———. "Paladino." In *Encyclopedia of Contemporary Italian Culture,* ed. Gino Moliterno. London: Routledge, 2000.

———. "Transavantgarde." In *Encyclopedia of Contemporary Italian Culture,* ed. Gino Moliterno. London: Routledge, 2000.

Statham, Paul. "Broadcasting." In *Encyclopedia of Contemporary Italian Culture,* ed. Gino Moliterno. London: Routledge, 2000.

———. "RAI." In *Encyclopedia of Contemporary Italian Culture,* ed. Gino Moliterno. London: Routledge, 2000.

Steele, Valerie. *Fifty Years of Fashion.* New Haven: Yale University Press, Conn., 1997.

———. "Italian Fashion and America." In *The Italian Metamorphosis,* ed. Germano Celant. New York: Solomon R. Guggenheim Museum, 1994.

Sturani, Federica. "Theatre." In *Encyclopedia of Contemporary Italian Culture,* ed. Gino Moliterno. London: Routledge, 2000.

Sullivan, Francis A. "The Doctrinal Weight of *Evangelium Vitae.*" *Theological Studies* 56 (1995): 560–65.

Sylvers, Eric. "Breaking Away, with a Sponsor." *The New York Times,* June 3, 2003.

———. "Grudge Match: Italy vs. the Bean Counters." *The New York Times,* November 11, 2003.

Tessari, Roberto. "Actor Training in Italy." *New Theatre Quarterly* 4, no. 14 (1988): 184–85.

Took, John. "Petrarch." In *The Cambridge History of Italian Literature,* ed. Peter Brand and Lino Pertile. Cambridge: Cambridge University Press, 1999.

Usher, Jonathon. "Origins and Duecento." In *The Cambridge History of Italian Literature,* ed. Peter Brand and Lino Pertile. Cambridge: Cambridge University Press, 1999.

Van Watson, William. "Gassman." In *Encyclopedia of Contemporary Italian Culture,* ed. Gino Moliterno. London: Routledge, 2000.

"Vittorio Gassman." *The New York Times,* June 30, 2000.

Wagstaff, Christopher. "Cinema." In *Italian Cultural Studies,* ed. David Forgacs and Robert Lumley. New York: Oxford University Press, 1996.

———. "The Media." In *The Cambridge Companion to Modern Italian Culture,* ed. Zygmunt Barański and Rebecca J. West. Cambridge: Cambridge University Press, 2001.

Ward, David. "Intellectuals, Culture and Power in Modern Italy." In *The Cambridge Companion to Modern Italian Culture,* ed. Zygmunt Barański and Rebecca J. West. Cambridge: Cambridge University Press, 2001.

Weaver, William. "Italian Theatre's Gifted Rebels With a Cause." *The Financial Times* (London), January 11, 1990.

White, Nicola. *Reconstructing Italian Fashion.* Oxford: Berg Publishers, 2000.

"Who Will Follow Him?" *The Economist,* October 4, 2003.

Willson, Perry R. *The Clockwork Factory: Women and Work in Fascist Italy.* Oxford: Clarendon Press, 1993.

Wood, Sharon, and Joseph Farrell. "Other Voices: Contesting the Status Quo." In *The Cambridge Companion to Modern Italian Culture,* ed. Zygmunt Barański and Rebecca J. West. Cambridge: Cambridge University Press, 2001.

Zewdou, Fassil. "Ridolfi." In *Encyclopedia of Contemporary Italian Culture,* ed. Gino Moliterno. London: Routledge, 2000.

Index

1968, 37, 52, 53, 55, 62, 63, 80, 85,
   131, 181, 207

Abbado, Claudio, 161–62
Abruzzi (Abruzzo), 2, 10, 11, 114,
   140, 145
Agriculture, 25
AIDS, 67, 88
Albertini, Filoteo, 200
Aleramo, Sibilla, 83
Alighieri, Dante, 5, 14, 23, 137–39
Alleanza Nazionale (AN or National
   Alliance), 39, 48, 129, 218
American influences, 36, 51, 59, 99,
   117, 166–67, 174, 178–81,
   184, 190, 193, 203, 205, 208,
   212, 215
   on architecture, 184
   on art, 179
   on Berlusconi government, 40
   during Cold War, 44
   on dance, 174
   on design, 178
   on economy, 190, 195, 204, 208
   on politics, 40, 190
   on popular culture, 50, 51, 80, 117,
      166–67, 169, 181, 201, 205,
      212, 215
   rejection of, 191
   on sport, 134
   on Vatican, 59
   during World War II, 98, 203
Andreotti, Giulio, 38
Anniversario della Liberazione (Liberation Day), 98, 100
Antonacci, Anna, 162
Antonioni, Michelangelo, 51, 203–6
Apennine mountains, 1, 2, 6, 7–11
Apulia (Puglia), 3, 12, 114
Architecture, 177, 183–89
   Architettura e città (journal), 189
   Archizoom, 187, 192
   BBPR, 183, 186, 187, 197
   Casabella (journal), 186
   Group 9999, 187
   IUAV, *Istituto Universitario di
      Architettura di Venezia* (Venice
      Institute of Architecture), 186
   neorealism, 184
   rationalism, 177

Superstudio, 187, 192
Torre Velasca, 187, 197
Argan, Giulio Carlo, 184
Armani, Giorgio, 193, 195
Arno River, 2, 7, 183
Aulenti, Gaetana, 188
Austrian influences, 1, 6, 25, 26, 28, 31–32, 35, 140
Auto Racing, 119–20, 122–23, 131–33
    Ferrari, Enzo, 132
    Mille Miglia, 123
    Nuvolari, Tazio, 122, 123
    Schumacher, Michael, 132, 136
    Scuderia Ferrari (team Ferrari), 131–32

Balbo, Cesare, 27
Balestrini, Nanni, 149
Bartoli, Cecilia, 99, 125, 162
Basilicata, 12, 96
Basketball, 134
Bassani, Giorgio, 148
Bellini, Mario, 188
Bellini, Vincenzo, 13, 157, 162–63, 165, 188
Bene, Carmelo, 171–72
Benetton, 120, 133, 195
Benigni, Roberto, 209–10
Bergonzi, Carlo, 162–63
Berio, Luciano, 159–61
Berlinguer, Enrico, 37
Berlusconi, Silvio, 39–40, 56, 64, 87, 127–29, 199, 209, 214–17
    AC Milan soccer team, 127–28
    and Bush administration policy, 40, 217
    Casa delle Libertà, 40
    conflict-of-interest charges against, 217
    and feminists, 87
    and film industry, 209
    and Fini, Gianfranco, 129
    Fininvest, 127–29, 215–16

Forza Italia movement, 216
    merger of media and politics, 199
    Polo delle Libertà, 39
    prime minister, 40, 216
    publishing, 216
    Publitalia, 216
    rise to power, 56
    and symbolism of sport, 129
    television, 214–16
Bertolucci, Bernardo, 204–9
Blasetti, Alessandro, 201, 205
Boccaccio, Giovanni, 137–38, 207
Bocelli, Andrea, 165–66
Bonaparte, Napoleon, 25–26, 28–29, 157
Bossi, Umberto, 39
Branzi, Andrea, 187
Broadcasting Act (Mammì law) of 1990, 215
Brunelleschi, Filippo, 24
Brusati, Franco, 207–8
Bruson, Renato, 162–63
Buonarroti, Michelangelo, 7, 24, 51, 101, 203
Busoni, Ferruccio, 158
Bussotti, Sylvano, 159

Calabria, 1, 12–13
Calendimaggio (May Day eve), 98
Calvino, Italo, 49, 51, 53, 137, 146, 148
Camerini, Mario, 201
Campania, 11–12, 96, 108, 114
Caporetto, Battle of, 32
Cappuccilli, Piero, 162–63
Carboneria, 26
Carducci, Giosuè, 137, 140
Carlo Alberto (Charles Albert), King of Piedmont, 27
Carlson, Carolyn, 174–75
Carnevale (Carnival), 91, 94–95
Casella, Alfredo, 158–59
Cassola, Carlo, 148
Catholic Action, 58–60, 62

Cavour, Count Camillo Benso di,
        27–28, 57, 106
Celant, Germano, 181
Centro Culturale Virginia Woolf, 88
Chailly, Riccardo, 161–62
Chia, Sandro, 182
Children, 79
Cinema, 167, 199–210
    Centro Sperimentale di
        Cinematografia, 200
    Cinecittà (Cinema City), 200–201
    Fascism and, 200
    Hollywood, 34, 126, 193, 200–4,
        208–9
    Peplum (toga) films, 205
CINES, 200
Clemente, Francesco, 182
Clementi, Aldo, 160
Cold War, 36–37, 47, 59–60, 123,
        143, 151, 178, 182, 185, 213,
        217
Commedia dell'arte, 155
Cooking
    Neapolitan, 113
    Piedmontese, 110
    Roman, 113
    Sardinian, 114
    Sicilian, 114
    Turinese, 110
    Tuscan, 107, 111
    Venetian, 110
Corelli, Franco, 156, 162–63, 166
Il Corriere della Sera (Milan), 215
Crispi, Francesco, 28–30
Croce, Benedetto, 7, 41–46, 49, 51,
        54–55, 101, 142
    and Hegel, 45
    historicism, 43–46, 54–55
    La Critica, 43, 44, 142
    Liberal Party, 43, 44
    philosophical idealism, 43–45, 54
    and Vico, Giambattista, 45
Cucchi, Emilio, 182
Cycling, 123–25

Bartali, Gino, 123–25
Coppi, Fausto, 122–26
Gimondi, Felice, 125
Giro d'Italia, 122, 124, 125
Milan-San Remo race, 124, 125
Pantani, Marco, 125
Tour de France, 122, 124, 125

Dallapiccola, Luigi, 159
Dance, 170, 173–75
    ballet, 173–74
    Carlson, Carolyn, 174–75
    Company Excursus, 175
    Danza libera, 174
    Fracci, Carla, 173–74
    Sosta Palmizi, 174–75
Dante (Alighieri), 5, 14, 23, 137–39
D'Azeglio, Massimo, 27, 29
DC (Christian Democratic Party),
        36–39, 42, 47, 48, 59–61, 64,
        67, 73, 84, 86, 123, 165, 171,
        178, 185, 190, 207, 212–17
    and anti-communism, 47
    and center-left coalition, 60
    collapse of, 64, 67
    control of media, 213, 215
    and corruption, 61
    and feminist agenda, 84, 86
    and housing construction, 185
    1948 victory, 47
    and Vatican, 42, 47, 59, 61
De Barentzen, Patrick, 194
De Benedetti, Carlo, 215–16
De Céspedes, Alba, 145–46
De Felice, Renzo, 56
De Filippo, Eduardo, 170–71
Della Mirandola, Pico, 24
De Sica, Vittorio, 49, 201–3, 208
Design, 189–97
    fashion, 193, 195
    furniture, 190–91
    Memphis group, 192
Di Stefano, Giuseppe, 162
Divorce, 204

Dolce (Domenico) and Gabbana (Stefano), 193, 196–97
Donatoni, Franco, 159
Donizetti, Gaetano, 157, 161, 163, 165
La Donna (Woman) (journal), 83–84

Eco, Umberto, 41, 51, 53, 55, 137, 149, 150, 152–53, 159
Enlightenment, 25, 41, 45–46, 55
Epifania (Epiphany), 94
Ethiopian War, 30, 35, 143, 201
Etruscan influences, 7, 16–17, 107, 180

Fabrizi, Aldo, 202
Family traditions, 71, 77, 95, 146
Fascism, 6, 30–36, 43–49, 56–60, 84, 92, 98, 109, 122–23, 129, 141–48, 158–59, 166, 170, 173, 177–79, 183–84, 189, 193, 199–203, 207–11
   1924 election, 33
   and anti-semitism, 35
   and architecture, 177, 184
   and censorship, 142, 144, 159, 170, 173, 210
   and cinema, 200–202
   Corporate state, 34
   creation of the Fascist state, 33, 44
   cultural policy, 166, 173
   fall of, 189
   Fascist Grand Council, 33, 36
   Fascist Union of Writers, 143
   and fashion industry, 193
   Gentile, Giovanni, 44
   March on Rome, 33
   PNF (Fascist Party), 33
   propaganda, 34, 47
   and radio, 211
   relations with the Vatican, 34
   Salò Republic, 36, 98
   Sport and physical education, 122, 123, 134
   squads, 32–33
   and traditional gender roles, 84

Fellini, Federico, 41, 51, 161, 202–9, 218
Feminism, 150
Ferragosto, 104
Ferrari, Enzo, 74, 119, 131–33, 136
Ferrari, *Scuderia* (team), 74, 119, 131–33, 136
Ferrè, Gianfranco, 193
Feste (festivals), 91–106
   Festa de' Noantri (Our own festival), Rome, 91, 103
   Festa di San Giuseppe (St. Joseph's Festival), 95, 98
   Festa di Santa Lucia (Festival of Saint Lucy), 105, 165
   Festa di Santa Maria Assunta (Festival of the Assumption of the Virgin Mary), 102
   Good Friday, 96
   Natale (Christmas), 105
   Ognissanti (*Tutti i Santi* or All Saints' Day), 104–5
   Palm Sunday, 95
   Pasqua (Easter), 91, 94–98, 161
   Pasquetta (Little Easter, Easter Monday), 97
   Scoppio del Carro (Explosion of the cart), 97
Festival dei Due Mondi (Festival of Two Worlds), Spoleto, 8, 99, 160
Fiat, 4, 38, 72, 74, 121, 126, 128, 133, 190, 215
Figini, Luigi, 185
Fiorucci, Elio, 194
Florence (Firenze), 2, 7, 16, 23–24, 40, 91, 97, 99, 101, 109, 111, 113, 117, 138–40, 143, 156, 172, 183, 186, 188, 193, 195, 210, 216
   Alighieri, Dante, 23
   Arno River, 2, 7, 183
   art and architecture, 7, 183, 186
   Boccaccio, Giovanni, 138
   Brunelleschi, Filippo, 24

Buonarroti, Michelangelo, 7, 24, 51, 101, 203
Calcio Storico Fiorentino, 91, 101
city-state, 23
Collettivo di Danza Contemporanea, 173
Dallapiccola, Luigi, 159
fashion design, 193–94
Festa di San Giovanni Battista (St. John the Baptist), 101
Florentine cooking, 107, 109, 111
Gassman, Vittorio, 171
liberated, 1944, 36
Maggio Musicale, 91, 163
Medici influences, 7, 23–24, 108, 109
Montale, Eugenio, 143
press, 210
radio, 214
Sanzio, Raffaello (Raphael), 24
Scoppio del Carro, 91, 97, 99
Vinci, Leonardo da, 4, 7, 24, 137, 139, 151
Fo, Dario, 41, 53, 168, 171–72, 213–14
Folliero de Luna, Aurelia Cimino, 83
Fontana Sisters, 180–81, 194
Food
    alta cucina (gourmet cooking), 108
    Bolognese, 107–8, 111
    French influences, 110
    Ligurian, 111
    Medici, Catherine de' and, 108–9
    Neapolitan, 113–14
    Parmigiano Reggiano, 111
    Roman, 113
    Sardinian, 114–15
    Sicilian, 114
    Tuscan, 107–8, 111
    Venetian, 110
Forquet, Federico, 194
Fracci, Carla, 173, 175
Francesconi, Luca, 160

French influences, 22–23, 25–27, 30–31, 35, 52, 57, 108–10, 193
    diplomatic, 34, 35
    on fashion design, 193
    on food, 107, 109, 110
    French Revolution, 25–26, 46
    military, 22, 24–28
    Napoleon Bonaparte, 25, 157
    Napoleon III, 28, 57
    Pope Clement V, 23
    on theater, 170
    World War II, 35
Freni, Mirella, 162
Fronte nuovo delle arti (New Front of the Arts), 179
Futurism, 31–32, 84, 141, 158, 173, 177, 182

Gadda, Carlo Emilio, 143–44, 153
Galatzine, Irene, 194
Gardini, Raul, 133, 216
Garibaldi, Giuseppe, 3, 27–28
Gassman, Vittorio, 171, 204
Gastronomia (preparation and consumption of food), 106–17
Gavazzeni, Gianandrea, 161
Gay rights movement, 82, 88–89
    Arcigay, 88
    Babilonia, 88
    Fuori, Fronte Unitario Omossessuale Rivoluzionario Italiano (United Italian Revolutionary Homosexual Front), 88
    Lambda, 88
Gazzelloni, Severino, 163–64, 166
Gender issues, 71, 82–89
Gentiloni Pact, 31, 58
Germi, Pietro, 204
Ghibellines, 22
Gigli, Romeo, 196
Ginzburg, Natalia, 137, 145–46, 148, 172
Gioberti, Vincenzo, 27–28, 57
Giolitti, Giovanni, 30–33, 43, 58, 84

Giorgini, Giovanni Battista, 193
Giulini, Carlo Maria, 161
Gobbi, Tito, 162–63
Gramsci, Antonio, 41, 43, 46–52, 55,
     144, 147
Grandparents, 81
Gruppo 63, 149, 152–53
Guarnieri, Adriano, 160
Gucci, 193, 195
Guelphs, 22
Guttuso, Renato, 49, 179–80

Industry, 3, 4, 6, 7, 8, 9, 11, 12, 13,
     30, 32, 34, 37, 48, 58, 72–75,
     81–83, 85, 110, 121, 128, 129,
     131, 143, 148–49, 177–78,
     187–97, 200, 204–5, 207–9,
     210, 212, 214, 217
  in architecture and design, 187–97
  and family, 72–75, 81
  and gender, 81–85
  in literature, 143, 148–49
  and mass media, 200, 204–5, 207–9,
     210, 212, 214, 217
  and sport, 121–22, 128–31
Italian Empire, 35, 201
Italian left, 47, 49, 56, 178

Kingdom of Italy, 4, 28–29, 57, 107
Krizia (Mariuccia Mandelli), 193, 195
Kuliscioff, Anna, 83

Lampedusa, Giuseppe Tomasi di, 1,
     148
Lateran Pact, 34, 59
Law of Papal Guarantees, 29, 57
Lazio, 9, 10, 16–17, 111, 113, 128–31
Lega Nord (Northern League), 39, 218
Leonardo (da Vinci), 4, 7, 24, 137,
     139, 151
Leoncavallo, Ruggiero, 158
Leone, Sergio, 145, 204, 208
Lesbianism, 88
Levi, Carlo, 49, 145

Liguria, 2, 3, 77, 111, 166
Lombardy (Lombardia), 3, 4, 24–28,
     110–11, 210

Machiavelli, Niccolò, 24
Maderna, Bruno, 159–61
Mafia, 29, 65–66, 151, 207, 208
Magazines, 211, 216
Maggio Musicale, Florence, 99, 175
Magnani, Anna, 202
Malpiero, Gian Franco, 160
Mammismo, 79
Mani pulite ("clean hands" movement),
     38
Manzoni, Pietro, 139, 141, 181
Marches (Le Marche), 8–9, 111, 113
Marriage, 71
Marshall Plan, 37, 59, 189, 190
Marxism, 42–51, 53, 144, 147,
     179–80, 206, 208, 214
  art, 178–79
  cinema, 206–7
  Croce, 44–45
  cultural influence, 44, 47–48, 56,
     144
  and Fascism, 46
  Gramsci, Antonio, 42, 43, 48,
     144
  neorealism, 49–50
  radio, 214
  Resistance movement, 47
  Soviet Union, 51
  Togliatti, Palmiro, 50
  and Vatican, 58
Mascagni, Pietro, 140, 158
Mastroianni, Marcello, 204
Matteotti, Giacomo, 33
Max-Mara, 194
Mazzini, Giuseppe, 26–28, 167
Media, 199, 210–18
  corporate consolidation of, 216
  Ferruzzi group, 120, 216
  Mondadori group, 215–16
  Rusconi group, 216

Medici family, 7, 23–24, 108–9
Menotti, Giancarlo, 99, 160–61
Metternich, Prince Klemens von,
       26–27
Michelangeli, Arturo Benedetti, 163
Michelangelo (Buonarroti), 7, 24, 51,
       101, 203
Michelucci, Giovanni, 186, 188
Milan (Milano), 4, 23, 30, 32, 36–38,
       53–55, 61, 62, 67, 73, 83, 89,
       110, 121, 123–25, 128–31,
       139, 141, 143, 147, 151,
       157–61, 163, 166, 168, 170,
       178–79, 181, 183, 185, 187,
       192, 195, 197, 210, 215
   architecture, 178, 183, 185–87, 192
   art, 179–80
   capital, western Roman Empire, 20
   church attendance, 62
   Committees of National Liberation
       (CLNs), 36
   Comunione e Liberazione (Commu-
       nion and Liberation, CL), 67
   design, 195–96
   destroyed by Frederick Barbarossa,
       22
   Duchy of, 25
   fashion industry, 74
   Fatti di Maggio (events of May
       1898), 30
   food, 110
   French occupation, 24
   gay rights movement, 88–89
   and industrial-commercial triangle,
       30
   language, 15
   Lombard capital, 110
   music, 142, 159, 163
   press, 210, 215
   radio, 214
   sport, 121, 123–24, 128–29,
       130–31, 134
   Tangentopoli scandal, 38
   theater, 170–71

Il Verri, 149
Visconti family, 23, 138
women's movement, 83
Minority populations
   Albanian, 15, 16, 107
   Greek, 15
   Slovenian, 15
   Yugoslav, 16, 123
Missoni, Ottavio and Rosita, 195
MLD, Movimento di Liberazione della
       Donna (Movement for the
       Liberation of Women), 86
Molise, 11
Montale, Eugenio, 137, 142–44, 147,
       150
Monteverdi, Claudio, 156
Montezemolo, Luca Cordero di, 74
Morante, Elsa, 89
Moravia, Alberto, 89, 137, 143, 146,
       179, 207
Morelli, Salvatore, 83–84
Moretti, Nanni, 141, 209
Moro, Aldo, 37, 133
Moschino, Gianfranco, 196
Mozzoni, Anna Maria, 83
Music, 156–69
   Italian Society for Modern Music,
       159
   jazz, 166, 169, 175
   opera, 122, 149, 161–62, 173
   rap, 168–69
   San Remo Festival, 3, 125, 166–68
Mussolini, Benito, 31–36, 44, 56,
       58–59, 84, 92, 109, 122–23,
       131, 134, 142, 144, 200, 211
   censorship, 142
   Corporate State, 34
   De Felice, Renzo, 56
   diplomacy, 34–35
   execution of, 36, 98
   Fascist movement, 32
   Lateran Pact, 34, 44
   Matteotti crisis, 33
   PNF (Fascist Party), 33

Il Popolo d'Italia, 31
prime minister, 33
propaganda, 34
and radio, 211
recreation and sport, 122, 134
removal from power, 36
Salò Republic, 36
schools, 59
Socialist Party, 31
Muti, Riccardo, 99, 161–62

Nannini, Gianna, 166
Napoleon (Bonaparte), 25–26, 28–29,
    157
Napoleon III, Emperor of the French,
    28–29
Natalini, Adolfo, 187
Nationalism, 31
Neorealism *(neorealismo),* 49–50, 144,
    184
Nervi, Pier Luigi, 4, 175, 185, 187
Newspapers, 210–11
    national, 210
    readership, 210
Nizzoli, Marcello, 190
Non expedit, 57–58
Nono, Luigi, 159

Olivetti, 120, 185–86, 188, 190, 192,
    216
Opera, 122, 149, 156–63, 173
Ortese, Anna Maria, 149

Paci, Enzo, 42, 54
Padre Pio, 63, 64
Painting, 178–82
    Arti Visive, 180
    figurative, 180
    Fronte nuovo delle arti (New Front of
        the Arts), 179
    Guttuso, Renato, 49, 179, 180
    ideologically driven, 180–81
    spatialism, 180
    Transavanguardia (transavantgarde),
        182

Venice Biennale, 172, 180–82, 186
Paladino, Mimmo, 182
Palio delle Contrade, 91, 102–3
Panorama, 211, 215–16
Papacy, 2, 21–24, 27, 29, 37, 42,
    57–64, 66, 96, 101, 139
    Pope John Paul II, 42, 62, 64–66
        Evangelium Vitae, 66
    Pope John XXIII, 37, 42, 60–61, 63,
        64
        Pacem in Terris, 61
        Second Vatican Council, 60–65,
            67
    Pope Leo XIII, 58, 60
        Rerum novarum, 58
    Pope Paul VI, 61
    Pope Pius IX (Pio Nono), 27, 29,
        57
        Non expedit, 57, 58
    Pope Pius XII, 59–61
    Pope Stephen II, 21
Papal States, 21, 23, 25–28, 57
Pareyson, Luigi, 42, 54
Parliament, 13, 28–29, 31–34, 36,
    38–40, 58, 62, 66, 86, 88, 89,
    128, 130, 140, 215–16
Pasolini, Pier Paolo, 41, 50–51, 53, 89,
    137, 147, 153, 160, 167, 171,
    204, 206–7, 209
Pavarotti, Luciano, 99, 162–63, 169
PCI, *Partito Comunista Italiano* (Com-
    munist Party), 36–38, 40,
    47–50, 52–53, 84, 86, 88, 145,
    179, 202, 213, 215–17
PDS, *Partito Democratico della Sinistra*
    (Democratic Party of the Left),
    37, 216
Pentecost, 98–99
Petrarca, Francesco (Petrarch), 137–
    39
Pezzana, Angelo, 88
Piedmont (Piemonte), 3, 4, 26–29, 77,
    109–11, 188
Pininfarina, 190
Pirandello, Luigi, 137, 140, 170

Pirelli, 4, 121, 187
Pizzetti, Ildebrando, 160
PNF, *Partito Nazionale Fascista* (Fascist Party), 33, 48, 143
Poetry, 140, 142
Il Politecnico, 50, 145–46
Pollini, Gino, 163, 185
Pollini, Maurizio, 163, 185
Pontecorvo, Gillo, 204, 206
Ponti, Gio, 4, 187, 190
Po River, 2–4, 6, 16, 101, 110
PPI, *Partito Popolare Italiano,* 32–33, 39, 64
Pratolini, Vasco, 49
Prodi, Romano, 39, 218
Prosperity, 20
PSI, *Partito Socialista Italiano* (Socialist Party), 30–32, 37–38, 61, 83, 215, 217
Pucci, Emilio, 193–94
Punic Wars, 17, 201
Purini, Franco, 188

Quasimodo, Salvatore, 137, 142, 147, 179

Radio, 159, 211–14, 217
  deregulation of, 214
  listenership, 34, 211, 213
  monopoly status, 211
  music, 159–60, 166
  political use of, 52, 56, 86, 213
  Radioballila, 211
  radio libere (free radio), 214
  radio pirato (pirate radio), 214
  resurgence, 217
  sport, 123, 211
  and standardization of language, 212
RAI *(Radio Audizioni Italia),* 159, 164, 212–17
Rame, Franca, 171–73, 213
Raphael (Raffaello Sanzio), 24
RC, *Rifondazione Comunista* (Communist Refoundation), 37, 39

Regionalism, 2–4, 14, 29, 74, 76, 78, 85, 105, 107, 109, 115, 130–31, 151, 153, 210–11
  auto ownership, 74
  food, 91, 107, 109, 115
  language, 14–15
  literature, 151–52
  religion, 62
  sport, 130–31
  stereotypes, 29
Renaissance, 4, 7, 16, 22–24, 41–42, 92, 108–9, 138, 139, 155, 172, 182–83, 189, 192
  Alighieri, Dante, 23
  Brunelleschi, Filippo, 24
  Buonarroti, Michelangelo 7, 24, 51, 101, 203
  city-states, 23, 92
  craftsmanship, 189
  drama, 155
  early, 22
  Florentine, 24
  food, 108–9
  humanism, 24
  literary, 138
  patronage, 23
  Roman, 24
  Sanzio, Raffaello (Raphael), 24
  Tuscan, 7
  Vinci, Leonardo da, 4, 7, 24, 137, 139, 151
La Repubblica (Rome), 210, 216
Rerum novarum, 58
Resistance, 47–50, 55–56, 85, 145–48, 159–60, 165, 178, 183, 189, 202
Respighi, Ottorino, 158
Ricciarelli, Katia, 162
Risorgimento, 4, 28–29, 31, 57, 60, 82, 158, 210
Rogers, Ernesto Nathan, 183, 186
Roman Catholicism, 9, 16, 20–23, 26, 29, 33–34, 41–42, 45, 52, 57–67, 82, 92–94, 96, 98, 101, 104–6, 121, 138, 147, 155

church attendance, 16, 41, 60
and Cold War, 178
culture, 60
and education, 34, 58–59
feste, 91–106
fundamentalism, 63
and Italian culture, 57, 62, 66
labor unions, 59, 62
and politics, 29–32, 36, 42, 57–58, 64
and socialism, 121
and sport, 121, 124
voluntary associations, 67
women's issues, 84
Roman Empire, 19–21, 41
Julius Caesar, 17–18
Octavian (Augustus), 19, 104
Roman Question, 29, 57
Roman Republic, 17–18, 27, 93
Ronconi, Luca, 171–72
Rosi, Francesco, 167, 204, 206–7
Rossellini, Roberto, 49, 144, 201–4, 213
Rossini, Gioacchino, 157, 162
Russolo, Luigi, 158

Samonà, Giuseppe, 186
San Gennaro (liquification of the blood), 63, 91
Sanguineti, Edoardo, 149
San Remo Festival, 3, 125, 166–68
Sanzio, Raffaello (Raphael), 24
Sardinia (Sardegna), 1, 3, 13, 14, 24–26, 104, 114
Scarlatti, Alessandro, 156
Scarlatti, Domenico, 4, 13, 151, 156, 167, 195, 196
Scarpa, Carlo, 186
Sciarrino, Salvatore, 159–61
Sciascia, Leonardo, 137, 151, 153, 209
Scotto, Renata, 162
Second Vatican Council, 60–61, 63–67
Secularism, 41

Severino, Emanuele, 53, 55–56, 163, 166
Sicily (Sicilia), 1, 2, 3, 12, 13, 16, 21–22, 25–28, 30, 65, 95, 96, 105, 114, 137, 151, 188, 205, 209
Arab invasion, 21
Bourbon control, 27
Byzantine invasion, 21
dialect, 14, 137
feste, 95, 101, 104
food, 114
German invasion, 22
Greek settlements, 16
in literature, 142, 144, 148, 151, 205
Mafia, 65
revolution of 1848, 27
Risorgimento, 28
Spanish control, 24
Silone, Ignazio (Secondo Tranquilli), 137, 145
Skiing, 133
Campagnoli, Deborah, 133
Olympics, 133
Tomba, Alberto, 133
Soccer (calcio), 125–31
AC Milan, 128–31
AS Roma, 121, 129
"Azzurri" (national team), 126, 129
foreign players, 126
indebtedness, 130
Inter Milan, 121, 129, 130, 131
Juventus, 121, 127–31
Lazio, 129, 130, 131
Lega Calcio, 129–30
Meazza, Giuseppe (Peppino), 126
Roberto Baggio, 126
Rossi, Paolo, 126
ultràs, 128, 129, 131
Socialism, 29–33, 44, 46, 49, 51, 58, 61, 83–84, 98, 121, 123, 140–41, 215
Marxism, 42–51, 53, 144, 147, 179–80, 206, 208, 214

PSI, Partito Socialista Italiano (Socialist Party), 30–32, 37, 38, 61, 83, 215, 217
Sottsass, Ettore, 192
Soviet influences, 37, 47, 147, 182
Spanish Civil War, 35, 143
Spanish influences, 11, 24–25, 107, 143
  empire, 24–25
  food, 107
  Treaty of Cambrai, 24
Sport, 119–35
  basketball, 120, 133–34
  commercialization of, 129
  cycling, 120–21, 124, 126
  early history, 119–24
  Fascism and, 123
  Olympic games, 122, 125–26, 133, 185
  racing, 74, 119–20, 122–23, 131–33
  skiing, 121
  soccer, 119–23, 125–27, 129–31
  yachting, 133, 196
La Stampa (Turin), 210, 215

Tangentopoli ("kickback city") scandal, 38, 199, 217
Taviani brothers, Paolo and Vittorio, 204, 207
Tebaldi, Renata, 162
Telemontecarlo, 215–17
Television, 208, 212, 217
  DC control of, 213
  experimental transmisisons, 212
  pay-per-view, 217
  RAI, 159, 164, 212–17
  Talk shows, 212
  telenovela (soap opera), 212
  videocrazia (videocracy), 208
Theater, 170–73
  avant-garde, 171
  commedia dell'arte, 95, 155, 170, 201
  Fo, Dario, 41, 53, 168, 171–72, 213–14
  Marxist, 53

Piccolo Teatro, 170
stabili, 170–71
  women's, 172
Tiber River, 2, 7, 9, 16, 108
Togliatti, Palmiro, 47, 49–50, 56
Totò (Antonio De Curtis), 201
Transavanguardia (transavantgarde), 182
Trentino-Alto Adige, 3, 4, 6, 110
Tuscany (Toscana), 3, 7, 25, 27–28, 40, 108, 138, 174

UDC, *Unione dei Democratici Cristiani* (Union of Christian Democrats), 64
UDI, Unione Donne Italiane (Italian Women's Union), 85, 86
Ughi, Uto, 163
L'Ulivo (Olive Tree coalition), 39, 40
Umbria, 7–8, 99, 111, 113, 166, 169
Ungaretti, Giuseppe, 142, 144, 147
Universities, 22, 34, 56, 166, 186, 188

Vacchi, Fabio, 160
Valentino (Valentino Garavani), 193–94
Vattimo, Gianni, 53–55
Veneto, 4–6, 14, 32, 62, 74, 110, 111, 153
Venice (Venezia), 2, 6, 21, 23, 40, 94, 98, 104, 111, 113, 160, 172, 179, 180, 182, 186, 188
  architecture, 188
  Austrian control of, 25, 27–28
  Carnevale, 94–95, 156
  cooking, 110
  dialect, 153
  economic importance, 5
  Festa di San Marco, 98
  Festival of Contemporary Music, 160
  film festival, 201
  harbor, 2
  La Regata Storica (the historical regatta), 104
  Medieval commune, 20

Medieval republic, 6
opera, 156–57
Renaissance city-state, 23
Risorgimento, 27, 28
Venice Biennale, 172, 180, 181, 182, 186
Venice Institute of Architecture, 186
Verdi, Giuseppe, 99, 142, 157–58, 161–63
Verga, Giovanni, 140–41, 144, 158, 203
Il Verri, 149
Versace, Gianni, 193, 195–96
Vespa motor scooter, 190
Vesuvius, Mount, 2, 12, 63
Vico, Giambattista, 45, 190
Vinci, Leonardo da, 4, 7, 24, 137, 139, 151
Visconti, Luchino, 23, 49, 99, 140, 144, 161, 194, 202–6
Vittorini, Elio, 49–51, 56, 144–46, 179
Vittorio Emanuele (Victor Emmanuel) II, King of Italy, 27–28, 30
Vittorio Emanuele (Victor Emmanuel) III, King of Italy, 30

Wertmüller, Lina, 207–8
Wines, 110–15
  Barbaresco, 110
  Barolo, 110
  Brunello, 111
  Cannonau, 115
  Chianti Classico, 111
  Corvo, 114
  Frascati, 113
  Marsala, 114
  Orvieto, 113
  Soave, 110
  Torgiano, 113

Valpolicella, 110
Valtellina, 110
Vernaccia di Oristano, 115
Vino Nobile di Montepulciano, 111
Women, 83–86, 96, 125, 133, 138, 142–43, 145, 150, 168, 173, 197
World War I
  impact on economy, 32
  impact on women, 84
World War II, 6, 35, 37, 40, 46–47, 55, 60, 72, 76, 82, 85, 125, 132, 143, 165, 174, 177, 180, 184, 189, 197–200, 202, 209, 213
and architecture, 184
broadcasting, 211
impact of, 55
invasion of France, 35
resistance, 85
and sport, 123, 125
Writers
  early twentieth century, 140–41
  feminist, 86, 151, 172, 195
  futurist, 141
  neo-avant-garde, 149, 150
  neorealist, 144–45
  novelists, 139–45, 148–53
  poets, 48, 50, 137–43, 147, 149–50, 153, 156–57, 160
  regional, 137, 151–53, 209
  women, 145–46

Yachting, 133
Young Italy (*Giovane Italia*), 26

Zeno, Apostolo, 141, 156
Zevi, Bruno, 184, 185
Zucchero, 166, 168

About the Author

CHARLES KILLINGER is Professor of History at Valencia Community College, Orlando, Florida, and the author of *The History of Italy* (Greenwood, 2002).

945.092   Killinger, Charles 7/05
KIL   L.

          Culture and customs
          of Italy.

$49.95

DATE			

BAKER & TAYLOR